The Literary Criticism of T. S. Eliot

The Literary Criticism of T. S. Eliot

New Essays
collected and edited by

DAVID NEWTON-DE MOLINA

. . . the criticism of a poet; not a dull
collection of theorems . . .

JOHNSON: *Life of Dryden*

UNIVERSITY OF LONDON
THE ATHLONE PRESS
1977

Published by
THE ATHLONE PRESS
UNIVERSITY OF LONDON
at 4 Gower Street London WC1

Distributed by Tiptree Book Services Ltd
Tiptree, Essex

USA and Canada
Humanities Press Inc
New Jersey

© University of London 1977

ISBN 0 485 11167 5

Printed in Great Britain by
WESTERN PRINTING SERVICES LTD
Bristol

Preface

These essays on aspects of T. S. Eliot's literary criticism were written at the editor's invitation and are published in the present volume for the first time.

It is a decade since T. S. Eliot's death and a generation or more since his extraordinary influence as poet-critic was at its zenith. The words are worn, but now may be a time to expect some fresh historical revaluations and reassessments. We see the gains and losses, the virtues and vices, the successes and failures of Eliot's critical oeuvre against a widening and deepening retrospect on Modernism. And some of the renewal and excitement that the seizing of new opportunities affords is part of the attraction of the revaluations and reassessments visible in these nine essays.

It is a commonplace that the period between 1910 and 1939 saw a renaissance in English literature worthy of comparison with those of 1590–1612, 1710–35 and 1798–1822. A revolution in poetry and in all other imaginative writing, the death of one world and the birth of another, released energies that fed an accompanying revolution in literary criticism. And the critical writings of T. S. Eliot were a cardinal feature, understood or mis-understood, in that critical revolution for nearly half a century as active forces. At present, as the twentieth century looks forward to its close, and as Eliot's critical writings enter their struggle for renewed life against the viewless prospect of futurity, the spirit of disinterested inquiry will be increasingly freed to look back to contemplate and understand afresh. We could borrow some of Eliot's own words (on Samuel Johnson) as a motto for the enigma of Eliot's current standing as critic. Written during the high-tide of his celebrity (in 1944) they carry a characteristic undertone of half-concealed ironic self-parody: 'we are always impressed by a reputation for influence, as influence is a form of power. But when the tide of influence, which a writer may set in motion for a generation or two, has come to its full, and another force has drawn the waters in a different direction, and when several tides have risen and fallen, great writers remain

of equal potentiality of influence in the future.' Our present
concern, at all events, is to envisage as lucidly as possibly the
changes in the complex relations between two complex questions,
questions that are aspects of a single double question in the ultimate light of history: the question of T. S. Eliot's all-pervasive
recent *influence* in literary criticism in English, and the question
of his true or distinctive *greatness* as a literary critic.

Naturally, prophecy is vain and time must bring in its changes.
Meanwhile, we could turn to Eliot's several meditations on the
vital mystery of the quick and the dead in all literary experience
and culture. From first to last, it was a theme that manifested
(as in the poetry) much of his creative and critical sincerity and
authenticity—or to use Eliot's own term, it was a theme that
manifested the symptomatic 'intensity' of realizing what *is* alive
(and dead) in all developments of literary taste. And why not
adapt some of Eliot's most celebrated phrases when we wonder if,
as literary critics, we are likely to know what is to be done unless
we live in what is not merely the present, but the present moment
of the past, unless we are conscious, not of what is dead, but of
what is already living in the noble creation that forms T. S.
Eliot's completed critical oeuvre?

It remains for me to thank F. W. Bateson, Denis Donoghue,
Graham Hough, Samuel Hynes, R. Peacock, William Righter,
W. W. Robson, Roger Sharrock and C. K. Stead for first making
the book a possibility, then a reality; for their disinterested
generosity and enthusiasm in the interests of a great poet-critic.

I also wish to thank the Board of the Athlone Press and their
staff for their co-operation and assistance. Without the Board's
foresight in encouraging the collection of the essays, and without
unfailing support in savage economic times, nothing would have
come to fruition.

My dearest debt was once again to my wife Marie-José:

> *Une femme est l'amour, la gloire et l'espérance;*
> *Aux enfants qu'elle guide, à l'homme consolé,*
> *Elle élève le cœur et calme la souffrance,*
> *Comme un esprit des cieux sur la terre exilé.*

University of Edinburgh   David Newton-De Molina
21 September 1975

Contents

Criticism's Lost Leader

F. W. BATESON

Just for a handful of silver he left us,
    Just for a riband to stick in his coat—
Found the one gift of which fortune bereft us,
    Lost all the others she lets us devote . . .

In spite of its boisterous vulgarity Browning's 'The Lost Leader'
has insisted on being remembered. The poem fills a gap in the
mythology or phrase-book of modern representative democracy
without limiting the concept too strictly to politics, to a *duce* or
a *Führer*. T. S. Eliot, who had been persuaded by Ezra Pound to
take Browning more seriously than most of us can do to-day,
realized at least once the possible applicability of the term to
himself. It will be found in *Thoughts after Lambeth* (1931), a
rumination upon the condition of the Anglican Church which he
thought sufficiently well of to include in the *Selected Essays*.
The passage runs as follows:

> One of the most deadening influences upon the Church in the
> past, ever since the eighteenth century, was its acceptance, by
> the upper, upper-middle and aspiring classes, as a political
> necessity and as a requirement of respectability. There are
> signs that the situation to-day is quite different. When, for
> instance, I brought out a small book of essays called *For
> Lancelot Andrewes*, the anonymous reviewer in the *Times
> Literary Supplement* made it the occasion for what I can only
> describe as a flattering obituary notice. In words of great
> seriousness and manifest sincerity, he pointed out that I had
> suddenly arrested my progress—whither he had supposed
> me to be moving I do not know—and that to his distress
> I was unmistakably making off in the wrong direction.
> Somehow I had failed, and had admitted my failure; if not a

lost leader, at least a lost sheep; what is more, I was a kind of traitor . . .[1]

Lost leader? Lost sheep? A kind of traitor? The alternatives, as Eliot presents them, are all three sufficiently bleak. But I suspect there was at least an element of truth in each of them. In its unspoken implications the obituary was not flattering at all.

I read the review when it came out. It carried an air of authority with it which suggested that it might have been by Middleton Murry, the one-time editor of the *Athenaeum*, to which Eliot had contributed many early essays and reviews. (Richard Aldington, who had been one of the original 'Imagist' group and was an assistant editor of Eliot's *Criterion* when it started, is another possibility.) I quote the passage from the review (*Times Literary Supplement*, 6 December 1928) which makes its 'obituary' character clear:

> . . . by accepting a higher spiritual authority based not upon the deepest personal experience . . . but upon the anterior and exterior authority of revealed religion, he has abdicated from his high position. But most of us . . . have gone too far to draw back. It is to the country beyond the Waste Land that we are compelled to look, and many will consider it emptier that we are not likely to find Mr. Eliot there. Recently he recorded his conviction that Dante's poetry represents a saner attitude towards 'the mystery of life' than Shakespeare's. Not a saner, we would say, but simply a different attitude, and to the majority, the great majority, to-day no longer a vital one.

In any case, however, the *TLS* reviewer, whoever he was, had not apparently been disturbed by the decline in critical quality that *For Lancelot Andrewes* displays as compared with *The Sacred Wood* (1920) and *Homage to John Dryden* (1924). But it was this that dismayed Eliot's humbler admirers such as myself at the time. Only one of the eight essays, that on Baudelaire, can be considered first-rate as literary criticism, and the long passage on Hobbes in the Machiavelli essay (which Eliot did not reprint later) is grotesque in its misrepresentations. No, what distressed the *TLS* reviewer was the religious about-turn that Eliot proclaimed in the preface to *For Lancelot Andrewes*. We had taken the gay anti-clericalism of earlier poems like 'Mr. Eliot's Sunday Morning Service' and 'The Hippopotamus' quite literally, at their face meaning of a sarcastic agnosticism—*not* as mere youthful indiscretions or rebelliousness. And it seems certain that we were right to do so; after all Eliot was a man of thirty or thereabouts when he wrote them. The scepticism that he shared with Ezra Pound and had learnt from Jules Laforgue and Remy de Gourmont, respectively the poet and the literary critic whom he found most congenial at the time when he wrote those poems, was serious and profound. As the essays collected in *The Sacred Wood* demonstrate over and over again it was this diffused scepticism that had made the early criticism possible. The later 'humility', about which he tended to protest too much, was basically (though not in all its manifestations) less of a moral advance personally than a general social surrender.

Eliot became a member of the Church of England in 1927 and a naturalized English citizen in the same year. The two acts must be seen in conjunction as aspects of a single conversion which —in spite of the denials of *Thoughts After Lambeth*—really amounted to a return to complete respectability; Eliot had signed up with the English Establishment. The Anglo-Catholicism which he now professed publicly was no doubt sincerely held, but the TLS reviewer was right—or so many of us believed at the time—to be distressed at the manner and consequence of its avowal. We, who had been the most ardent admirers both of the poems (with some exceptions, of course) and of almost all the literary criticism, felt ourselves let down.

The preface to *For Lancelot Andrewes* had included a defiant declaration by Eliot to the effect that he was not only a classicist in literature but also a 'royalist' in politics as well as an anglo-catholic in religion. The background to the enunciation of this unhappy tripartite formula is provided in 'To Criticize the Critic', the last of Eliot's essays of any substance (originally it had been a lecture at Leeds, delivered in 1961). It seems that Irving Babbitt, the Harvard teacher 'to whom I owe so much', had dined with Eliot in London shortly before the academic year 1927/28 began:

I had not seen Babbitt for some years, and I felt obliged to acquaint him with a fact unknown to my small circle of

readers . . . that I had recently been baptized and confirmed
into the Church of England. I knew that it would come as a
shock to him to learn that any disciple of his had so turned his
coat . . . But all Babbitt said was: 'I think you should come out
into the open.'[2]

Eliot admits that he was nettled by Babbitt's comment, and
that his classicist—royalist—anglo-catholic reaction was too
extreme. His profession of classicism may have been partly intended to ingratiate Babbitt, whose deflation of romanticism in
Rousseau and Romanticism (1919) and elsewhere has a certain
crude negative merit. The royalism is more difficult to excuse.
Eliot was flirting at the time and later, as the articles he accepted
for publication in the *Criterion* show, with the authoritarian
concepts of monarchy of which Charles Maurras was the prophet
and the *Action Française* with its absurd 'Camelots du Roi' the
vulgar expression. His comment in 'To Criticize the Critic' that
he was still, thirty years later, 'in favour of the maintenance of
the monarchy in all countries which have a monarchy' is therefore somewhat less than frank. The nearest after all that the ideas
of Maurras got to political fulfilment was in the Vichy régime
of Pétain and Laval, and not in the decorative constitutional
monarchies.

But Browning's historical butt in 'The Lost Leader' was not in
fact a political turncoat or traitor. The poem really portrays a
great poet, the poet Wordsworth, who incidentally was still alive
when Browning wrote it. As he explained to one friend, it was a
Wordsworth 'purposely disguised, retaining certain characteristic traits and discarding the rest'. Under the political accoutre-
ments of a successful politician who has allowed his early ideals
to be corrupted in middle age Browning was describing the
undeniable if gradual deterioration of Wordsworth's poetry. And
he was also suggesting that the literary deterioration was in some
sense the consequence of the public corruption. Wordsworth had
at one time been an enthusiastic supporter of the French Revolution, but his revolutionary period *preceded* the composition of his
best poems; when he did in 1813 accept the Government's offer
of a virtual sinecure as Distributor of Stamps for Westmorland
and parts of Cumberland, this *followed* the best poems by some

ten years or more. The two events were—it seems fair to say—one the premature, the other the belated symptom of subjective conditions other than themselves, though no doubt personal and social causes were interrelated and interdependent. As I have argued at length elsewhere, the central cause underlying the sudden flowering of Wordsworth's poetry in the years 1797 to 1802 was the obscure emotional intimacy throughout this period with his sister Dorothy. In Eliot's case the emotional causes were almost certainly equally private and equally undefined.[3] It is reasonable to connect them (i) with the death of Jean Verdenal, the French friend drowned or killed in the Anglo-French naval operation launched unsuccessfully in the narrows of the Dardanelles in 1915. (Eliot had proclaimed his affection for Verdenal in hyperbolic terms in the *Prufrock* volume's dedication.) And (ii) with the marriage to Vivien Haigh-Wood later in 1915. Too little is known, one is told, about either Verdenal or the early years of the marriage to make possible more than an intelligent guess or two of their relevance to either the poetry or the criticism. Agreed. But a passage in the lecture 'Shakespeare and the Stoicism of Seneca' (1927) does make it clear that Eliot was fully aware of some such private connections:

> . . . I am used [Eliot told his first audience, the London Shake-speare Association] to having cosmic significances, which I never suspected, extracted from my work . . . by enthusiastic persons at a distance; and to being informed that something which I meant seriously is *vers de société*; and to having my personal biography reconstructed from passages which I got out of books, or which I invented out of nothing because they sounded well; and to having my biography invariably ignored in what I *did* write from personal experience . . .[4]

The final clause makes the crucial admission. So, having eliminated the cosmological meanings, the bits from books, etc.—not too difficult as the critics and source detectives get busier—there *is* a residuum of personal experience in what was written before 1927. What was it—for one thing, what could it possibly not have been, if not at any rate in part the Verdenal affair (which has been documented in two acute and sympathetic articles by John Peter)?[5] (Why is April the cruellest month? *Because* it was

in April Verdenal was reported *mort aux Dardanelles*.[6] And the
impact of Vivien is even clearer.[7] In the early years of the marriage it was her gaiety that impressed their friends and this quality is surely reflected, at least in part, in the sophisticated
comedy of the Sweeney poems and such literary conundrums as
the epigraph prefixed to 'Burbank with a Baedeker: Bleistein
with a Cigar' (the clue connecting the quotations is 'Venice').
But, for reasons that have only been proposed so far by more or
less irresponsible gossip (such as drugs, or the brief affair with
'Mr. Apollinax', alias Bertrand Russell) Vivien became nervy
and edgy, ultimately indeed almost mad.

The parallel with Wordsworth is at least suggestive. In 1802,
as Dorothy's affection for her brother became more clearly sexual,
an explosive situation had built up in Dove Cottage which
Wordsworth solved by the desperate remedy of marrying Mary
Hutchinson. But the poetry from then on became increasingly
conventional. For Eliot, trapped after his day's work was done for
Lloyd's Bank with a half-mad wife in a small London flat, no such
solution was available. The inevitable consequence was the break-
down in the autumn of 1921 and the three months' sick-leave
that was immediately granted him by the Bank. In a curious
letter to Aldington, written on November 6, he pooh-pooed the
collapse: '. . . my "nerves" are a very mild affair, due not to
over-work but to an aboulie and emotional derangement which
has been a life-long affliction.'[8] The 'aboulie' seems to be a mis-
spelling of *aboulia*, a medical term for loss of will-power, though
Eliot may have used the word in some such sense as loss of nerve.
But the breakdown was far from being 'a very mild affair'. Less
than three months after the completion of his treatment in
Lausanne (where *The Waste Land* was finished except for the
tidyings-up by Pound), Eliot began 'going to pieces' again and
Vivien's condition also got worse. Somehow he struggled on, but
a typed letter describing his difficulties of 12 March 1923 ends in
ink 'I am worn out, I cannot go on'.[9] On April 26, to the same
correspondent, it is 'I feel pretty well knocked out; the shock of
thinking seven or eight times over that my wife was at the point
of death was enough in itself'.[10] In the end Eliot became a publisher and Vivien entered a mental home, but the price of his
survival was a new dependence upon props offered him by

society, especially aristocratic English society and that of the Bloomsbury intellectuals.

Wordsworth celebrated his return to conformity in the 'Ode to Duty'. Duty is a 'Stern Lawgiver', but

Thou dost preserve the stars from wrong;
And the most ancient heavens, through thee, are fresh and
                            strong.

Eliot's verse can provide no exact equivalent to Wordsworth's cosmic confidence (except *Ash-Wednesday?*), but 'What the Thunder Said', the final section of *The Waste Land*, was perhaps intended to have some such comparable function. In a letter to Bertrand Russell of 15 October 1923 Eliot described it as not in his opinion 'the best part, but the only part that justifies the whole, at all'.[11] This is no doubt true but, as Eliot seems to recognize here, the religious passages should have been better written if they were to carry the weight they are expected to bear. It was the last part of *The Waste Land* to be written and the poetic deterioration—which lasts at least until *Four Quartets*—had already set in.

It was my great good fortune to be one of Eliot's earliest readers. Though I only met him twice, I was (I suppose) on the outer fringe of his inner circle. My reading began in 1919 when I was briefly at Oxford trying my luck in the annual scholarship examinations. Between the papers I explored the bookshops and found odd copies of the little magazines—*Art and Letters, Coterie, The Chapbook*, etc.—that exploded in London before or soon after the 1918 Armistice. 'T. S. Eliot' was a name I found in all of them—either contributing critical articles in a manner and prose style I had not known before, or as the author of poems excitingly different from any of those I had found in the consecutive volumes of *Georgian Poetry* which had satisfied my salad days at school. In 1920 I met Robert Graves at a tennis party and we discovered common interests and that we had been at the same house at Charterhouse. (It was from Graves I learnt that Eliot was an American.) And in October 1920 the *Athenaeum* printed my first poem—a very bad one, I am afraid, which tried to blend the Graves manner with Eliot's.

I apologize for this autobiographical name-dropping. The point

I wish to establish is simply that I was in it all almost at the beginning. *The Sacred Wood* was published in the November of my first term at Oxford. I read it immediately; I remember the *TLS* review of it[12] which I read as soon as it came out; I can even remember that the first sentence of that review began by quoting Eliot's dictum that 'Criticism is as inevitable as breathing'. I did not read the 1920 *Poems* until 1921 or perhaps 1922; there was apparently only one copy of it in Oxford, which belonged to Jean de Menasce, an elegant Egyptian Jew at Balliol who not only lent me the precious volume but insisted on my dining with him and Eliot *à trois* in Oxford's Carlton Club. (An embarrassing meal: Eliot's one preoccupation was not to miss the next train back to London.)

And so when A. Walton Litz, the editor of *Eliot in His Time* (1973), describes himself and the other contributors to this useful semi-centenary celebration of *The Waste Land* as 'the last generation' capable of reading the poem as a contemporary artifact, I rub my eyes. Litz himself can only just have been born in October 1922 (when *The Waste Land* appeared in the first number of Eliot's *Criterion*) and even Dame Helen Gardner, who is the oldest member of his team, may still have been in pigtails. They belong to the post-*Waste Land* generation. But to those of us who were about twenty in 1922 *The Waste Land* had to be judged in a context already created by the 1920 *Poems* and *The Sacred Wood*. (We read the *Prufrock* volume rather later.) In such a context, as the sequel to such brilliantly lucid poems as 'Sweeney Among the Nightingales' and 'Burbank' which Eliot rightly told his brother Henry (in 1920) were both 'intensely serious' and 'among the best that I have ever done',[13] *The Waste Land* came as a great disappointment. It was, indeed it still is, chaotic and pretentious, though admittedly a few passages in it, particularly the superb Dantesque vision of the crowds of the dead swarming over London Bridge—are among the master-pieces of English literature. But approaching it as we had done through the quatrain poems *The Waste Land* was a flawed work of genius—as the necessity of Pound's surgery has now demonstrated. 'Sweeney', 'Burbank', even 'Gerontion', are self-sufficient, as *Ash-Wednesday* and large areas in the *Four Quartets* are not. Eliot's poetry lost something of special splendour in the breakdown of September 1921 that it never wholly recovered.

Is this also true of the criticism? I think it is. I believe that the literary essays and reviews up to and including the end of the summer of 1921—'The Metaphyical Poets', though not printed until the *TLS* of 20 October 1921, was presumably written several weeks before—decline in quality in much the same way. This is not to say that there are not occasional passages with the earlier brilliance in the later work, but they are rare exceptions. The general level is of a respectable interestingness; a specialist will read it all, but the common reader is, I suggest, under no such obligation. He can pick and choose. If the eyes close, as they will do fairly often, he need not be unduly ashamed.

Shelley has described Wordsworth's decline as a poet in the Dedication to the still under-valued *Peter Bell the Third* as occurring in four stages:

> Peter [=Wordsworth] changes colours like a chameleon, and his coat like a snake . . . He was at first sublime, pathetic, impressive, profound; then dull; then prosy and dull; and now dull—O, so very dull! it is an ultra-legitimate dulness.

By 'ultra-legitimate dulness' Shelley meant the torpor that descended upon Europe with the return of the Bourbons and Habsburgs to the thrones of their ancestors. We may translate it in Eliot's case to 'Ultra-Establishment'. That his criticism became duller—less original, less lively—is not likely to be denied by those who have struggled through *On Poetry and Poets* (1957), though it is agreeable to be able to report that the essays included in this collection which were composed in the 1950s are decidedly less soporific than those of the 1940s.

And here one more parallel with Wordsworth suggests itself. No-one, I suppose, is likely to deny that the Preface to the second edition of *Lyrical Ballads* (1800) is Wordsworth's critical masterpiece. The two Prefaces to the 1815 *Poems* are of considerable interest, but they are not of the same acute theoretic quality. And there is no later criticism at all—except sporadically in the letters or the accounts of his own poems that he dictated to Eliza Fenwick. Eliot's counterpart to the *Lyrical Ballads* preface would generally be agreed to be 'Tradition and the Individual Talent'

(1919), which has been reprinted in critical anthologies and discussed by other critics more often than any of his other essays;
Eliot gave it the pride of place in the *Selected Essays* (1932),
though it is true he disparages it, for no obvious reason, in 'To
Criticize the Critic'. Now Wordsworth was only thirty-one
when he wrote the famous Preface, and Eliot must have been
exactly the same age (thirty or thirty-one) when he completed
'Tradition and the Individual Talent'. The coincidence is striking,
but what I find even more significant is the composition of
their critical masterpieces when they were still so comparatively
young. Dryden was 69 when he wrote the brilliant Preface to his
Fables; Johnson was 70 or more when he wrote the *Lives of the
Poets*. And Aristotle, Horace, Quintilian, Dante, Montaigne,
Lessing, Coleridge, Goethe, Sainte-Beuve, Arnold are other examples of critics whose critical prime was in middle or later life.
If Wordsworth and Eliot are exceptional in beginning their
critical careers with their masterpieces in the genre, may it not
be that their finest creative work also came early, and that their
best criticism is essentially devoted to expounding and justifying
what their own poetry merely implies?

Eliot was content to make just this distinction in his own case
without raising the further problem of earliness versus lateness.
'The Music of Poetry' (the W. P. Ker lecture delivered at Glasgow
in 1942 and subsequently included in *On Poetry and Poets,* spells
it out. On the one hand, 'the critical writings of poets . . . owe a
great deal of their interest to the fact that the poet, at the back of
his mind, if not as his ostensible purpose, is always trying to
defend the kind of poetry he is writing'; on the other hand, there
is 'the more detached critic' who supplies 'impartial judgment'.
Apart from Ker no names are produced, but it is clear that Eliot
puts himself among the 'practitioner-critics' as against such
'scholar-critics' as Ker. What was implied in 'The Music of Poetry'
becomes explicit in the much later 'To Criticize the Critic' (1961).
Having (he assures us) re-read all of his earlier criticism he can
now say out loud of his earlier essays that 'in writing about
authors who had influenced me, I was implicitly defending the
sort of poetry that I and my friends wrote'.

Was he right? Was he primarily a poet or a critic? Eliot had
no doubt himself that he was one of those writers 'who are

primarily creative but reflect upon their own vocation and upon
the work of other practitioners' (To *Criticize the Critic*, p. 25).
My own view is the exact opposite of this. I regard him as an
interesting, even good minor poet (more American than English)
who was a major literary critic (an *English* critic and of the
stature of Johnson, Coleridge and Arnold). The case of Henry
James is a partial parallel.

It is only necessary to consult Donald Gallup's splendid
T. S. Eliot: a Bibliography (1969) to see how much more easily
criticism came to him than poetry. Excluding such preliminary
matter as title-pages and dedications Eliot's poems, including the
Poems written in Early Youth, the strange suppressed 'Ode'
(1920), and the original parts of *The Waste Land* that Pound
persuaded him to excise, the poems add up to about 240 short
pages. (Translated into the smaller type and longer lines and
pages of *Selected Essays* it would be not much more than a
hundred pages.) On the other hand, the critical essays and intro-
ductions—even excluding the deplorable *After Strange Gods*
(1934), on which *Tantum religio potuit suadere malorum* is
perhaps a sufficient comment—add up in the collections author-
ized by Eliot himself to some 1250 pages. I have excluded the
plays from these calculations; apart from the short *Sweeney
Agonistes* and perhaps *The Family Reunion* I cannot take them
seriously. (Here too the parallel with James re-asserts itself.) The
social and religious pamphlets also fall outside these statistics,
though some of them are of considerable interest.

Eliot will certainly survive both as literary critic and as poet.
But was the direction his criticism took influenced to the extent
he himself believed by the need to defend or justify either his
own poems or the poems of the Imagist group? An important
passage on the interrelationship of the two faculties, creative and
critical, occurs in 'The Function of Criticism' (1923). Matthew
Arnold, he tells us there, overlooked 'the capital importance of
criticism in the work of creation itself':

Probably, indeed, the larger part of the labour of an author in
composing his work is critical labour; the labour of sifting,
combining, constructing, expunging, correcting, testing: this
frightful toil is as much critical as creative. I maintain even

that the criticism employed by a trained and skilled writer on
his own work is the most vital, the highest kind of criticism;
and . . . that some creative writers are superior to others solely
because their critical faculty is superior.[14]

Whether Eliot had himself in mind in that final sentence is
not easily demonstrated, but the circumstances of the essay's
composition certainly suggest it. *The Waste Land* had been published in the first number of the *Criterion*, Eliot's ambitious new
review that was intended to create an English climate of literary
opinion similar to that created in France by the *Nouvelle Revue
Française* (originally edited by Jacques Rivière[15] but the brain-
child of André Gide and including Marcel Proust, Giraudoux and
Albert Thibaudet among its regular contributors). 'The Function
of Criticism' dominated the first number of the *Criterion's* second
volume (October 1923), as *The Waste Land* had dominated that
of the first volume. Here was the new journal's declaration of
intent, its manifesto—which, as compared with its French model,
is much more self-consciously critical and also much more class-
conscious. Its title alone had nailed the flag of criticism to its
mast. If the sneers at Matthew Arnold ('one whose place, on
the whole, is with the weaker brethren') and the wrangle
with Middleton Murry over the Inner Voice (essentially the
Romantics' doctrine of 'inspiration') are irritating, and the conclusion that 'any note in *Notes and Queries,* which produces a
fact even of the lowest order about a work of art' is superior
critically to Coleridge on *Hamlet* is grotesque, one message does
come through: some creative writers are better than others
because they are better self-critics—and better self-critics, it
seems, because with only the fewest exceptions they are better
educated. The passage about 'this frightful toil' of 'sifting, combining, constructing, expunging, correcting, testing' anticipates
passages in *Four Quartets*:

> Words strain,
> Crack and sometimes break, under the burden,
> Under the tension, slip, slide, perish,
> Decay with imprecision, will not stay in place,
> Will not stay still.   (*Burnt Norton*, v, 13–17)

So here I am . . .
Trying to learn to use words, and every attempt
Is a wholly new start . . .   (*East Coker*, v, 3–5)

The word neither diffident nor ostentatious,
An easy commerce of the old and the new,
The common word exact without vulgarity,
The formal word precise but not pedantic . . .
                              (*Little Gidding*, v, 6–9)

Closest of all is *East Coker's* 'the intolerable wrestle/With words
and meanings' (ii, 20–1), which is almost a paraphrase of 'this
frightful toil' in 'The Function of Criticism'. It is true 'Twenty
years largely wasted, the years of *l'entre deux guerres*' (*East
Coker*, v, 2) separate the critical anticipation from its poetic use,
but that may be because Eliot was right about himself and the
twenty years between *The Waste Land* and *Four Quartets*. They
were 'largely wasted'. The fact that 'The Function of Criticism'
preceded the creative use of his own verbal labours and difficulties
remains as a challenge—one that (I believe) none of Eliot's
numerous critics has so far met. A single passage in prose had
here anticipated several excellent ones in verse. Was this—to
think in prose and later translate the prose into verse—what it
really meant to be a 'classicist'?

A similar case is the prosodic one of Eliot's loose blank verse.
The critical beginnings will be found in 'Reflections on *Vers
Libre*', the earliest article to be allowed into the *corpus*, which
the *New Statesman* had printed in March 1917 and which has
now been reprinted in *To Criticize the Critic*. The article is uncertain in tone, but almost all of Eliot's later unrhymed verse is
implicit in the conclusion that is reached:

> . . . the most interesting verse which has yet been written in
> our language has been done either by taking a very simple
> form, like the iambic pentameter, and constantly withdrawing
> from it, or taking no form at all, and constantly approximating
> to a very simple one.[16]

The examples Eliot gives of the two possibilities are in fact all of
withdrawals from the iambic pentameter—six from Jacobean
tragedy (Webster, Middleton) and one each, if I am not mistaken

(Eliot gives no references) from T. E. Hulme ('The Embankment') and Pound ('Near Perigord'). Of the second type, Eliot gives an example from 'H.D.', an original Imagist with Pound and Eliot, (her poem was 'Hermes of the Ways'), pointedly dovetailing it with several lines from Arnold's 'The Strayed Reveller'. 'Gerontion', which was not to be written for another two years, would have been a good example of the first type:

> Here I am, an old man in a dry month,
> Being read to by a boy, waiting for rain.

Ten syllables in each line, but only scannable as iambic pentameters by complicated inversions and forcings of the accent.

And *The Waste Land*? Is not its style essentially a versification of 'Tradition and the Individual Talent', with its plea for 'the whole of the literature of Europe' as well as 'his own generation' somehow in the good author's bones? Two lines from *The Waste Land* will exemplify what was presumably meant by the poet's need for this special historical sense:

> There I saw one I knew, and stopped him, crying: "Stetson!
> You who were with me in the ships at Mylae!"

To be called Stetson in the early twentieth century was to identify oneself as a modern American; J. Alfred Prufrock would have worn a Stetson hat. And those who were 'in'—rather than 'on' or 'with'—the ships at the naval battle at Mylae (probably that of 260 B.C.) were the poor devils of slaves who propelled the triremes of either the victorious Romans or the defeated Carthaginians. Whether Stetson stands for Conrad Aiken (who lunched with Eliot two or three times a week when much of *The Waste Land* was being written), and whether the Carthaginian defeat has some connection with Phlebas the Phoenician (=Verdenal) are considerations I must leave to literary detectives, an honourable profession to which I once belonged.

Significantly, an anticipation in prose of the unsavoury class-consciousness which later disguised itself as 'royalism' makes its first entry into the literary criticism in 'The Function of Criticism', the essay which as I read it divides the sceptical Eliot of the early essays from his more conformist successor. The mode of entry was via Murry's Inner Voice:

The inner voice, in fact, sounds remarkably like . . . 'doing as one likes'. The possessors of the inner voice ride ten in a compartment to a football match at Swansea, listening to the inner voice, which breathes the eternal message of vanity, fear, and lust.

The 'ten in a compartment', the football match, the selection of Swansea as the destination, are all sheer snobbery. May not the same message have been breathed to or from a rich friend of Eliot's, Lady Rothermere for example, riding alone in a first-class compartment to the Riviera? C. S. Lewis took up the point in that long-drawn argument he had with E. M. W. Tillyard called *The Personal Heresy*. Tillyard had applauded Eliot's disgust at the philistinism of what we might now call Commuter Land —all that is typified in this line from one of the choruses in *The Rock*,

> The land of lobelias and tennis flannels . . .

To Lewis, on the other hand, Eliot's whole attitude here was deplorable. This 'dismissing some tens of thousands of my fellow citizens' shocked and revolted him. When he returned to the passage and its key-line later in the argument it was to be even more dismissive:

> . . . for the proper pleasure of personality, that is, for love, we must go where it can be found—to our homes or our commons, to railway carriages and public houses, or even (for you see I am one of the vulgar) to the 'land of lobelias and tennis flannels.'[17]

Though no Lewisite I too am one of the vulgar.

In these examples, which could easily be multiplied, the prose has anticipated the poetry. Does the poetry also tend to be the *product* of the criticism? This is an approach that is the reverse of what Eliot would seem to be appropriating for himself in 'The Music of Poetry', though there is a contradiction in the implications of that essay that has been overlooked.

We begin by agreeing with him there that a valid distinction can be drawn between the practitioner-critic and the scholar-critic. W. P. Ker can no doubt typify the latter. It is the practitioner-critic who creates the difficulties. The recurrent thesis in 'The Music of Poetry' is that 'poetry must not stray too far from the everyday language which we use and hear' (p. 29), that 'Every revolution in poetry is apt to be . . . a return to common speech' (p. 31), that 'the task is to catch up with the change in colloquial speech' (p. 35), 'At a time like ours, when a refreshment of poetic diction similar to that brought about by Wordsworth had been called for' (p. 35), and that 'if the work of the last twenty years is worthy of being classified at all, it is as belonging to a period of search for a proper modern colloquial idiom' (p. 38). The essay is not unintelligent, but it becomes sleep-inducing as the same formulas turn up over and over again. And they beg the question of the changes in method and style in Eliot's later poetry. Since 1919 the sentence structure if not the vocabulary of his verse had in fact become less and less colloquial. How far if at all, one has to ask, are the formulas relevant to the poems Eliot was in fact writing at the time of his Glasgow homily?

The lecture was delivered in 1942, the year of the first edition of *Little Gidding*, *The Dry Salvages* having been published in 1941, *East Coker* in 1940, and *Burnt Norton* in the *Collected Poems* (1936). In other words, 'The Music of Poetry' belongs to the end of the *Four Quartets* period. In that context its doctrine of the desirability of a modern colloquial mode of speech in poetry can only be seen as a confession of personal error by Eliot comparable to the 1947 essay on Milton in which Eliot 'recanted' his 1936 depreciation. The point can be made more forcibly. From 1923 the poetry develops *independently* of the criticism—a non-relationship that may help to explain the general inferiority of both the later criticism and the later poetry. (I regard the status of *Four Quartets* as still an open question. There are, of course, some brilliant moments—notably the Dantesque air-raid episode in *Little Gidding*—but the writing is in general slack and tired, and too often merely pretentious, groping towards profundity by contortions of repetition.)

A characteristic of the later criticism is that it abhors specificity. It is all much too much up in the air. There is not enough concrete evidence produced at any one time. Thus in a volume that calls itself *On Poetry and Poets* one would expect the essays to be dotted, as the earlier poetic criticism had been, with quotations, however short, to illustrate or enforce the point under discussion. But in 'The Social Function of Poetry', 'The Music of Poetry', 'What is Minor Poetry?', and the second Milton lecture, all of them lectures of some length that must have taken nearly an hour to deliver, not one single line of poetry is quoted. 'What is a Classic?', one of the more interesting of the later essays, gets by without quoting a line until the very end, when we are dismissed with three valedictory lines from Dante. A few poets' names are occasionally inserted in this lecture, but it is always in the most casual way, and 'maturity', the concept on which the whole argument hinges, by not being illustrated is never properly defined. There are degrees of rarefication in the other pieces in the volume, one of the best surprisingly being on Kipling, but in general any quotations that do occur in the whole collection are not *used*. The situation is similar in the later collection *To Criticize the Critic* in which three of the six essays on literary topics do not offer us even one quotation. The two early items in this collection—'Ezra Pound: His Metric and Poetry' (originally a booklet published separately in New York) and 'Reflections on *Vers Libre*'—that were added 'In response to many requests'—illustrate immediately the difference between Eliot's earlier and later critical methods. The Pound piece (of 21 pages) quotes 124 lines of poetry and the short *Vers Libre* essay quotes 40 lines in its 7 pages.

The statistics I have just presented go some way to clarify a radical difference between the early and later criticism. The early essays derive their sceptical force from the continuous invitation in them to dig below the verbal or conventional surface. The Swinburne essay in *The Sacred Wood* is typical:

> . . . agreed that we do not (and I think that the present generation does not) greatly enjoy Swinburne, and agreed that (a more serious condemnation) at one period of our lives we did enjoy him and now no longer enjoy him; nevertheless, the words which we use to state our grounds of dislike or indifference cannot be applied to Swinburne as they can be to bad poetry.[18]

Eliot points out that to call Swinburne 'diffuse' in any pejorative sense simply won't do. That the material used in 'The Triumph

of Time' should have released 'such an amazing number of
words' *is* a kind of genius. And Swinburne's words, as Eliot makes
us look hard at them, are indeed very odd. (They excite enormously but with the minimum of meaning, all connotation with
practically no denotation.) Similarly, the essay on Massinger
begins by calling attention to the difference of kind between
some phrases of Shakespeare and Massinger's imitations of them.
Elsewhere in *The Sacred Wood* there is a differentiation of Marlowe from Spenser by comparing his plagiarism of a stanza from
The Faerie Queene with the Spenserian original. In the Dryden
essay parallel stanzas from him and Shelley are instructively
compared. And so on.

This mode of criticism naturally demanded the frequent use of
quotation. The young Eliot was primarily, as R. P. Blackmur once
pointed out,[19] a *technical* critic. But the technical analysis was
used to impose a more general re-assessment resulting eventually
in a dethronement of the conventional or Arnoldian values.
Behind the innovations of critical method, though Blackmur did
not realize it, there was in reality the propagation of a sceptical
social philosophy—one that had been nourished in verse by
Laforgue and in prose by Remy de Gourmont—that might have
seemed to herald the arrival of a new Voltaire. The explosive
possibilities of *The Sacred Wood* and the three *TLS* articles of
1921, published in 1924 as *Homage to John Dryden*, remain to
tantalize us. As things turned out these early essays—together
with those others still uncollected, which Valerie Eliot is
rumoured to be reprinting shortly (the best appeared in the
Athenaeum)—became unfortunately the ancestral gods of the
non-political I. A. Richards and the dead-end critics of American
'explication'. It need not have been so, if Eliot had not had the
break-down in September 1921.

In some ways the essay on Blake provides the best example in
The Sacred Wood of the enormous extra-literary potentialities of
Eliot's early criticism. Blake's peculiarity, it will be remembered,
was what Eliot called his honesty, 'which, in a world too
frightened to be honest, is peculiarly terrifying'. The world con-
spires against it, preferring to the *Songs of Experience* the so-
called Prophetic Books written after Blake too had himself become
too terrified to be honest. But Blake's ultimate greatness is proved,

in Eliot's remarkable words, by his best poetry having 'the un-
pleasantness of great poetry'. It was a novel, indeed revolutionary
criterion and it points the way Eliot's criticism might have developed after 1921 if he too had not succumbed—for entirely
intelligible reasons with which it is impossible not to sympathize
—to the embrace of our terrified world.

2

Eliot and the *Criterion*

DENIS DONOGHUE

There is pretty general agreement that the *Criterion* failed in its purposes and that the failure is not fully explained as one small instance of the immense failure of Europe in the years between 1922 and 1939. The failure is more immediate and personal than such an account would imply. The standard by which the enterprise may be judged a failure is indicated by pointing to the *Nouvelle Revue Française* under Jean Paulhan from 1925 to 1940 and *Scrutiny* under F. R. Leavis from 1932 to 1953 as examples of success however qualified. I am aware that the sense in which NRF and *Scrutiny* may be said to have succeeded is not self-evident and that the qualifications which ought to be attached to that judgement are considerable in each case, but I have no doubt that the judgement could be sustained. It will be agreed, I suppose, that a magazine is a success in the sense we have in mind if its principles are serious in themselves and continuously tested by specific judgements and provocations. The influence of a magazine upon the minds of its readers and thereafter upon the minds of people who have read it casually or not at all is often a matter of luck. Some magazines have failed in practice which would not have failed if principle and intelligence were sufficient to ensure success. But it would be absurd to claim success for a magazine which had little or no influence upon its readers. Leavis's *Scrutiny* and Paulhan's NRF in their different ways demanded from their readers not the mild assent which attends upon urbanity but a responsiveness commensurate with the urgency of their editors. By this standard, which makes energy a moral principle, Leavis and Paulhan succeed where Eliot fails. Readers of the *Criterion* do not regularly feel themselves impelled to care.

The magazine began in October 1922. At the end of the first volume Eliot defined the purpose of a literary review:

A literary review should maintain the application, in literature, of principles which have their consequences also in politics and in private conduct; and it should maintain them without tolerating any confusion of the purposes of pure literature with the purposes of politics or ethics.

In the common mind all interests are confused, and each degraded by the confusion. And where they are confused, they cannot be related; in the common mind any specialized activity is conceived as something isolated from life, an odious task or a pastime of mandarins. To maintain the autonomy, and the disinterestedness, of every human activity, and to perceive it in relation to every other, require a considerable discipline. It is the function of a literary review to maintain the autonomy and disinterestedness of literature, and at the same time to exhibit the relations of literature—not to 'life', as something contrasted to literature, but to all the other activities, which, together with literature, are the components of life.

(i. 421)

The reference to 'pure literature' is odd, and it points to a certain insecurity of principle beneath the ostensibly strict categories. If you read literature it is as literature that you must read it, and not as another thing: well and good. But there is an obscure place between that position and the defence of literature in terms of its autonomy and disinterestedness. When literature is most compelling, these are not the terms we feel inclined to invoke in its defence. In January 1926, when Eliot's magazine appeared as the *New Criterion*, he moved away from the idiom of autonomy and disinterestedness to note 'the impossibility of defining the frontiers, or limiting the context of "literature"':

Even the purest literature is alimented from non-literary sources, and has non-literary consequences. Pure literature is a chimera of sensation; admit the vestige of an idea and it is already transformed. (iv.4)

The particular idea or value which Eliot invoked on that occasion was 'classicism', which he described as a tendency 'toward a higher and clearer conception of Reason, and a more severe and serene control of the emotions by Reason', a tendency exemplified in such works as Sorel's *Réflexions sur la violence*, Maurras's *L'Avenir de l'intelligence*, Benda's *Belphégor*, T. E. Hulme's *Speculations*, Maritain's *Réflexions sur l'intelligence*, and Irving Babbitt's *Democracy and Leadership* (iv.5). These books, and the tendency which Eliot admired and welcomed in them, stimulated him to name other books which represented 'that part of the present which is already dead': H. G. Wells's *Christina Alberta's Father*, Shaw's *St Joan*, and Bertrand Russell's *What I Believe*. The autonomy and disinterestedness of literature ceased to be a major theme in Eliot's magazine at this stage. Instead, the *New Criterion* was offered in January 1927 as a vehicle 'for the various, divergent or even contradictory opinion of a widening group of individuals in communication' (v.2). This programme led to the experiment of running the magazine as a monthly: it became the *Monthly Criterion* in May 1927, but reverted to its proper name and condition in June 1928 as a quarterly, the *Criterion*. The magazine continued to be a literary review, but only in the sense in which such a review publishes essays on politics, religion, history, as well as literature. In its later years the *Criterion* became in something of the old sense a 'quarterly review'. In January 1936 Eliot defined the function of such reviews as concerned 'with political philosophy, rather than with politics, and with the examination of the fundamental ideas of philosophies rather than with the problems of application' (xv.265). One reason for the failure of the magazine is that it never fully knew itself, it did not understand the nature of its talent. Classicism, which the *Criterion* undertook to define and serve, failed to become the spirit of the age. When that failure became clear, the nobility and austerity of Eliot's purposes could not save the magazine from eccentricity: at the end, in 1939, it was clear that the values which Eliot sponsored were in chaos.

The purposes are clear; the only pity is that they were bound to fail. Eliot's aim in the *Criterion* was to bring to bear upon the individual talent of his English readers and writers the force of tradition as manifested in 'the mind of Europe': the whole enterprise was conceived as an attack upon native provincialism. In August 1927 he welcomed 'the European Idea' and the diversity of its forms: it may include, he said, 'a meditation on the decay of European civilization by Paul Valéry, or a philosophy of history such as that of Oswald Spengler', or it may appear 'allied with an intense nationalism as in the work of Henri Massis' (vi.98). In any version the European Idea was a response to the Russian Revolution, 'for the Russian Revolution has made men conscious of the position of Western Europe as (in Valéry's words) a small and isolated cape on the western side of the Asiatic Continent: and this awareness seems to be giving rise to a new European consciousness' (vi.98). The European Idea was congenial to Eliot not only because of its intrinsic value and the opulence of its content but because it enabled him once again to employ, at least in theory, a fundamental paradigm of his mind: bringing to bear upon the matter in hand the force of a larger perspective, an ancient discipline. The matter in hand was the state of contemporary English culture: the ancient discipline included a true sense of the past, a response to other cultures, other times, Greece and Rome, the mind of Europe. The critic's aim is to bring 'the art of the past to bear upon the present, making it relevant to the actual generation' (the *Egoist*, May 1918). In the *Athenaeum* (1 August 1919) Eliot wrote of discipline in the same spirit. 'We suppose', he said,

> a mind which is not only the English mind of one period with its prejudices of politics and fashions of taste, but which is a greater, finer, more positive, more comprehensive mind than the mind of any period. And we suppose to each writer an importance which is not only individual, but due to his place as a constituent of this mind.

Eliot took pride, therefore, in publishing in the *Criterion* essays by various critics on Flaubert, Joyce, Mallarmé, Balzac, Proust, Chekhov, Kipling, Virginia Woolf and Laforgue: translations of Dostoevsky, Benda, Pirandello, Valéry, Rivière, Hofmannsthal, Cavafy, Maritain, Maurras, Scheler, Montale; and setting these items beside work by Yeats, Pound, Joyce, Forster, Ford, Lawrence, Wyndham Lewis, Middleton Murry, Herbert Read, Clive Bell, I. A. Richards, Aldous Huxley, Gertrude Stein, T. Sturge Moore, T. E. Hulme, Hart Crane, Chesterton, Harold Laski, Allen Tate. The dispute about Romanticism and Classicism

which agitated Eliot and the *Criterion* from 1924 to 1926 arose
not only from the influence of Babbitt and the exacerbation of
Middleton Murry's recourse to the Inner Voice but from Eliot's
tendency to see each occasion as a symptom of vanity and
provincialism: the only cure was the discipline of a grand perspective. In October 1923 he spoke of the difference between
Classicism and Romanticism as 'the difference between the complete and the fragmentary, the adult and the immature, the
orderly and the chaotic' (ii.34). The romantic 'is deficient or un-
developed in his ability to distinguish between fact and fancy,
whereas the classicist, or adult mind, is thoroughly realist—
without illusions, without day-dreams, without hope, without
bitterness, and with an abundant resignation' (ii.39). In the same
spirit Eliot asserted that '*all* European civilisations are equally
dependent upon Greece and Rome—so far as they are civilisations
at all' (ii.104). Our categories of thought, he maintained, are
largely the outcome of Greek thought, our categories of emotion
largely the outcome of Greek literature. 'Neglect of Greek means
for Europe *a relapse into unconsciousness*' (iii. 342). Hence
the question Eliot posed in April 1926: 'Are there enough
persons in Britain believing in that European culture, the Roman
inheritance, believing in the place of Britain in that culture,
and believing in themselves?' (iv. 222). Provincialism was
Britain's low dream: what Eliot invoked was the high dream of
Europe:

> The peculiar position of Britain is this: that she is on the one
> hand a part of Europe. But not only a part, she is a mediating
> part: for Britain is the bridge between Latin culture and
> Germanic culture in both of which she shares. (viii.194)

Against the Whiggery of the Inner Voice, therefore, Eliot proposed to set the mind of Europe: imperial Virgil, Classicism,
Order, the categories of Greece and Rome, Dante's precision and
lucidity, and ultimately that 'pattern laid up in Heaven', the
City of God.

This is not the place in which to examine yet again Eliot's
sense of Tradition: it has been severely treated by several critics
and notably by Graham Hough in his *Image and Experience*.
I will make only a brief comment on the matter. A reader of

Eliot ought to take seriously the idea of a tradition in some enabling relation to a writer's individual talent; if not, he must settle for the wisdom of the inner voice. Eliot's particular notion of tradition is vulnerable not in principle but in practice; not because its constituents, when he chooses to produce them, are eccentric or ignoble—they are not—but because he failed to bring them to bear upon any matter in hand. The mind of Europe and the mind of Britain are negotiable ideas, but Eliot deployed them as parallel lines of force, one superior to the other, and they never meet. The *Criterion* published a respectable list of French and German writers, but it did not find or make a point of contact where one force would really impinge upon another. The problem inherent in every form of thought which invokes the figures of perspective is that the mind finds it easier to gain altitude than to retain contact with the particular details of experience. It is quite possible to distinguish between political philosophy and politics and to concern oneself with the first rather than the second. Eliot did not edit a daily newspaper or a weekly magazine, he was not obliged to offer a judgement upon every theme or event. Many events are properly judged by time and by the tendency of one event to supersede another. But the distance between Eliot's mind and daily events was congenial to him, a temperamental choice rather than a matter of chance, True, he was agile in its defence, and very often he was in the happy position of pointing to the absurdity of those who had rushed forward with premature opinions and allegiances. But often, in the presence of an event which could not be ignored, recourse to a grand perspective merely silenced Eliot or consigned him to the ablative state of being neither fish nor flesh.

Take for instance Eliot's position in January 1937 when the Spanish Civil War was an inescapable concern, dividing men into Left and Right. The British Government insisted upon remaining neutral. Most of the intellectuals supported the Popular Front, *New Writing* was about to appear, the *Left Book Club* was to concentrate the force of feeling against the National Front. Auden, Beckett, Spender, Ford, Middleton Murry and many other writers spoke and wrote for the Popular Front, composing battle hymns for the Republic. A few voices spoke for the National Front; a few stayed neutral, notably Pound, Wells and

Eliot. It is still possible to argue that neutrality was the wisest position to hold. Much of the rhetoric lavished upon Left and Right now appears silly. But Eliot's version of neutrality is chilling, because it is facile in the assumption of a perspective far beyond the fray. 'One might think', he said,

> after perusing a paper like the *New Statesman*, that the elected Government of Spain represented an enlightened and progressive Liberalism; and from reading *The Tablet* one might be persuaded that the rebels were people who, after enduring with patience more than one would expect human beings to be able to stand, had finally and reluctantly taken to arms as the only way left in which to save Christianity and civilization.

Eliot then posited 'an ideally unprejudiced person with an intimate knowledge of Spain' who would be in a position to arrive at a proper judgement. Excusing himself from these qualifications, he maintained that 'so long as we are not compelled in our own interest to take sides, I do not see why we should do so on insufficient knowledge: and even any eventual partisanship should be held with reservations, humility and misgiving'. Up to this point the argument is reasonable; though it raises a doubt about the merit of pursuing the study of political philosophy if it must retire at the first touch of a political situation. The next paragraph—I am still quoting from Eliot's 'Commentary', January 1937—is shrewd in its assessment of both Fronts:

> Whichever side wins will not be the better for having had to fight for its victory. The victory of the Right will be the victory of a secular Right, not of a spiritual Right, which is a very different thing; the victory of the Left will be the victory of the worst rather than of the best features; and if it ends in something called Communism, that will be a travesty of the humanitarian ideals which have led so many people in that direction. And those who have at heart the interests of Christianity in the long run—which is not quite the same thing as a nominal respect paid to an ecclesiastical hierarchy with a freedom circumscribed by the interests of a secular State—have especial reason for suspending judgement. (xvi. 290)

But there is one sentence which defines Eliot's perspective as a point of view far higher than that required for the discharge of a plague upon both Fronts:

> That balance of mind which a few highly-civilized individuals, such as Arjuna, the hero of the *Bhagavad-Gita*, can maintain in action, is difficult for most of us even as observers, and, as I say, is not encouraged by the greater part of the Press.
> (xvi. 290)

The irony which sets the *Bhagavad-Gita* as a rebuke to 'the greater part of the Press' is exorbitant if not gratuitous: the *Bhagavad-Gita*, 'the next greatest philosophical poem to the *Divine Comedy* within my experience', as Eliot reported in his essay on Dante (*Selected Essays*, 1951, p. 258). The third section of 'The Dry Salvages' paraphrases Krishna's advice to Arjuna as part of the admonition to

> consider the future
> And the past with an equal mind.

The passage, glancing at Cantos II and VIII of the *Bhagavad-Gita*, reads as follows:

> 'At the moment which is not of action or inaction
> You can receive this: "on whatever sphere of being
> The mind of a man may be intent
> At the time of death"—that is the one action
> (And the time of death is every moment)
> Which shall fructify in the lives of others:
> And do not think of the fruit of action.
> Fare forward.
>   O voyagers, O seamen,
> You who come to port, and you whose bodies
> Will suffer the trial and judgement of the sea,
> Or whatever event, this is your real destination.'
> So Krishna, as when he admonished Arjuna
> On the field of battle.
>   Not fare well,
> But fare forward, voyagers.
> (*Collected Poems* 1909–1962, p. 211)

This is convincing in the poem because a justifying place has been prepared for it; we are possessed by the spirit of the *Four Quartets* as a whole, responsive to a superior perspective thoroughly earned. In the *Criterion* commentary the reference to Arjuna is not earned, it is set down on a page which has done nothing to justify it. The moral superiority which it claims cannot appear as anything but bleak indifference, pointing not toward the grandeur of the *Quartets* but toward a lesser work of this period, *The Family Reunion*, and to the snobbery of a hero, Harry Monchensey, for which Eliot later apologised. As it happens, we have fairly close at hand an example of precisely the kind of application of political philosophy to a political situation which a man in Eliot's position might reasonably have been expected to produce on the occasion of the Spanish Civil War. Jacques Maritain contributed a preface to Alfred Mendizabal's account of the origins of the War, *Aux Origines d'une Tragédie*. Eliot arranged to have the book reviewed by Middleton Murry, who praised it and particularly welcomed Maritain's preface for its application of principles of moral theology to the problems of modern politics (*Criterion*, xvii.721). Eliot himself mentioned the matter when Maritain was attacked by Serrano Suner, Franco's Minister of the Interior, for refusing to endorse the claim that the war of the Franquistas was 'a holy war' (xviii.58). Clearly, Maritain emerges more impressively than Eliot from this episode. It was entirely proper of Eliot to praise Maritain and to rebuke Suner: let that be acknowledged. But Maritain's effort to concentrate his mind and bring the force of Christian philosophy to bear upon a complicated situation in Spain is a noble enterprise, and it makes Eliot's stance appear morally lazy rather than lofty or disinterested. The separation of political philosophy from politics seems to me in this case a stratagem rather than a principle. I suspect that Eliot was drawn to make the separation mainly because he could not find any secure means by which the mind could intervene in history. History whose 'cunning passages, contrived corridors' are delineated in 'Gerontion' was fatally obscure to Eliot. I do not mean that his historical sense was weaker than anyone else's, but that he regarded history as a cave of error, its very elements obscure. The second part of 'The Dry Salvages' refers to

The backward look behind the assurance
Of recorded history, the backward half-look
Over the shoulder, towards the primitive terror.

Eliot was peculiarly sensitive to the primitive terror and regarded
the assurance of recorded history as vanity, Madame Sosostris's
connivance with our 'whispering ambitions'. If history is what
happens to politics, politics is bound to be deceptive, mostly
bogus, alien to those who would consider the future and the past
with an equal mind. I am not accusing Eliot of triviality or
evasiveness. I am offering an explanation for the recourse to
perspectivist thought, principles cut adrift from applications and
circumstances, and Eliot's insecurity in the presence of a political
act.

The insecurity shows itself most clearly in the editorial aspects
of the magazine, the relation between general policy and its embodiment in poems, essays, reviews. Eliot always set his face
against coterie-journals, he had no ambition to use contributors
as mere extensions of himself. He wanted contributors who
would be bound together by a very loose act of fellowship and
communication. In practice, this meant not bound at all. The
editor's hand upon the *Criterion* is a feeble thing, so far as it is
exerted in the choice of contributors and themes: it is much
stronger when it is felt in relation to Eliot's own writing. The
most valuable essays in the *Criterion* are Eliot's Commentaries.
They may appear random, often devoted to matters which not
even Eliot's most vivid prose has been able to keep alive, but it is
precisely their occasional nature which keeps the commentaries
strong. Eliot was addressing himself not to major international
events which he could bear to contemplate only from the heights
of Arjuna, but to rather small-scale themes provided by the
events of the day, week, month. He had no difficulty in effecting
entry to these themes, he had merely to apply his intelligence to
the matter in hand. The distinction between political philosophy
and politics did not arise: in most cases Eliot was commenting
upon local events as symptoms of the general state of affairs in
the cultural life of England. The themes I recall include the
destruction of London's churches, plans for the extension of
Westminster Abbey, the idea of a national theatre, Bertrand

Russell, Diaghilev, F. H. Bradley, Yeats, Conrad, Shaw, the substitution in the new Prayer Book of 'infinite' for 'incomprehensible' and of 'eternal' for 'everlasting', the question of censor-
ship, Kipling, Arnold, Marxist criticism, Irving Babbitt, Paris,
anthologies, monarchy, A. R. Orage, the National Trust. There
are only a few Commentaries which meditate upon larger questions; notably a crucial essay on the nature of belief (xii.468–73)
and another one, equally important, on the relation between past
and present. I shall make one or two comments on this latter
essay.

The occasion was the publication of a book by Ernst Robert
Curtius, *Deutscher Geist in Gefahr,* a collection of essays on
sociology and humanism. Eliot was particularly interested in
Curtius's essay on Karl Mannheim, 'a contemporary sociologist
named Mannheim, of whose work I am ignorant', he confessed
(October 1932), 'and who has hitherto been only a name to me'.
Curtius remarked that for Mannheim and many other thinkers
there appeared to be a crude antithesis between Change and
Value on the one side and Permanence and Valuelessness on the
other. Eliot took up the theme at that point, associating the antithesis with the year 1910, 'the pleasant essays of William James
(as popular a writer for his time as are Eddington and Jeans in
ours) and with the epidemic of Bergsonism'. The antithesis was
also seen in the popularity of a distinction between 'static' (bad)
and 'dynamic' (good). The common tendency, Eliot argued, was
to misrepresent the relation between the eternal and the transient, and therefore to lend exaggerated value to our own time.
The doctrine of progress, 'while it can do little to make the future
more real to us, has a very strong influence towards making the
past less real to us':

The notion that a past age or civilization might be great
in itself, precious in the eye of God, because it succeeded
in adjusting the delicate relation of the Eternal and the
Transient, is completely alien to us. No age has been more
ego-centric, so to speak, than our own; others have been ego-
centric through ignorance, ours through complacent historical
knowledge. Everything in the past was a necessary evil—evil
in itself, but necessary because it led up to the present. Thus

we take ourselves, and our transient affairs, too seriously.
(vii. 75)

Eliot then applies this consideration to the question of criticism:

All great art is in a sense a document on its time; but great art
is never merely a document, for mere documentation is not art.
All great art has something permanent and universal about
it, and reflects the permanent as well as the changing—a
particular relation in time of the permanent and the transient.
And as no great art is explicable simply by the society of its
time, so it is not fully explicable simply by the personality of
its author: in the greatest poetry there is always a hint of
something behind, something impersonal, something in relation to which the author has been no more than the passive
(if not always pure) medium. A good deal of brilliant criticism
seems to me wasted labour just because it ignores the enduring
in favour of the topical. (xii.76–7)

Eliot turns at this point to the question of Communism, but there
is no need to follow him, he says what we would expect him to
say. The sentences about the relation between past and present
may be read as parts of an argument which Eliot deploys in
'Tradition and the Individual Talent' (1919), the essays on
Babbitt and Humanism (1928–9), the comments on Secularism
in 'Religion and Literature' (1935) and later work on the idea of
a Christian society and the definition of Culture. Or they may be
read as a prose gloss upon the lines about progress in the second
part of 'The Dry Salvages'. Or we may ask ourselves to what
extent the argument of these sentences is still valid. The sentences were written in 1932, we are reading them or re-reading
them in 1977: are they still alive? It seems clear to me that our
time is just as egocentric as Eliot's was and that our alienation
from the past is just as extreme. Ours is not a generation noted
either for its historical sense or for its respect for gone times.
It is difficult to describe the spirit of an age and it may be that in
emphasizing the movements of contemporary thought which are,
however vaguely, structuralist in tendency, we are mistaking the
ephemeral for the significant. But structuralist thought certainly
presents itself as congenial to the age in maintaining that the
crucial questions about literature and society are structural and

synchronic, concerned primarily with the enabling relation between a writer's imagination and the linguistic codes which are available to him. It is widely maintained that these codes mark the outer limit of a writer's expression. *Parole* is a subdivision of *langue*. I recite these commonplaces only to make the point that structuralist thought connives with anyone who wishes to disown the past. The relations deemed to be important are not those which require on the writer's part either a sense of the past or an ethical scruple in the use of language. Structuralist assumptions have no place for that 'something permanent and universal' to which Eliot refers, or for the 'something behind, something impersonal, something in relation to which the author has been no more than the passive (if not always pure) medium'. The last phrase may prompt us to say that the force of that 'something' is exerted, for structuralist thought, by language; as if language were entirely capable of exerting the same pressure upon individual talents which Eliot construed as being exerted by tradition. This is simply not true. Graham Hough has argued that tradition, however we choose to define it, is acquired, even by major poets, in a much more selective way than Eliot's account of it implies: that Keats, for instance, got from Milton and two or three favourite poets as much nourishment as his art needed or could assimilate. Poets do not move among masterpieces as Erich Auerbach or Ernst Robert Curtius did. The point is well taken, but it does not alter the essential argument. Eliot uses the idea of tradition to stir our consciences, reminding us of values which we have ignored, forgotten, or abused. Tradition in his sense is not a Great Books course, it is designed to do the work of ethics rather than of knowledge or learning. Indeed, if Eliot's idea of tradition is to be resented or repudiated, it must be because he deploys it like a moral terrorist, not because he is naive in prescribing a course of reading for poets. Because the single fact which can be established in regard to Eliot's idea of tradition is that he has in mind a preferential structure of values. Indeed, the most accurate comparison I can suggest would associate Eliot's idea of tradition not with an ethically neutral concept of language but with the idea of ecclesiastical dogma. It is significant that in his later writings Eliot ascribed to orthodoxy the work he had once ascribed to tradition. Continuity between these two

terms makes it clear that the central meaning of tradition in
Eliot's use of the term makes it, to start with, a secular version
of dogma or doctrine, a structure of values, choices, preferences
and commitments. When he became a Christian he merely trans-
posed the term into a specifically doctrinal idiom. I have referred
to the central meaning of the term, because I am aware that on
some occasions Eliot used the word tradition to mean the loose
system of habits and assumptions which a man acquires by being
born and growing up in a particular place. It would not be
difficult to show, however, that on the whole Eliot favoured a
definition of tradition which makes it something we have to
labour to acquire rather than something we acquire naturally
and thoughtlessly. The 'something behind, something impersonal' to which he refers is therefore nothing as permissive as a
structuralist's 'language' but a force of ethical or quasi-ethical
choices and preferences: it is that to which one's conscience
listens, when it is active and scrupulous. Of course there is more
to be said on this theme. My account is designed merely to
suggest how Eliot's sentences may be read for their present bearing rather than as footnotes to 'The Dry Salvages'.

I have laboured the recourse to perspectivism in Eliot's editing
because it accounts for the favourite gestures of his rhetoric.
When two ideologies are ostensibly opposed, he declares that the
differences are accidental. Communism and Capitalism 'are only
forms of the same thing' (xii.642). 'We should learn', Eliot
asserted, 'that one kind of sham is offered to the public when
decadence is in vogue, and another when *revolution* is in vogue;
and that they may be at bottom the same old sham' (xii. 470).
In October 1930 the Labour Government's policy appeared to
differ from the previous Conservative Government's policy: no,
'it is the same old policy after all' (x.2). Deploring the General
Election of 1929 as an 'undesirable luxury', Eliot predicted that
the results would include 'the usual waste of time, money and
energy, a very small vote in consequence of the increased number
of voters, and the return, known to Dryden, of "old consciences
with new faces"' (viii.377). When people were exercised about
Communism and Capitalism, or it might be about nearly any
ideological rivalry, Eliot's temper inclined him to say: 'the combat
of Tweedledum and Tweedledee is not likely to lead to any

millenium' (x.715). Spending a Commentary upon Harold Laski's *An Introduction to Politics* and Lord Lymington's *Ich Dien: The Tory Path*, Eliot mocked Laski for the intellectual shoddiness of his Socialism, and mocked Lymington equally for thinking of Toryism as 'something to be revived, instead of something to be invented'. Socialism and Conservatism, if these authors gave true accounts of their creeds, were absurdly shallow answers to Bolshevism. 'The Bolsheviks at any rate believe in something which has what is equivalent for them to a supernatural sanction; and it is only with a genuine supernatural sanction that we can oppose it' (xi.71). This marks a common pattern in Eliot's rhetoric. Take two forces between which public opinion appears to be divided. Show that each is in its own way defective, and not only defective but demonstrably inferior to some gross ideology (Communism, Fascism, or whatever). Then triumph over the winning ideology by recourse to a higher creed, 'a genuine supernatural sanction', Christianity. Eliot's liveliest Commentaries are those in which this rhetorical pattern is most powerfully active.

But it is impossible to escape the conclusion that Eliot's work on the *Criterion* declined in buoyancy as the years went on. Indeed, the plain facts are that his magazine dealt with real issues between 1922 and 1939 and yet that its engagement with these issues became increasingly helpless. Eliot's own themes make the point. He begins with Marie Lloyd, 'the expressive figure of the lower classes', praised mainly because she embodied the virtues of the only class in England that had any real virtues to define, the middle classes being 'morally corrupt' and the aristocracy scared (i.194). But Eliot's sense of lower-class vitality did not amount to a conviction that a genuine culture would flower from that soil. Within a short time he was immersed in a sense of 'the political and economic anarchy of the present time': that was 1927, the year in which the *Criterion* occupied itself with the question of Intelligence and Intuition, Middleton Murry's question being answered in various idioms by Eliot, Martin D'Arcy, Ramon Fernandez, T. Sturge Moore and Charles Mauron. The question was exacerbated by further considerations of the issue of Romanticism and Classicism, the terminologies of Order, and in 1928 the Vatican's condemnation of the *Action*

Française. From 1929 to the end the *Criterion* concerned itself mainly with Fascism, Communism, Humanism and Religion (More, Foerster, Fernandez again, and Chesterton), Property, Money, Economics, the theory of Value, and Literature pitched rather desperately into these contexts. On most of these questions Eliot's attitudes, when they declare themselves, seem to me entirely worthy. On Fascism, for instance, he argued that it did not contain any idea of general interest, and as a religious faith it was 'humbug'. Admittedly, the question he chose to ask about Fascism was not the one which would now seem to have been most urgent in December 1928: 'whether Fascism is the emergence of a new political idea or the recrudescence of an old one'. In July 1929 he maintained that Fascism as an idea was utterly sterile, 'the natural idea for the thoughtless person'; nothing more than 'a combination of statements with unexamined enthusiasms'. 'In the *success* of a man like Mussolini (a man of "the people") a whole nation may feel a kind of self-flattery; and the Russian people deified itself in Lenin', Eliot argued. 'Both Italy and Russia seem to me to be suffering from Napoleonism' (viii.690). It is clear that Eliot, faced in England with a society which had not entertained a new political idea since Fabianism, was asking whether or not there was anything new and useful in Fascism. His answer was: no. He confessed that he preferred the Fascist form of unreason to the Communist form of unreason, but he thought his own form of unreason more reasonable than either. He made no bones about his feeling that democratic government in England was already 'watered down to nothing'. 'From the moment when the suffrage is conceived as a *right* instead of as a privilege and a duty and a responsibility, we are on the way merely to government by an invisible oligarchy instead of government by a visible one.' This is at least an arguable position, there is nothing stupid or vicious in Eliot's words. Now that the question of democratic government and its consequences has emerged again from the current political and economic crisis as something that must be discussed, Eliot's observations should be examined in a more objective spirit than critics have been willing to produce. 'The modern question,' he wrote, 'as popularly put is: "democracy is dead; what is to replace it?", whereas it should be: "the frame of democracy has been des-

troyed: how can we, out of the materials at hand, buil.. a new
structure in which democracy can live?".' But as one reads
through the subsequent volumes of the *Criterion* one finds it
increasingly clear that Eliot could not think of building anything
from the materials at hand. The 'Commentary' for October 1930,
for instance, should be read in full as evidence that Eliot despised
what passed for 'life' in England and detested those politicians
who conspired to enforce, instead of genuine spiritual values, the
mechanical criterion of 'the standard of living'. Eliot was dis-
gusted by the form in which the debate was presented: to engage
in debate on those terms meant yielding up the only terms, quali-
tative and spiritual, in which he was really interested. In 1936
when the public air was dense with arguments about war and
peace, he was irritated by special pleading on the concept of a
just war. At one point the Bishop of Durham asserted that 'it is
the quite evident duty of English Christians to support the
Government in whatever efforts and sacrifices that policy may
involve'. Eliot was exasperated by the euphemistic cant of
'efforts and sacrifices' when the plain meaning was 'war', and he
enquired, barely restraining his impatience with the whole
debate:

> Then which comes first: the 'quite evident duty' to support the
> Government, or the duty, previously enjoined by the Bishop,
> of every man to 'follow his conscience at all hazards'? And if
> the Bishop falls back, as he does, on the Latin text of the
> XXXVIIth Article, are there not two interpretations of *licet*
> ('it is lawful') possible? Surely it is possible for the Latin or
> even the English to mean, merely that a thing is *permissible*,
> without being (as the Bishop seems to take it) *obligatory*. The
> former meaning seems, according to dictionaries, to be more
> primitive and radical. I have found no guidance in the Bishop
> of Durham's letter. (xv.664)

In happier times Eliot would have enjoyed breaking a lance
against the Bishop and consulting the respectable Latin diction-
aries for sanction, but his heart was not engaged in the dispute,
he could not rid himself of distaste for an age in which a sensible
man was obliged to waste his spirit upon such matters. It is clear
from the remainder of the Commentary (July 1936) that Eliot

wanted to turn a shoddy story of crime and punishment into a drama of sin and expiation: another occasion for moving to the higher perspective of theology and truth:

> It is almost impossible to say anything about the subject with-
> out being misunderstood by one or both parties of *simplifiers*.
> (Yet Aeschylus, at least, understood that it may be a man's
> duty to commit a crime, and to accomplish his expiation for it.)

One parenthetical sentence removes the debate to a higher ground; or rather, to a ground where it can no longer be carried on as a debate but pursued, each man for his own salvation, in terms of penance and humility:

> The economic causes are the most accessible and the most
> amenable; even though they are only abstractions from the
> general stupidity and sinfulness of mankind. The problem of
> conscience towards war is far too deeply rooted in the general
> problem of evil to be settled by letters to *The Times*. (xv.665)

In such a perspective very few topics of the day are worth discussing. Eliot was already moving to a situation in which it would appear pointless to continue issuing the *Criterion*.

The magazine ceased in January 1939, the 71st number. The local reason was that the imminence of the war made further publication impossible. But that reason is not convincing; *Scrutiny* managed to continue during the war. The real reason is that Eliot was too depressed to continue, he had lost enthusiasm for the work, he felt himself going stale. In October 1938 he said that 'there seems no hope in contemporary politics at all' (xviii.60). It was not merely that the Labour Party and the Conservative Party were equally futile, but that the idea upon which the *Criterion* was sustained had obviously collapsed. 'The mind of Europe', 'which one had mistakenly thought might be renewed and fortified', Eliot wrote in the final *Criterion*, 'disappeared from view'. There was another factor:

> For myself, a right political philosophy came more and more to
> imply a right theology—and right economics to depend upon
> right ethics: leading to emphases which somewhat stretched
> the original framework of a literary review. (xviii.272)

Otherwise put: it was time to take to the hills and continue the
fight by altering its rules.

In 1946 Eliot gave three broadcast talks with German listeners
in mind: they are printed in an Appendix to *Notes Towards the
Definition of Culture* (1948). In the first, speaking of the unity of
European culture', he referred to three elements which an artist
would find himself acknowledging: 'the local tradition, the
common European tradition, and the influence of the art of one
European country upon another' (p. 114). In the second talk
Eliot reviewed the history of the *Criterion*, starting with its original aims, to bring together 'the best in new thinking and new
writing in its time, from all the countries of Europe that had
anything to contribute to the common good', and 'to establish
relations with those literary periodicals abroad, the aims of which
corresponded most nearly to my own', the list including the
Nouvelle Revue Française, the *Neue Rundschau*, the *Neue
Schweizer Rundschau*, the *Revista de Occidente*, and *Il Con-
vegno*. Eliot then described the common basis of these magazines,
including the *Criterion*, as 'a common concern for the highest
standards both of thought and of expression . . . a common curiosity and openness of mind to new ideas' (p. 117). 'For the health
of the culture of Europe', he said, 'two conditions are required:
that the culture of each country should be unique, and that the
different cultures should recognise their relationship to each
other.' This recognition is possible 'because there is a common
element in European culture, an interrelated history of thought
and feeling and behaviour, an interchange of arts and of ideas'
(p. 119). The failure of the *Criterion* Eliot attributed 'to the
gradual closing of the mental frontiers of Europe', and its 'numb-
ing effect upon creative activity within every country' (p. 116).
The moral of the story is that 'a universal concern with politics
does not unite, it divides: it unites those politically minded folk
who agree, across the frontiers of nations, against some other
international group who hold opposed views; but it tends to
destroy the cultural unity of Europe' (p. 117). In the third talk
Eliot spoke of the constituents of culture, and emphasised 'the
common tradition of Christianity which has made Europe what
it is' (p. 122).

The history of the *Criterion* falls with desolate precision into two periods. From 1922 to about 1930 the magazine sustained itself upon the general sense of a new literature: *The Waste Land, Ulysses, The Magic Mountain,* the later volumes of *A la recherche du temps perdu, Charmes, Harmonium,* and Pound's early Cantos. Even when Eliot's magazine wrote of other things or remained silent upon some of these things, its buoyancy was animated by a sense of contemporary bearing, its presence at the centre. After seven or eight years the exhilaration of taking part in a new movement of feeling wearied of itself, the magazine began to confuse itself between a desperate knowledge of its purposes and another knowledge, only more desperate, that it was faced with forces which it could not assimilate to the idiom of political philosophy. In 1931 Ezra Pound thought the *Criterion* had gone soft: 'Far be it from me to deny or affirm or in any way uncriterionisticly to commit myself on the subject of Mr. Fletcher's ignorance or the reverse . . .' (x.730). In the following year F. R. Leavis referred to 'the general regret that the name of the *Criterion* has become so dismal an irony and that the Editor is so far from applying to his contributors the standards we have learnt from him' (*A Selection from Scrutiny,* 1968, i, p. 174), It may be said that Eliot, lest the *Criterion* become a coterie-magazine, hoped that a general fellowship of interests would make it unnecessary for him to apply to his contributors, in anything like Dr Leavis's sense, the standards he defined and exemplified in *The Sacred Wood.* A somewhat blunt comment must also be included, that Eliot himself was not trained or otherwise fitted to act with the full resources of his mind upon the level of high and general principles which he proposed to occupy. He was a trained philosopher, highly competent in the finer points of philosophical idealism. He was a poet of genius. But he was not versed in political philosophy, if by that phrase we mean the discipline of thought we find in Michael Oakeshott, Hannah Arendt, Karl Popper. By temperament, Eliot's interest was in the definition of principles: when we refer to a grand perspective we refer also to the patience which its occupation enjoins. But he failed to establish in the *Criterion* a genuine relation between principle and particular, between orthodoxy and the daily madness of events.

These general phrases add up to a symptom rather than a cause. Even when we have taken the force of Eliot's enterprise

and registered in some degree the severity of his purpose in the
Criterion, we still feel that the whole effort was somehow artificial, a function of his will at odds with his talent. It may be
possible to account for this impression by recourse to a bizarre
sentence in Eliot's *Egoist* essay on Henry James, published in
January 1918. Eliot has been praising James's treatment, in
The American, of such characters as Noémie Nioche and the
Bellegardes, and he goes on to say that James's best American
characters 'have a fullness of existence and an external ramifica-
tion of relationship which a European reader might not easily
suspect'. He then comments on the presentation of Tom Tristram:

> In all appearance Tom Tristram is an even slighter sketch.
> Europeans can recognise him; they have seen him, known him,
> have even penetrated the Occidental Club; but no European
> has the Tom Tristram element in his composition, has anything
> of Tristram from his first visit to the Louvre to his final remark
> that Paris is the only place where a white man can live.
> It is the final perfection, the consummation of an American to
> become, not an Englishman, but a European—something which
> no born European, no person of any European nationality, can
> become. Tom is one of the failures, one of nature's misfortunes,
> in this process.

Recall that Tristram's failure to become a European reveals
among its symptoms not only the Occidental Club, poker-
sessions, his hideous sociability, and his ability 'to be degenerate
without the iridescence of decay', but also the characteristics
which allow James to dispose of him in a sentence: 'and then he
was idle, spiritless, sensual, snobbish'. Predictably, Tristram's
reference to America, now that he is living in the Avenue d'Iena,
compel Christopher Newman to express himself as vexed 'to see
the United States treated as little better than a vulgar smell in
his friend's nostril'. Tom, as Eliot says, is one of the failures in
the process by which an American makes himself a European.
Well and good: but if Tristram is a gross failure, who is a success
in the same process? I shall risk the vulgarity of saying that Eliot
himself pursued success in the art of making himself a European
and that while 'the Tom Tristram element' did not figure as a
grossness in his ambition it marked its presence by forcing him to

pursue his object with the insistence of principle. I put the case in
a monstrous form: an American poet sets out to achieve the final
perfection, the consummation of an American, to become a
European sage. But if the formula is monstrous, we have only to
take some of the harm out of it, soften its harshness, to make
it decent. It is enough then to say that when the editor of
the *Criterion* appeals for sanction to 'the mind of Europe', there
is a clear if silent claim that he has earned the right to make
that appeal, he has taken the mind of Europe unto himself.
I am not referring to the simple claim of having read Plato,
Virgil, Augustine, Dante, but to the more daring claim of having
grasped the spiritual entity of which these writers are constituents. For the occasion of my argument it is not necessary to
maintain that Eliot's silent claim is outrageous: even if the claim
were precisely valid it would still attach to itself an air of failure
in the degree to which its very success would be a *tour de force*.
We hear a good deal these days about the American Eliot and the
American element in his poems: it is true and important. But the
editor of the *Criterion* presents himself as the European he has
made himself. What shows, for the most part, is the strain. There
is something strained, willed, and therefore grim in the official
concerns of Eliot's public life, the programme or regimen by
which he moves from literature to society to religion to Christen-
dom toward the City of God. I list these concerns not to mock
them but to say that the movement from one to another is not
an unfolding or a natural development but a function of friction
and will. The *Criterion* documents not only the grandeur of
Eliot's ambition, but its exorbitance. By comparison, the enter-
prises of Arnold or Leavis appear natural, familiar, continuous
with the native qualities of their talent. *Culture and Anarchy*
and *Scrutiny* do not strike us as having an oblique or aberrant
relation to the native temper of their authors, they are at one
with themselves. But in the *Criterion* we are continually aware
of severances and disjunctions between one tone and another,
insecurities of feeling and the desperate labour of transcending
them.

3

The Poet as Critic

GRAHAM HOUGH

One of the tedious automatisms of literary history is the hostility, real or alleged, between poetry and criticism; and every age needs a poet-critic sufficiently powerful in both spheres to transcend such civil strife. For our time it has been Eliot who has filled this role, and if we look into the enabling conditions of his influence we shall find that one of them is the moderate nature of his claims. It has not always seemed so. In his early days it became the fashion, largely owing to the influence of Ezra Pound, to deprecate all criticism except that of the poets themselves; and Eliot was not unaffected by this attitude. As late as 1961 we find him writing 'The nearest we get to pure literary criticism is the criticism of artists writing about their own art'.[1] Pound had put it more bluntly: 'Pay no attention to the criticisms of men who have never themselves written a notable work'. This sounds exclusive and extreme, and it is open to the logical objection that we cannot know who the poets are or what works are notable without prior critical activity. At worst it consigns poetry to a closed group who live by taking in each other's washing. There is of course a rival doctrine, best expressed by Northrop Frye. For Frye criticism is the systematic anatomising of literary art, from which the poet as such is excluded by his nature and his function. It is an axiom of criticism that the poet 'cannot talk about what he knows'. The arts, including even the art of words, cannot explain themselves. They are beautiful but dumb, and the critic who is also a poet is simply another critic, possessing no special authority even in relation to his own work.

But Eliot's position is not really exclusive and extreme. If we survey his remarks on this matter, scattered over forty years, we find that on the whole they profess no more than to be a definition of his own tastes, and they incorporate some quite specific limitations of the poet-critic's range:

> I am, I admit, much more interested in what other poets have written about poetry than in what critics who are not poets have said about it.[2] (1961)

> I believe that the critical writings of poets, of which in the past there have been some very distinguished examples, owe a great deal of their interest to the fact that the poet, at the back of his mind, if not as his ostensible purpose, is always trying to defend the kind of poetry he is writing, or to formulate the kind that he wants to write . . . He is not so much a judge as an advocate . . . What he writes about poetry, in short, must be assessed in relation to the poetry he writes.[3] (1942)

We can see quite clearly, in a number of pronouncements belonging to his middle years, that it is within these limits that Eliot wished his own criticism to be remembered.

I think it will be agreed that his most vital critical work is of this kind—but it is not all of this kind. There is a fair body of formal and ceremonial lectures, retrospects and *pièces d'occasion*, that were instigated in quite different ways. The retrospects especially give an unexpected view of Eliot's literary operations. It is as if he were looking back from the farther shore on his most active years, and had assumed a different persona for the purpose. Sometimes he seems almost to be writing his own obituary. There is hardly a characteristic utterance of the twenties and thirties that has not later been qualified, deprecated, renounced, or reduced to relative unmeaning by diluting it in a wider context. Critics of other persuasions have been tempted to irritated remonstrance against some of Eliot's early dogmatisms; but in the end it has always turned out that the remonstrance was hardly worth making, for he has done it himself. An exploratory, challenging, and sometimes incautious literary condottiere has been annotated by a well-balanced man of letters, decorous sometimes to the point of tedium. But they happen to be the same man. Hence, of course, the common dichotomy between the proto-Eliot, commander of the vanguard, and the deutero-Eliot, a lost leader. But this will not really do. As a matter of straightforward chronology and literary history, the penetrating 'creative' critic survives at least into the early fifties, in 'Poetry and Drama' and 'The Three Voices of Poetry', for instance; and the anodyne academic revisionist appears as early as 1932, in parts of *The Use of Poetry*. The latter was implicit in the former from the start, and the two can be seen deadlocked in muted combat, in the paradoxes about tradition of his earliest and most celebrated essay. Nor were these rivals ever inaccessible to each other. Each was well aware of the other's existence; sometimes they found it convenient to go by without recognition, but a tip of the hat in passing, or even a dig in the ribs, occurred quite often enough to keep up communication. And to see Eliot as a critic at all justly is to see them both, in their uneasy union. The spectacle is a fascinating one, and it is of permanent importance to the remaining few who care about the development of our literary consciousness. Eliot ranks with Dryden, Johnson, Coleridge and Arnold as directors of that wayward progress. And though we are now less certain than he once was that anything to be properly called 'the mind of Europe' still exists, if it does it is something that would be incomplete without his contribution.

His influence was probably at its greatest between 1930 and 1950, and it was the influence of his poetry and criticism combined. It is often thought that they developed concurrently, as Austin Warren suggests in his fine essay on the continuity of Eliot's criticism.[4] That is encouraged by dates of publication; but in fact the poetry came first, as Eliot himself always affirmed. 'Prufrock', 'Portrait of a Lady' and 'La Figlia che Piange' were written between 1910 and 1912; 'Tradition and the Individual Talent' not till 1919. The essays on Jacobean dramatists are mostly subsequent to the poetry that had been modelled on their example. 'Poetry and Drama' (1951) came after the best plays had been written. This is the general truth, but actually the situation is more complicated and it needs qualification. Eliot was a self-conscious poet; he formed his practice on study and previous models. The study was in the interests of the poetry, and it made the poetry possible; after that it gave rise to a critical effort of a partly different and more generalised kind. And once, in the early 'Dialogue on Dramatic Poetry' (1928), the criticism shows the embryonic formation of a project not to be developed till many years later.

We should remind ourselves too of Eliot's material circumstances. He wrote the criticism to make money, and the need was pressing; but like most substantial writers he had the strength to organise a difficult life in the service of a continuing purpose. What he wrote from necessity and under pressure was worked into his *Lebensplan* with considerable skill. He needed the guineas from the *Times Literary Supplement*, but his poetry needed apologia and explanation; a climate of thought and feeling had to be created in which it could be read with understanding; and the mere tactics of a literary career became insensibly part of a grand strategy. Even so, his criticism was subject to cross-winds and inconsistencies, disconcerting to those who think of criticism as philosophical argument—like others I have often been disconcerted—but we can see now how much of its vitality depends on these accidents. Conscious development of a style, study of carefully chosen models—these are only one side of Eliot's criticism. As we could at any time have seen, but as he himself only made clear quite late ('The Three Voices of Poetry', 1953) his poetry was always radically dependent on unconscious and uncontrollable processes—'he does not know what he has to say until he has said it'—and these play their part in his criticism too. Then beyond all this and to some extent outside it, there is the development of his religious and social ideas. They exercise a continued but intermittent pressure and, since he never made up his mind quite clearly about how much and what kind of pressure they ought to exercise, they are apt to irrupt capriciously and not always happily into literary discussion.

2

It would not be very profitable to attach particular critical essays to particular poems, especially as the obscure processes of gestation are not reflected in ascertainable dates; but inquiry can be focussed by some rough groupings. 'Reflections on *Vers Libre*' and 'Ezra Pound: his Metric and Poetry' are contemporary with the publication of 'Prufrock', and until recently were little known.[5] While readers of poetry were digesting 'Prufrock',

'Gerontion' and The Waste Land they were also digesting The
Sacred Wood, Homage to John Dryden and the earlier essays on
Elizabethan and Jacobean dramatists. A new phase began with
For Lancelot Andrews in 1928 and Ash-Wednesday two years
later; and at that stage students of Eliot had to readjust their
ideas. But broadly speaking the Selected Essays of 1932, which
include most of the content of the earlier collections, form a
comprehensible whole, and they are the critical accompaniment
to the poetry before Four Quartets. It is largely by them that
Eliot's position as a critic was established. Quite early they came
to constitute a canon, and when Eliot's criticism is discussed it is
even now this collection that is mainly thought of, in spite of
revisions and distinguished additions later on.

Like other canons this one has been credited with a consistency
and authority that the writings which compose it could never
have originally claimed; and like other canons, it is a distillation
from much more extensive and miscellaneous material. The
Selected Essays are simply a selection from a large body of
periodical criticism written by Eliot over a period of fifteen years.
They are mostly brief and mostly book-reviews. So what has been
received as a considered literary programme was in origin something far more fortuitous. Since in our time no one can make a
living by poetry the poet has several possibilities before him. He
can adopt some entirely irrelevant profession—market-gardener
or civil servant. He can become an academic, he can become a
layabout, or he can settle for being a man of letters. Eliot chose
the first and the last of these courses. But even during his eight
years in Lloyd's Bank the best part of his energy was going into
literary work of various kinds. For the rest, his civil status was
that of literary journalist, publisher and editor of a review; and
that is the milieu from which his criticism sprang. 'Literary
critic' nowadays tends to indicate an academic addressing a pre-
selected audience of teachers and students: Eliot was a critic in
the old sense, like Johnson or Hazlitt. His criticism had to make
its way in the ordinary literary traffic of the time.

This was surely of great advantage to him. An alien and a
lonely man, he needed to belong to a literary community. A man
with something less than a voracious appetite for life, he needed
the stimulus of vicarious experience. The poet writes about what

has happened to him, but he also writes about what has not happened to him, what he hopes or fears might happen, what is happening to others around him. The relation between poetry and the experience of life in a richly endowed poetic nature is so various and many-sided that it can even accommodate Eliot's doctrine of impersonality without too much strain. The same shifting relationships are likely to be found in a poet's criticism also; and like Spinoza, the typewriter and the smell of cooking, these diversities may positively contribute to his poetry. He may write propaganda for his own work and that of his friends; he may write against tendencies that he thinks stultifying or deadening; but he may also exalt ideals that he has conspicuously failed to attain, or praise out of historical nostalgia a kind of poetry that could not be written in his age at all. It may be necessary for him to do all these things; and the sheer miscellaneous quality of periodical criticism gives him the opportunity to do so. To read Eliot's uncollected contributions to the *Egoist* and the *Athenaeum* between 1917 and 1920 is to see him in process of defining himself, not according to a predetermined programme, but as the result of chance encounters, appreciations and revulsions that were unforeseeable and far more fertilising than the narrowly chosen channels of university criticism could ever have been. He reviewed current poetry, novels, philosophy in the austerely technical sense, works of criticism and scholarship. Some of these were of no permanent interest; but sometimes the offered topic and the progress of his own thought ran together, and the commissioned essay congealed into the statement of a lasting conviction. These are the pieces reprinted in *Selected Essays*; but it would be a mistake to forget the background from which they sprang.

At all times, even in his bread-and-butter writing, Eliot is an admirable craftsman. The *Egoist* must be one of the liveliest little reviews ever published; the *Athenaeum* was a finely serious and responsible journal; and in this good company Eliot's contributions still stand out for their thoughtfulness, their concentration, and a quality I can only describe as intellectual charm. Because they are book-reviews they must be comparatively short: Eliot contrives a way of treating substantial questions in little space. Because they are periodical essays it is required that they may be read with pleasure: Eliot evolves a kind of grave wit that is extraordinarily attractive. A short sentence takes two un-expected twists that both define a situation with exactitude and keep the reader awake: 'Tennyson had a brain (a large dull brain like a farmhouse clock) which saved him from triviality.' A chance comparison between America and Russia, long before this collocation was a commonplace, reveals vistas beyond the merely geographical: 'There are advantages indeed in coming from a large flat country which no one wants to visit: advantages which both Turgenev and James enjoyed.' At times a kind of solemn impertinence is used to make a serious point: 'Because we have never learned to criticize Keats, Shelley and Words-worth (poets of assured though modest merit), Keats, Shelley and Wordsworth punish us from their graves with the annual scourge of the Georgian Anthology.' It is not difficult to see how the exercise of qualities such as these played their part in the formation of Eliot's literary attitude; and in this the development of his poetry must be included.

It was partly good luck, partly good management that enabled him to weave a coherent literary outlook out of his miscellaneous writing. It was not all luck: he had discerning and sympathetic editors who sent him the books he wanted. But sheer good luck made some striking contributions. The three essays reprinted as *Homage to John Dryden* now look like a considered manifesto for the poetry of wit. They were in fact three separate contribu-tions to the *TLS*, and their existence depended entirely on the arrival within eight months in 1921 of Grierson's *Metaphysical Lyrics and Poems of the Seventeenth Century*, Mark van Doren's *John Dryden*, and the Marvell tercentenary. Three unrelated external events served to focus and concentrate a train of thought that was of central importance to Eliot. The essays on Elizabethan and Jacobean dramatists extend from 1919 to 1934; seven out of the eleven were contributions to the *TLS*; most were reviews of new editions or critical studies. But here we have a continuing and deliberate policy. Eliot established himself as something of a critical authority in this field, and Bruce Richmond, the editor to whom he has more than once paid tribute, allowed him to take charge of it. Only one of the *Egoist* and *Athenaeum* articles is a spontaneous critical discussion, without the stimulus of reviewing. It is 'Tradition and the Individual Talent'; and it has always stood somewhat apart from the other essays. The question that naturally arises is how far this miscellaneous and externally motivated critical activity is a separate thing, and how closely it is related to the poetry.

3

It is hard to recall now the depths of unsophistication from which the aspiring common reader of the thirties attempted to rise to the challenge of *The Sacred Wood* and the *Selected Essays*. Few people realised that they were reprinted book-reviews. The heterogeneous content was overlaid by a magisterial manner; and the two combined to suggest the existence of an unsuspected pantheon, inhabited by the veiled figures of Irving Babbit, Remy de Gourmont, Marie Lloyd and Lancelot Andrewes, whose decrees seemed strongly authoritarian but impossible to bring together under any known banner. What is more, they seemed to have no discernible relation to 'Prufrock', 'Gerontion', or *The Waste Land*. As time went on some features of this obscure terrain became clearer. None of Eliot's poems, it is true, looked much like Donne or Marvell: but the identification of a line of wit in English poetry plainly had something to do with the quatrain poems of the 1920 volume. The related contention that satire could be poetry—an unfamiliar and unwelcome idea to many at that time—was seen in the end to stake out a claim for large areas of Eliot's own verse. The rehabilitation of intellectual play and the antiseptic value of negative emotions in poetry—these were implicitly anti-Romantic positions; and the explicitly anti-Romantic, anti-nineteenth-century bias of many passages was consistent with it. Consistent too with the urban imagery of the poems, the absence of sympathy between man and his environment, the glimpses of so many defeated and unheroic lives. These revulsions from the Romantic heritage were distasteful to the ordinary reader, for whom the archetypes of poetry were the 'Ode to a Nightingale' and 'Adonais'; distasteful and disturbing —but after a short interval of numbness most realised that they had been ready for the shock. Almost imperceptibly the Romantic heritage had been dissipating itself for a generation or more. The last of the old actors were leaving the stage, their gestures hopelessly outmoded. The 'impersonal' theory of poetry pointed in the same direction. Since Romantic art had been the apotheosis of the individual sensibility the new art must play it down, by making a sharp cut between the artistic emotion and the emotions of life, must place the weight on a craftsmanship divorced from subjectivity and confession, on the disinfectant irony of 'Portrait of a Lady' and 'Sweeney Erect'. So much soon became obvious; and gradually it was seen that Eliot had performed a remarkable feat. He had written a body of criticism that did intelligent and astringent justice to its ostensible objects, and at the same time given this miscellany a centralising, unifying reference to his own poetic development. We were reading about Swinburne or Donne or Jonson because we sought enlightenment about Swinburne or Donne or Jonson. And we found it. Regardless of his opinions, Eliot's sheer critical intelligence, the originality and vigour of his judgements, gave us something that was simply not to be found either in the scholarship or the amiable belles-lettres that then divided the field between them. And at the same time we were being insensibly nudged and sidled towards a novel conception of poetry—of which Eliot's own poetry turned out to be the exemplar:

> ... The twentieth century is still the nineteenth, although it may in time acquire its own character. The nineteenth century had, like every other, limited tastes and peculiar fashions; and, like every other, it was unaware of its own limitations.[6]

> [The virtue of wit] is absent from the work of Wordsworth, Shelley, and Keats, on whose poetry nineteenth-century criticism has unconsciously been based ...

> > . . .

> this modest and certainly impersonal virtue—whether we call it wit or reason, or even urbanity ... is something precious and needed and apparently extinct; it is what should preserve the reputation of Marvell. *C'était une belle âme comme on ne fait plus à Londres.*[7]

But perhaps, when the twentieth century has acquired its own character and emancipated itself from the standards of Wordsworth, Shelley and Keats, this modest and impersonal virtue will prove not to be entirely extinct, and come into its own? Is it not possible that even now another *belle âme*, its sensibility re-associated, not quite like that of Marvell but endowed with some of the same qualities, is even now forming itself in London? If such a being exists, must it not be the author of 'Prufrock', 'Portrait of a Lady' and 'La Figlia che Piange'? The suggestions are so discreet as to be virtually imperceptible; but like subliminal advertising they did their work.

There is a slight tincture of mystification in all this—an element not infrequent in Eliot's prose, and a good deal more evident in the uncollected pieces than in those he has preserved. It is hard to believe that he did not take a sly pleasure in writing serious and objective criticism on a diversity of subjects, while simultaneously propagating the tendencies by which he expected his own poetry to live. But this undercurrent of self-reference led him into some strange inconsistencies, and perhaps to a temporarily mistaken estimate of the nature of his own talents. Within a few pages of the *Selected Essays* we find the Metaphysical poets commended for diametrically opposite qualities:

> It is to be observed that the language of these poets is as a rule simple and pure; ... The *structure* of the sentences, on the other hand, is sometimes far from simple ... (p. 285)

> ... a method curiously similar to that of the 'metaphysical poets', similar also in its use of obscure words and of simple phrasing. (p. 289)

It looks at first as though he is fascinated by Metaphysical poetry but does not quite know why. It turns out however that in the second of these two places he is hardly thinking of the Metaphysicals at all; he is thinking of Laforgue. Immediately after it he quotes in illustration a long passage—'Géraniums diaphanes, guerroyeurs sortilèges' etc.—without indication of authorship. It is a bewilderingly allusive catalogue of some of the grislier aspects of bourgeois marriage, quite out of key with the general tone of the discussion in hand, and utterly unlike any writing by any Metaphysical poet. It comes from Laforgue's *Derniers Vers*. Here the underground concern with his own poetry has prevailed over the criticism. He has been influenced by the Metaphysicals, he has been influenced by Laforgue, so he finds them 'curiously similar'. But there is no similarity at all. The only link is through his own work, which is never mentioned.

Laforgue and Corbière are referred to in the next paragraph as 'nearer to the school of Donne than any modern English poet'. This need not be very near; but apart from their meeting in Eliot's creative process there is no reason for the collocation at all. Perhaps we are to understand 'Nearer than any modern English poet except one'. In 1961, when all his poetry had long been written, Eliot made an almost posthumous acknowledgement to Laforgue—'to whom I owe more than to any one poet in any language'. But he wrote no criticism of Laforgue's work, and during his active years allusions to it are brief and glancing. There is something here of the phenomenon (well known to examiners of academic dissertations) of citing all sources except the one to which you really owe most. Eliot has often taken a mischievous pleasure in sending his critics to bark up the wrong tree; and the more or less open acknowledgement of kinship to the English Metaphysicals is used to obscure the far closer kinship to the French Symbolists. Both influences are real: when Eliot praises the 'bright hard precision' of Metaphysical imagery, the re-creation of thought into feeling, 'the heterogeneity of material compelled into unity by the operation of the poet's mind', he is praising things that he not only admired but imitated and practised himself. But the other aspect of Metaphysical poetry that he commends—the 'tough reasonableness', the almost syllogistic arrangement of Donne's and Marvell's arguments— is utterly alien to Eliot's procedure. The most striking and disconcerting feature of his poems is that they have no rational structure at all. From what we know of their method of composition they could hardly have had any. They are brilliant collages, patterned by unity or contrariety of moods. No one knows what 'A Cooking Egg' is about to this day. Sometimes moods and images cluster round a 'plot' that is never stated but can be more or less divined. Sometimes even this submerged plot is absent. Yet the riddling 'modernist' organisation in the poetry is partnered in the criticism with obeisance to Aristotle, to clarity, rationality and the 'classical' virtues. Readers of Eliot wasted much energy in trying to reconcile these irreconcileables, while a very brief study of Laforgue's *Complaintes,* or still better, his last poems, would have shown the real nature of Eliot's method. But the slight clues in the published criticism were not picked up—were hardly meant to be picked up; while the partial debt to the Metaphysicals was excessively acknowledged.

This is puzzling. Are we then to give up the idea of Eliot's criticism as a disguised exegesis of his poetry? I do not think so; but we must realise its limits. Like the Tractarians, Eliot had a considerable belief in the economy of truth. He never intended to provide a pass-key to all the chambers of his mind. His readers and critics are to be allowed to see as much as they are likely to accept, or perhaps just a little more: they could not be driven farther without revolt, so if they are to go farther they had better find the way for themselves. The real difficulty of Eliot's poetry was never in its texture, its imagery or its rhythms—not to anyone who could read. The difficulty was in the structure—the absence of anything that by traditional standards could reasonably be called structure at all. To provide a set defence of these novel principles of organisation would have required an intolerable deal of casuistry, and would probably have failed. Very well then; let the critics be outfaced by a blankly contradictory declaration of 'classical' principles; and while they are worrying their heads over that paradox the poetry can quietly make its way. This manoeuvre was brilliantly successful. Eliot wished to provide himself with an English poetic ancestry, a place in the English poetic tradition. He was willing, even eager, to proclaim the necessity of nourishment and cross-fertilisation from the wider European stream; he was for a time dazzled by Pound; but he had in reality little of Pound's passion to 'make it new'. Still less had he the desire to appear as the disciple of a little-known modern French poet, a poet who by French standards was not even of the first rank. Among Eliot's early poems written at Harvard are several pastiches of Laforgue—at the clever-under-graduate level and no more. It was not that aspect of himself that he wished to perpetuate. He was quite prepared to conduct a campaign against nineteenth-century poetics which was in any case overdue, but he was not prepared to go farther in iconoclasm than that. Having thrown out Wordsworth, Shelley and Keats he prefers to claim kinship with an older, and as he sees it, a more enduring English tradition. The startling appearance of classicism in conjunction with royalism and anglo-catholicism in the celebrated announcement of 1927 was an adaptation from Maurras. It was a socio-political rather than a literary transplant, which Eliot hoped to acclimatise on English soil. In this he signally failed.

The word 'tradition' has now made its appearance; and as we know almost too well, it becomes prominent in Eliot's critical apparatus with the essay 'Tradition and the Individual Talent'. This first appeared in two numbers of the *Egoist*, September and December 1919. It is Eliot's first independent critical pronouncement, and in its idea of an impersonal art of poetry, subject to the whole tradition of European letters, it belongs with the prevailing anti-Romantic strain of the early criticism. We are apt to associate the ideas of 'Tradition and the Individual Talent' with the political and religious traditionalism of a rather later stage in Eliot's career; but the root of these reflections was strictly literary and closely connected with his own situation. It was the problem of novelty in poetry—the problem of 'modernism' in a literary climate that was still that of the nineteenth century. The subject had been on his mind two years before. In 'Reflections on *Vers Libre*' (*New Statesman*, March 1917) there is a passage which looks like the germ of the later essay:

> In an ideal state of society one might imagine the good New growing naturally out of the good Old, without the need for polemic and theory; this would be a society with a living tradition. In a sluggish society, as actual societies are, tradition is ever lapsing into superstition, and the violent stimulus of novelty is required.[8]

Here we see a mind divided; but there is no doubt where Eliot's sympathies lie; they are with the pre-lapsarian state where the violent stimulus of novelty is unnecessary. The problem however is to distinguish enduring tradition from mere acquiescence in the status quo. In an *Egoist* article of a few months later we find him veering in the other direction:

> All the ideas, beliefs, modes of feeling and behaviour which we have not time or inclination to investigate for ourselves we take second-hand and sometimes call Tradition.

And he supports this piece of decorous disrespect with a footnote:

> For an authoritative condemnation of theories attaching
> extreme importance to tradition as a criterion of truth, see
> Pope Gregory XVI's encyclical *Singulari nos* (July 15, 1834),
> and the Vatican Council canon of 1870, *Si quis dixerit* ...
> *anathema sit.*

As might be suspected, this is a leg-pull; the documents cited, so
far as they are relevant at all, have precisely the opposite tendency. But Eliot's leg-pulls are not without significance. The notes
to *The Waste Land* are a joke, but they suggest that he would
be quite willing to be edited like an ancient classic. Here we see
him cutting a solemn caper between excessive deference and
excessive disrespect for traditional authority—and the polarity
is quite serious and quite real. Two years later he has worked it
out and come to terms with it. A famous passage in 'Tradition
and the Individual Talent' resolves the conflict in an ingenious
synthesis that does simultaneously justice to both tradition and
innovation:

> The existing monuments form an ideal order among them-
> selves, which is modified by the introduction of the new (the
> really new) work of art among them. The existing order is
> complete before the new work arrives; for order to persist after
> the supervention of novelty, the *whole* existing order must be,
> if ever so slightly, altered; and so the relations, proportions,
> values of each work of art toward the whole are readjusted and
> this is conformity between the old and the new.

This is a wise saying, one that the student of modern poetry cannot recall too often; but apply it to Eliot's own poetry and there
is a little sleight-of-hand about it all the same. A good deal of
special pleading would be required to show how the structure of
The Waste Land achieves conformity between the old and the
new; and Eliot never undertakes it. His criticism tends always to
underline the links between his own practice and the practice of
the past. The really subversive elements are left to explain themselves, until an unexpected genetic explanation of them appears
in 'The Three Voices of Poetry', thirty years later.

4

Essentially the activity we have just been inspecting was a strategy for presenting his poetry. Poetry does not exist in a vacuum; it needs a setting, a literary climate, and in default of others, Eliot is changing the climate for himself. In other places we find him at a different task—working out his own technical principles, finding models and deciding how they are to be used. 'Reflections on Vers Libre' is not a good essay on free verse. Its contention is that all free verse is an approach to or a recession from a regular metre. This describes vers libéré not vers libre, and it leaves the ultimate free verse quite unaccounted for. But it describes with perfect accuracy the verse of 'Prufrock', published in the same year. It is quite simply an exposition of the principles on which his own early versification is based. The same is true of much in the essays on Elizabethan and Jacobean dramatists. These are scholarly critical essays in their own right, and very fine ones; and they have other interests too. But the detailed concern with the technique of blank verse in the essays on Marlowe, Tourneur and Ford is a technical study whose importance to his own verse Eliot has acknowledged, and whose influence is immediately evident in 'Gerontion' and The Waste Land. The Marlowe essay reveals Eliot's conviction that:

> blank verse within Shakespeare's lifetime was more highly developed, that it became the vehicle of more varied and more intense feeling than it has ever conveyed since, and that after the erection of the Chinese wall of Milton, blank verse has suffered not only arrest but retrogression.[9]

He goes on to say that the blank verse of Tennyson, 'a consummate master of this form in certain applications, is cruder ... than that of half a dozen contemporaries of Shakespeare; cruder, because less capable of expressing complicated, subtle, and surprising emotions'.

This is a passage pregnant with implications for Eliot's own practice. In spite of his oft proclaimed aversion from nineteenth-century poetry, his juvenilia are quite obviously based on Swinburne and the fin-de-siècle. His earliest mature verse, 'Prufrock'

and 'La Figlia che Piange', still has a base in the iambic verse of
the late nineteenth century, as Harvey Gross has pointed out;
Browning's in 'Portrait of a Lady', Tennyson's in 'La Figlia'. In
these poems far greater liberties are taken with the iambic
decasyllable than the nineteenth century allowed—and the
liberties are mostly those sanctioned by or extrapolated from late
Elizabethan blank verse. Short lines, reversal of accent, redun-
dant syllables, single 'prosaic' lines not amenable to normal
scansion—all these are to be found in the practice of Webster,
Tourneur and Middleton. One device he even seems to have
copied from the accidental mislineations of the seventeenth-
century printing house; it is the embedding of regular 'iambic
pentameter' in longer lines that give a different punctuation and
a different movement. This is not a study of Eliot's metrics, but
if it were it would be possible to follow up all the passing remarks
on versification in the Elizabethan essays and show how the
features observed have contributed to his own practice. In
'Gerontion', as has often been noted, this becomes a positive and
deliberate echo of Tourneur and Middleton, just as the opening
of 'A Game of Chess' in *The Waste Land* echoes late Shakespeare.
Eliot remarks particularly on the individual note that each of the
dramatists discussed is able to give to his blank verse, as though
his greatest interest is in the variety (at that time an unsuspected
variety) of which the form is capable. A well-known idiosyncratic passage from the essay on Massinger shows clearly enough
not only what he has found in the writers of this period, but
what he has learnt from them:

> ... Tourneur and Middleton exhibit that perpetual slight
> alteration of language, words perpetually juxtaposed in new
> and sudden combinations, meanings perpetually *eingeschach-
> telt* into meanings, which evidences a very high development
> of the senses, a development of the English language which we
> have perhaps never equalled.[10]

The Elizabethan essays have of course a far wider interest than
that. Along with the 'Dialogue on Dramatic Poetry' which
comes in the middle of them, they are concerned with some of
the main problems of poetic drama. They discuss the limits of
realism, the need for a convention, the relation of 'poetry' to

'drama', the moral quality of the play, revealed both in single characters and in the clash of one character on another. Even earlier is the brief fragment 'Rhetoric and Poetic Drama' (1919); and all these pieces show Eliot making a close study of the drama long before his own dramatic work began.

The incursion into poetic drama was evidently the result of a long incubation and much preparatory thinking. It was not pure criticism, for dramatic poetry more than any other is dependent on social habit, even on the minor social habits that we call fashions. Poetic drama can only function freely when there is a generally acceptable convention ready to embrace it. Eliot is acutely aware from the beginning that no such convention exists in our century, and most of his thinking about the drama is concerned with the possibility of creating one. Yeats found himself in the same dilemma, and masterfully devised a special convention of his own. Eliot in the end resigned himself to some of the conventions of the West End stage, already beginning to be out of date. But it was only after much heart-searching and experiment, and much study of English drama in its great period, when a happier state of affairs prevailed.

But his most substantial treatment of the subject belongs with the retrospects. It is the lecture 'Poetry and Drama' of 1951. By that time he had *Murder in the Cathedral*, *The Family Reunion* and *The Cocktail Party* behind him; and the principles he outlined here were not to change in his last two plays *The Confidential Clerk* and *The Elder Statesman*. Because it came at a time when his position was long established, and because it has had no particular influence on the course of things, this piece has been less noticed than some of his earlier criticism. Actually it is one of Eliot's finest essays, both for its masterly untendentious statement of general principles and for the unaffected candour with which it describes his own problems and endeavours. The core of the general argument is that dramatic prose with any just claim to the title is as artificial as verse, and hardly nearer to the formless speech of common life. What is called poetic drama in prose, except in special cases like Synge's, is even more limited by convention than poetic drama in verse. It ought to be possible to devise a form of verse sufficiently flexible and unobtrusive to deal with the ordinary circumstances of modern life, and yet capable, on due occasion, of 'reaching the border of those feelings which only music can express'. Then follows the account of his own experiments in that direction and the evolution of his own dramatic versification. This was something quite deliberately devised, different in principle from most of the earlier verse spoken in his own voice. Yet it was to become one of the cadences of his own voice, for the same principles were to serve for the staple verse of the *Four Quartets*.

5

In this essay it is as though with the approach of old age the stratagems and obliquities of his earlier criticism had melted away. They had often been necessary and fruitful in the past, but now Eliot speaks with a directness and simplicity that is particularly engaging and persuasive. The same is true of the slightly later essay 'The Three Voices of Poetry' (1953). The forbidding reserve and the gnomic allusiveness have gone, replaced by an unembarrassed plain speaking:

> The first voice is the voice of the poet talking to himself—or to nobody. The second is the voice of the poet addressing an audience, whether large or small. The third is the voice of the poet when he attempts to create a dramatic character speaking in verse; when he is saying, not what he would say in his own person, but only what he can say within the limits of one imaginary character addressing another imaginary character.[11]

When he comes to elucidate this formula he speaks quite openly from personal experience. 'I think that the best way for me to try to make my three voices audible, is to trace the genesis of the distinction in my own mind.' Because the tone here is so near to the graceful accessibility of old-fashioned belles-lettres it has been rather assumed that in these later writings Eliot has not much to say. In fact in this essay, written very freely and apparently without too much forethought, he makes the most important confession about the genesis of his own poetry to be found in all his critical work. Mr C. K. Stead has noticed this, and put it to admirable use in his book *The New Poetic*; but otherwise it has passed largely unremarked.

Eliot speaks at length about the third voice, supplementing in a slightly more discursive fashion the technical considerations raised in 'Poetry and Drama'. Incidentally he makes some of the acutest comments ever made on the dramatic monologue—applied directly to Browning, and equally applicable to the author of 'Prufrock' and 'Portrait of a Lady'. But it is in the discussion of the first voice, the voice of the poet talking to himself, what is commonly and inexactly called 'lyric', that the most illuminating and disarming observations occur. We cannot doubt that it is the first voice that is at the heart of Eliot's poetry, whatever reputable employment he may have found for the other two. And for many years readers and critics, both friendly and unfriendly, had felt a discrepancy between the actual tone of that voice and the critical pronouncements that accompanied it. Classicism, respect for tradition, tough reasonableness, wit—only by prayer and fasting could even the devoutest disciples get themselves into a state of mind where these could be seen as the dominant virtues of Eliot's poetry. Now in this late essay a whole array of critical defences is simply passed by. The Maginot line is doubtless impregnable, but it hardly matters for it is so easy to walk round the end.

Eliot approaches the question of lyric by citing a lecture of Gottfried Benn in which Benn finds the lyrist's starting point in an inert embryo or 'creative germ', initially formless and not open to examination:

> He has something germinating in him for which he must find words; but he cannot know what words he wants until he has found the words; he cannot identify this embryo until it has been transformed into an arrangement of the right words in the right order.[12]

Eliot is willing to go farther than this: in non-didactic verse the poet may be concerned *solely* to bring to birth this obscure embryo. 'He does not know what he has to say until he has said it; and in the effort to say it he is not concerned with making other people understand anything'. So much for tradition and the community of European letters. The endeavour is a purely private affair between the poet and the dark forces within him. And the passage goes on:

He is oppressed by a burden which he must bring to birth in
order to obtain relief. Or, to change the figure of speech, he is
haunted by a demon, a demon against which he feels power-
less, because in its first manifestation it has no face, no name,
nothing; and the words, the poem he makes, are a kind of form
of exorcism of this demon . . . And when the words are finally
arranged in the right way—or in what he comes to accept as
the best arrangement he can find—he may experience a
moment of exhaustion, of appeasement, of absolution, and of
something very near annihilation, which is in itself indescrib-
able.[13]

This is language of a kind that Eliot has never used before, and
it seeks to penetrate into the intimacies of the creative process in
a manner quite foreign to the earlier criticism. This is far
removed from wit, that modest and impersonal virtue, and from
poetry *pour distraire les honnêtes gens*. But he is not repudiat-
ing his former attitudes. He has simply reached a stage at which
it can be tacitly confessed that they were not fundamental. They
were regulative ideals, negative prescriptions, genuinely felt and
necessary both for himself and others; but they did not touch the
essential source of poetry. That is situated in another region
altogether, in a region not accessible to consciousness and not
amenable to intellectual control.

This seems at first sight to wipe out the sustained critical
endeavour of many long years, but in fact it still maintains a
place for it. The German word *aufheben* can mean both to nul-
lify and to preserve. We have no such convenient ambiguity, and
we cannot find a single word to describe what Eliot is here doing
to his earlier criticism. In effect he is showing that that criticism,
for all its seriousness and patience, is to some degree external; it
applies to the more outward and accessible areas of the poet's
activity. The climate of Eliot's earlier thinking had been per-
meated with a distrust of the inner voice; and indeed what is
appealed to here is still not the inner voice—it is the inner
silence. In his earlier formulations he had been perhaps excessively willing to stop short of any traffic with the unconscious;
but in this passage he drops his guard and says plainly that it is
in this inarticulate region that the poet's conscious activity

begins. Perhaps this hardly tells us anything new about the
genesis of his own poetry; but it circumvents some obstacles; and
it ratifies and sets his own seal upon what his more attentive
readers must have always in some sense have known.

At this point we reach one of the greatest unsettled questions
in poetic theory—the relation between conscious and unconscious, between the poet's expressed intentions, cultural or technical, and the deep roots of poetry in an area of the mind that
cannot be examined—and is perhaps not a property of the individual mind at all. Eliot himself has said little about it, and this
is not the place for a foray into that dark wood. But the impression we have remarked on, of an inconsistency between his for-
mulated programme and the actual nature of his poetry, does
give rise to some reflections. Freud remarks somewhere that in
classic art he looks for the unconscious, in romantic for the conscious—one of those penetrating obiter dicta that this unliterary
thinker not infrequently contributes to literary discussion.
Freud's observation suggests that a conflict between intention
and achievement is inherent in the creative process; and this is
possibly true. In the post-Symbolist period to which Eliot belongs
it was particularly likely to be true. Poe's literary theory placed
an equal weight on the obscure promptings of the soul and a
deliberate self-conscious craftsmanship. Sketchily and inade-
quately expressed as it is, Poe's critical thought is one of the
foundations of the Symbolist aesthetic in France. Eliot has more
than once paid a reserved tribute to it, and to its influence on his
own masters. Poe's elaborate justification of artifice and contriv-
ance is well known, but what is equally important is his realisa-
tion that the unconscious really is unconscious, that the obscure
depths of the soul really are obscure, and that images from this
region are unbiddable demons, not to be coaxed, solicited or
dragged out at will. The function of intellectual labour, willed
and fully self-aware, is at a later stage of the creative process. This
is the stage where concern for cultural tradition, the health of
the language, and the development of poetic technique can properly be active; and it is the only stage that is really open to discussion. It is with these matters that the great body of Eliot's criticism is concerned. 'The Three Voices of Poetry' stands out as
the clearest recognition that what is open to critical discussion is

only a part of the territory of poetry. Beyond it lies the obscure creative embryo invoked by Benn—which is never accessible to inspection.

Some of the ceremonial and commissioned essays—'The Classics and the Man of Letters' and 'The Aims of Education'—show how deeply uninspiring Eliot can be when he moves too far away from his own poetic concerns. In one case we find him obliged to write an encomium on a figure who had always been antipathetic to him, and the result is the perfunctory and unworthy lecture 'Goethe as the Sage'. We may admire the sixty-year-old not-so-smiling public man, but it is hardly to him that we go for the special kind of illumination that only the poet-critic can bring. Perhaps it is true of Eliot as a critic too, when he is at his best, that he 'does not know what he has to say until he has said it'. Perhaps it is fortunate that he did not always know, for what he knew he was going to say was not the unique thing he came into the world to say. Other men could have said it as well. It was sometimes interesting, generally worthy of respect—but how much of it would we have cared to listen to if it had not been the utterance of a man who had also said quite other things, in a quite different tone of voice? While he is building a persona of devotion, intellectual duty and ordered public activity—with the accomplished competence that attends most of his endeavours— his poetry and the criticism that is nearest to his poetry moves in another dimension. The glimpses are not always easy to discern, but the white sails still fly seaward, the lost heart stiffens and rejoices, and the spirit quickens to rebel, more often than would be suspected from the disciplined surface of his prose writing.

4

The Trials of a Christian Critic

SAMUEL HYNES

> A man's theory of the place of poetry is not independent of his view of life in general.
>
> *The Use of Poetry and the Use of Criticism*

Let us begin with Eliot's Matthew Arnold: *Eliot's* Arnold, not the man himself, for as often happens when a critic of decided convictions chooses an antagonist, Eliot looked into the mirror of Arnold and saw there a cautionary image of himself. His Arnold is a mixture of qualities—a critic of great virtues and of gross inconsistencies, an influential thinker who was incapable of connected reasoning, 'in some respects the most satisfactory man of letters of his age', but an undergraduate in philosophy and theology and a Philistine in religion.[1] Every time Eliot mentioned Arnold he conceded a worthiness, and then took it back; what we are left with is a man of contradictions, a high-minded man who hated what was hateful and praised what was best, but whose moral and rational limitations coarsened the idea of Culture that he cherished.

These contradictions revealed themselves most clearly, in Eliot's view, when Arnold assumed the role of social critic. 'He wasted his strength', Eliot wrote in *The Sacred Wood*,

> as men of superior ability sometimes do, because he saw something to be done and no one else to do it. The temptation, to any man who is interested in ideas and primarily in literature, to put literature into the corner until he has cleaned up the whole country first, is almost irresistible.[2]

Arnold succumbed to that temptation, and so made himself an example of the man of letters who takes society to be his subject. Indeed he was the *only* modern example of such a man at the time that Eliot began writing. But to Eliot, Arnold's example was a warning—he was a critic who had misjudged his gifts and had cast himself in a public role that society needed, but that he was ill-equipped to play. It is not surprising that the example of Arnold was much on Eliot's mind during the years when he was yielding to the same temptation to reach beyond literature; for if Eliot turned to cultural issues, he would be making himself the Arnold of his generation.

And that is clearly what he proposed to do. When he wrote of Arnold, in 1920, 'if he were our exact contemporary, he would find all his labour to perform again', and in 1927, 'it is not to say that Arnold's work was vain if we say that it is to be done again',[3] what was he saying, if not that *he* would pick up the fallen torch of culture? Like Arnold, he saw something to be done and no one else to do it. That is part of the temptation, to be persuaded that *you* are the only champion of your cause. Another part—so seductive to the intellectual—is the conviction that though your cause is just, it can never win: 'We must know in advance,' Eliot wrote, 'if we are prepared for that conflict, that the combat may have truces but never a peace . . . we fight rather to keep something alive than in the expectation that anything will triumph.'[4]

That image of the defence of culture as a crusade without a victory was written in 1927, the year that Eliot complicated his role as the twentieth-century Arnold by becoming a Christian. If a critic becomes a Christian, presumably he becomes a Christian critic, for surely belief should enter into every aspect of a believer's life, and most visibly, perhaps, if he is a convert. But it was difficult to see just what the consequences of conversion would be: what exactly would a Christian critic *do*? English criticism provided Eliot with no obvious answers. Certainly Arnold could be of no help here; on the contrary, his notion of the relation between poetry and religion was a crucial part of the problem, which the Christian critic would have to refute, whatever else he did.

But though the practices of a Christian critic might be unclear, Eliot's determination to be one was clear enough. In the year after he was received into the Church he wrote prefaces to two volumes of his essays, and in them he made his commitment explicit. One, the preface to *For Lancelot Andrewes*, has

been much quoted for its terse declaration of Eliot's point of
view: 'classicist in literature, royalist in politics, and anglo-
catholic in religion'. The other, a preface to a new edition of *The
Sacred Wood*, has received less attention, but is, to my mind, the
more important statement. Here Eliot announced that he had
'passed on to another problem not touched upon in this book:
that of the relation of poetry to the spiritual and social life of its
time and of other times'. And at the end of the preface, after
acknowledging that a poem 'in some sense, has its own life', Eliot
concluded:

> On the other hand, poetry as certainly has something to do
> with morals, and with religion, and even with politics perhaps,
> though we cannot say what . . . And in these questions, and
> others which we cannot avoid, we appear already to be leaving
> the domain of criticism of 'poetry'. So we cannot stop at any
> point. The best that we can hope to do is to agree upon a point
> from which to start. . .[5]

These statements are narrower in range than the sentence in *For
Lancelot Andrewes*, but they promise more. What they promise
is a new critical direction, which is in a general sense the direction of Matthew Arnold, beyond the domain of criticism of
'poetry'. Characteristically Eliot declines to say exactly what
that direction is, but the phrase 'the spiritual life', and the mention of religion, indicate the nature of the change. At this point,
in the first year of his conversion, Eliot was giving notice that he
recognized that a transformation of critical concerns must follow
upon his new faith, though he was still unsure of what that
transformation would be.

These years of the late twenties and early thirties were a time
when Eliot was trying to determine the consequences of his conversion in many areas of thought—in politics, in economics, in
philosophy—and was testing his ideas in the pages of the *Criterion*. In his literary criticism he was doing the same thing, trying out answers to the question: what is a Christian critic?
Clearly the central issue was the relation between literature and
belief, and Eliot's principal critical essays during these years are
focussed on that issue in various ways. There are theoretical
questions to be posed: how does belief enter into the creation of

poetry (is there a Christian imagination?) and how does it affect the reading of poetry (does a Christian read a poem as a non-Christian does?). Then there are questions of application: is this or that a Christian poem, is this poet a Christian, and what does the term mean when applied to poetry? Perhaps there are also terminological questions: is there a Christian language of criticism? can the critic bring literature and belief together by assimilating the language of religion? In the years between 1927 and 1934 Eliot struggled with all of these questions, sometimes clumsily and tentatively, mixing one with another, testing and revising ideas; what the critical writing of this period records is not anything like final, or even adequate answers to these questions, but rather the course of Eliot's efforts, and the difficulty that he found in determining how a Christian critic should perform his role.

He turned to the theoretical issue first—indeed his first statement on the subject pre-dated his formal conversion by some six months. 'A Note of Poetry and Belief' was written in response to an essay by I. A. Richards which Eliot had published in the *Criterion* in 1925, and which is the beginning of the whole poetry/belief debate that went on being argued well into the thirties. In describing the modern state of mind, Richards had written:

A sense of desolation, of uncertainty, of futility, of the baselessness of aspirations, of the vanity of endeavour, and a thirst for a life-giving water which seems suddenly to have failed, are the signs in consciousness of this necessary reorganisation of our lives. [By 'reorganisation' Richards meant the acceptance of a scientific view of the world, what he called 'the neutralisation of nature'.]

To this sentence the following footnote was attached:

To those familiar with Mr Eliot's *The Waste Land*, my indebtedness to it at this point will be evident. He seems to me by this poem, to have performed two considerable services for this generation. He has given a perfect emotive description of a state of mind which is probably inevitable for a while to all those who most matter. Secondly, by effecting a complete severance between his poetry and *all* beliefs, and this without

any weakening of the poetry, he has realised what might otherwise have remained largely a speculative possibility, and has
shown the way to the only solution of these difficulties.[6]

It is only a passing reference, dropped into a footnote, but it is
nevertheless important both in the history of modern criticism
and in the critical history of *The Waste Land*. For Richards had
devised a theory of modern poetry in terms of which Eliot's poem
was a key example and a model, and his interpretation of the
poem as a document of unbelief for a time of unbelief very
quickly became the common one. Eliot did not protest the interpretation in 1925, when he accepted Richards's essay for publication, nor in 1926, when it was reprinted in *Science and Poetry*
as 'Poetry and Beliefs'; but one can see why he had to speak up
in 1927, for he was then on the verge of conversion, and from his
new point of view Richards's admiration could only be an embarrassment. Reading over Richards's footnote, Eliot must have felt
like a general who has lost his artillery to the enemy, and is being
shelled by his own guns.

In his reply, Eliot took exception to Richards's second point,
both on general theoretical grounds ('I cannot see that poetry can
ever be separated from something which I should call belief') and
on personal grounds: 'As for the poem of my own in question',
he wrote,

> I cannot for the life of me see the 'complete separation' from
> all belief . . . A 'sense of desolation,' etc. (if it is there) is not a
> separation from belief; it is nothing so pleasant. In fact, doubt,
> uncertainty, futility, etc., would seem to me to prove anything
> except this agreeable partition; for doubt and uncertainty are
> merely a variety of belief.[7]

This is not quite a Christian critic speaking—Eliot is scrupulous
to identify himself as a doubter—but the position is a religous
one in that it asserts a necessary connection between the creating
imagination and some form of belief; and the example to which
he limits himself is *Christian* belief, an historical line that he
draws from Dante to Crashaw to Christina Rossetti and, by shy
implication, to himself. The argument in support of this position
scarcely exists in the essay; Eliot simply denies Richards's view,

and associates himself with another, believing position. It is as though at this point, just before his conversion, Eliot recognized that the question of poetry and belief would be an important one for him, and knew where he would have to take his stand, but did not yet have a theory to stand on.

One other point in Eliot's 'Note' is important to notice. In the course of his attack on Richards, Eliot wrote: 'Mr. Richards seems to me to be slightly under the sentimental influence of Matthew Arnold.'[8] It was an influence that Richards was eager to claim; his essay in its first version began with a quotation from an Arnold poem, and *Science and Poetry* begins and ends with Arnold: the epigraph is the passage from 'The Study of Poetry' in which Arnold claims for poetry the role in human life previously played by religion, and the final essay imagines a future as prophesied by Arnold: 'We shall then be thrown back, as Matthew Arnold foresaw, upon poetry. It is capable of saving us . . .' Like Arnold, Richards took the death of religious belief as a given:

> Countless pseudo-statements—about God, about the universe, about human nature, the relations of mind to mind, about the soul, its rank and destiny—pseudo-statements which are pivotal points in the organisation of the mind, vital to its well-being, have suddenly become, for sincere, honest and informal minds, impossible to believe. For centuries they have been believed; now they are gone, irrecoverably . . .[9]

This argument, linking the most influential of Victorian critics with one of the most influential of modern, was one that Eliot *had* to attack, whatever else he did, for if the Arnold-Richards idea of the relation between poetry and belief was correct, then belief (in Eliot's sense) did not exist at all—it was simply poetry pretending to be something else.

The 'Note' was a tentative first approach to a theoretical problem that would concern Eliot the Christian critic for many years. It was tentative, partly perhaps because Eliot doubted in himself the 'power of connected reasoning' that he found lacking in Arnold, and partly because he could not yet speak as a Christian. Consequently it touches on only one aspect of the problem, on which Eliot might be assumed to have some superior insight— the necessity of belief of *some* kind as a condition of the creating mind. Two years later he returned to the subject with a good deal more confidence in 'Dante', a long essay in which the greatest Christian poet is dealt with *as* a Christian, and therefore as a necessary case of the problem of poetry and belief as it affects the reading of poetry. Eliot is careful not to attack this problem immediately—the early pages of the essay are concerned with questions of understanding and appreciation—but it is nevertheless the central issue. The thrust of Eliot's argument is that belief exists in the *Divine Comedy*, that it is an informing element that must be recognized and responded to, but that recognition and response do not necessarily imply assent to the truth of the belief. The correct critical state of mind, Eliot concludes, is one in which 'one sees certain beliefs, as the order of the deadly sins, in which treachery and pride are greater than lust, and despair the greatest, as *possible*, so that we suspend our judgment altogether'.[10] This is not the Arnold-Richards line—belief stands as belief, and not as poetry or pseudo-statement—but it is an attempt to avoid dogmatism, while retaining the sense of the importance of belief as a part of the work.

The theoretical basis for this argument is not developed in the essay and Eliot must have felt that this was so, for he attached to it a long footnote in which he set forth his general theory, noting as he did so that it was 'still embryonic'. The note is an example of the way Eliot worried over critical problems during these years, returning to earlier formulations, revising, expanding or compressing, as though he was continually uncertain as to whether he had found the right, the *Christian* way of putting it. In this case he was revising his 'Note on Poetry and Belief', starting once more from Richards, and working toward a theory of his own that would allow to poetic belief the *authority* of belief. Even Richards's offending passage on *The Waste Land* is quoted again, to be dismissed in a single sentence: 'Mr. Richards' statement . . . that a certain writer has effected "a complete severance between his poetry and *all* beliefs" is to me incomprehensible.'

The argument of Eliot's embryonic theory consists mainly in the offering of two apparently contradictory views of the relation between poetry and belief, which Eliot argues are nevertheless both true:

it must be possible to have full literary or poetic appreciation without sharing the beliefs of the poet;

and

It is possible, and sometimes necessary, to argue that full understanding must identify itself with full belief.[11]

If you deny the first, Eliot argues, you deny the existence of both poetry and criticism, for both then become sub-categories of philosophy or theology; if on the other hand you deny the second, you deny the power of belief to alter consciousness, and this Eliot cannot allow. The contradiction is not resolved, and as an argument the note is not much of a contribution to the theoretical problem. But in terms of Eliot's understanding of the problem it was an advance in two ways: he recognized that the extreme opposing positions were contradictory, and that both were untenable, and he recognized that the problem involved the reader as well as the writer of poetry. In his earlier note Eliot had argued that belief necessarily figures in the creative process; that being so, he assumes here that it must figure also in the reader's response. But neither aspect of the issue is dealt with conclusively and the note is more an acknowledgement of problems than an urging of solutions. 'I have tried', Eliot modestly concludes,

to make clear some of the difficulties inhering in my own theory. Actually, one probably has more pleasure in the poetry when one shares the beliefs of the poet. On the other hand there is a distinct pleasure in enjoying poetry as poetry when one does *not* share the beliefs, analogous to the pleasure of 'mastering' other men's philosophical systems. It would appear that 'literary appreciation' is an abstraction, and pure poetry a phantom; and that both in creation and enjoyment much always enters which is, from the point of view of 'Art,' irrelevant.

That states the problem well enough; but it leaves all the hard questions unanswered.

Eliot returned to the question again a year later in 'Poetry and Propaganda', an essay which is a sort of footnote to the 'Dante' note. 'In a note to a recent essay which I have published on

Dante', he wrote, 'I made a first attempt to criticize both views [the two contradictory positions], and to find some way of mediation between the truth of both. I am now making a fresh start.'[12] This fresh start begins with the analogy between poetry and philosophy that Eliot had made in the Dante note quoted above, and elaborates on it in two ways. The first argument is that philosophical poetry does not *prove* ideas, but merely lends them an aesthetic sanction. If I understand Eliot correctly here, he is saying that even though we may not be able to accept a philosophy as true, we will not altogether despise it if we see that it can be used in a good poem; the poem will demonstrate, simply by existing, that its ideas 'are valid not merely in theory, but can be integrated into life through art'. But one must object that that last phrase begs the entire question; for what we are asking, if we discuss this issue at all, is *how* does art integrate belief into life?

Eliot's second point follows from the first. 'We must remember', he writes,

> that part of the *use* of poetry for human beings is similar to their use for philosophy. When we study philosophy as a humane discipline we do not do so merely in order to pick out one which we shall adopt as 'true,' or either to confect a philosophy of our own out of all philosophies. We do so largely for the exercise in assumption of entertaining ideas; for the enlargement and exercise of mind we get by trying to penetrate a man's thought and think it after him, and then passing out of that experience to another. Only by the exercise of understanding without believing, so far as that is possible, can we come in full consciousness to some point where we believe *and* understand. Similarly with the experience of poetry.[13]

This notion of the use of poetry avoids some of the problems connected with poetic belief, but it raises others. If poetry, like philosophy, merely demonstrates that other worlds of thought are possible, then it is initially independent of belief, though it will guide us toward belief. But as we move toward that point, what becomes of our experience of poetry? Apparently we leave most of it behind: 'We aim ideally', Eliot says, 'to come to rest in some poetry which shall realize poetically what we ourselves believe . . .' *Come to rest* is an odd phrase. Does it mean that Eliot imagines a point in life at which one stops reading new poems, or at least poems that do not express one's own beliefs, and settles down to re-read the safe, familiar ones until senility sets in? Another passage in the essay seems to confirm this interpretation:

> We do tend, I think, to organize our tastes in various arts into a whole; we aim in the end at a theory of life, or a view of life, and so far as we are conscious, to terminate our enjoyment of the arts in a philosophy, and our philosophy in a religion—in such a way that the personal to oneself is fused and completed in the impersonal and general, not extinguished, but enriched, expanded, developed, and more itself by becoming more something not itself.[14]

Here again is the curious notion that the experience of art has not simply an *end* (in the sense of a goal), but an *ending*. Whether *terminate* means to cut off, or to arrive at a destination, the sense is the same: art leads to philosophy, and philosophy leads to religion, which is the final term in the sequence. Having arrived there, one is at rest. This is certainly Eliot the Christian speaking, finding an instrumental role for poetry in the shaping of belief, though at the expense of the autonomy of both poem and poet. What he seems to be postulating is an orthodoxy of belief. This is not an altogether satisfactory resolution of the problem, but it is as far as Eliot got, and his later references to the problem (as for example his remarks on Shelley in *The Use of Poetry and the Use of Criticism*) essentially repeat this position.

At the same time that Eliot was theorizing about poetry and belief he was writing essays on Christian writers, demonstrating belief *in situ*. Some of his subjects, Dante for example, and Pascal, are obvious choices, but others are rather more surprising and show more interestingly the possible consequences, for a critic, of becoming a Christian. Take, for example, the two essays on Baudelaire. The first, written in 1927, the year before the *Sacred Wood* preface, seems intended as a demonstration of what Eliot had meant by 'the relation of poetry to the spiritual and social life of its time and of other times.' The occasion, a review of a translation by Arthur Symons, gave Eliot an opportunity to consider Baudelaire in his own time, in the nineties, and in the nineteen-twenties. For Eliot the constant in Baudelaire is that 'he was essentially a Christian, born out of his time'; the variable is what other times have made of his Christianity. Symons, reading him with the blind sensibility of his nineties generation, is partly right, partly wrong.

> what is right in Mr. Symon's account is the impression it gives that Baudelaire was primarily occupied with religious values. What is wrong is the childish attitude of the 'nineties toward religion, the belief—which is no more than the game of children dressing up and playing at being grown-ups—that there is a religion of Evil, or Vice, or Sin.[15]

Whereas 'we' (meaning Eliot) recognize in Baudelaire a self-made Christian, to whom the notion of Original Sin and the need for prayer came spontaneously, a kind of saint who in his solitude attained the greatest of the Christian virtues, the virtue of humility. It is a conception of Baudelaire that reflects Eliot's ideas as much as Symons's reflects the nineties—a Baudelaire for believers.

The second essay, written three years later, is a longer and more elaborately argued version of the first—another example of how Eliot returned to and revised his criticism. Whereas in the first essay he had simply stated that Baudelaire was essentially a Christian, in the second he hedged that assertion round with reservations:

> It was once the mode to take Baudelaire's Satanism seriously, as it is now the tendency to present Baudelaire as a serious and Catholic Christian . . . I think that the latter view—that Baudelaire is essentially Christian—is nearer the truth than the former, but it needs considerable reservation.[16]

(The principal example of the latter view of course is Eliot's own earlier essay, but here de-personalized, reduced to the status of an approximate truth, a first draft.) The reservation that Eliot proposes in this new version is that Baudelaire's religious understanding was only a part of Christianity; what he had discovered for himself was the reality of Sin and the sense of Evil. And, the argument goes, if the critic shares that sense, he will have a route to an understanding both of the poet and of the age that he represents.

The Baudelaire essays, and particularly the second, are important examples of Eliot performing as a Christian critic, using his own religious sense to discover that sense in another poet. Baudelaire was useful to him, as for example Hopkins was not, simply because his Christianity was *not* explicit. To Eliot, his case seemed to demonstrate that a poet sensitive to the spiritual condition of his time might arrive intuitively at a Christian position, and that a Christian critic would detect that intuited Christianity.

As Eliot continued to think about poetry and belief, and about Christian literature, it is not surprising that the terminology of religious discourse, and especially discriminative terms such as *orthodoxy* and *heresy*, began to turn up in his writing. Take, for example, this passage from the 'Dante' note:

> In short, both the view I have taken in this essay, and the view which contradicts it, are, if pushed to the end, what I call heresies (not, of course, in the theological, but in a more general sense). Each is true only within a limited field of discourse, but unless you limit fields of discourse, you can have no discourse at all. Orthodoxy can only be found in such contradictions, though it must be remembered that a pair of contradictions may *both* be false, and that not all pairs of contradictions make up a truth.[17]

The 'views' here are the contradictory ideas about poetry and belief that I discussed above: I cannot see how they can be regarded as *heresies*, even if we take that term in a 'general sense'. Do they promote division and schism? Are they contrary to the opinions of the community? Or are they simply opposing views in an argument over literary theory? As for *orthodoxy*, it seems to me quite meaningless to say that it can only be found in such contradictions, as though one arrived at the orthodox by striking an average between heresies, nor do I understand what sort of orthodoxy is being described: *religious* orthodoxy? Surely not. *Critical* orthodoxy? But what could that term possibly mean?

Such language is scattered through Eliot's critical writings of the period: one finds it for example in a review of a book on D. H. Lawrence and again in *The Use of Poetry and the Use of Criticism*, where Lawrence appears among 'the great heretics of all times', a category that seems also to include Wordsworth, Shelley and Goethe (the reference of pronouns is somewhat unclear).[18] In no case does this terminology clarify the point at issue; indeed when it appears it is more likely to reveal Eliot's failures of definition and logic. But I take it that Eliot's reason for using such terms was rather a matter of strategy than of logic: when he called the other side of an argument *heresy*, and his own *orthodoxy*, he was simply defining the ground on which he chose to fight his critical battles. It was a way of announcing that the critic engaged in this judgement must be taken as a *Christian* critic.

2

In 1932 Eliot travelled to the United States to give two series of lectures: the Norton lectures at Harvard (published as *The Use of Poetry and the Use of Criticism*) in the winter of 1932–3, and the Page-Barbour lectures at the University of Virginia (published as *After Strange Gods*) in the autumn of 1933. The two series are Eliot's most elaborate performances as a Christian critic and together they demonstrate the critical implications of the position at which he had arrived.

In the Harvard series Eliot is more nearly the conventional literary critic dealing with a literary subject; nevertheless, one finds in the lectures all the Christian concerns that I have been discussing: the problem of poetry and belief, the judgement of Christian subjects, examples of heresies, even a passing remark on the devil in modern literature. And the central thesis of the lectures is a religious one: that is, it is a proposition about the relations between poetry and religious faith—that as ideas of religion have changed, corresponding changes have taken place in ideas of the use of poetry. It is the subject that Eliot announced in his *Sacred Wood* preface: 'the relation of poetry to the spiritual and social life of its time'. As Eliot in the lectures moves chronologically through English literature, the judgements he offers belong as much to religious as to literary history: in the age of Addison 'theology, devotion and poetry fell fast into a formal-

istic slumber'; Wordsworth brought a 'profound spiritual revival'; Arnold represents another decline, in which 'the best
poetry supersedes both religion and philosophy'; and in the
twentieth century I. A. Richards is another Arnold.

What the lectures amount to is a history of English criticism
as seen by a Christian critic. It is Christian criticism in that it
takes as its primary variable the state of faith in England, and
relates changes in criticism to it. It is also, perhaps necessarily, a
polemic: for it implies an ideal condition in society, in which
poetry and faith interact, but keep their own domains. This condition is not exemplified in any historical period covered by the
lectures, and least of all by the present which is represented
chiefly by the heresies of Arnold and Richards; indeed it seems,
as one reads through it, that Eliot must have written the book
mainly for the opportunity it provided of winding up with his
two antagonists and refuting yet again Richards's judgement of
The Waste Land.

Eliot was not satisfied with his Harvard performance; the
result, he said, was only 'another unnecessary book'. What he
meant by this he explained in a letter to his friend Paul Elmer
More:

> The subject of 'The Use of Poetry' was undertaken merely
> because it seemed the one on which I could write with the
> minimum of new reading and thinking; the field of 'After
> Strange Gods' was one to which my real interest had turned.
> I therefore feel more regret at the inadequacy of the latter than
> of the former.
>
>   I am painfully aware that I need a much more extensive and
> profound knowledge of theology, for the sort of prose work
> that I should like to do—for pure literary criticism has ceased
> to interest me.[19]

Most of us would not call *The Use of Poetry* 'pure literary criticism', but it seems clear that to Eliot it was a book that failed to do
what he had set as his intention back in the *Sacred Wood* preface,
to leave 'the domain of criticism of "poetry" '. It was therefore,
to his mind, a less important work than the series of lectures that
followed, and he was anxious to defend the seriousness of *After
Strange Gods* against its critics. When Ezra Pound suggested in a

review that of the two books *The Use of Poetry* was the better,
Eliot protested in a letter to the editor:

> Mr. Pound has done your readers a disservice in suggesting
> that a book of mine, which is an unsatisfactory attempt to say
> something worth saying, is more neglible than another book of
> mine which is an unsatisfactory attempt to say a variety of
> things most of which are not worth saying.[20]

One recognizes the self-denigrating tone as Eliot's characteristic
public attitude toward his own work, but in this case I think we
take him literally; he did apparently think that both books were
inadequate. But of the two, *After Strange Gods* was the one to
be defended. It was an attempt to say something that mattered,
something that was in the field of Eliot's real interest. What that
field was should be clear enough: Eliot had described it in the
1928 preface to *The Sacred Wood*, and had been tilling it ever
since, or trying to. It was simply a kind of criticism that would be
integrated by the critic's beliefs, and the religious tradition to
which he belonged, a criticism that would turn away from the
idea of autotelic poetry, from the separation of the man who
suffers from the poet who creates, and which would urge the
relevance of a religious view of life both to the making and to
the experiencing of literature. 'A man's theory of the place of
poetry is not independent of his view of life in general', he had
written in *The Use of Poetry*; *After Strange Gods* is his culmina-
ting effort to demonstrate the critical consequences of that conviction.

Eliot first described his intentions for the book in a letter to
More, written while he was revising the lectures for publication:

> I have had to turn to the revision of my Virginia lectures
> which have to be published in the spring. Again, an unsatis-
> factory piece of work. A good subject, I think: fundamentally
> a criticism of the lack of moral criteria—at bottom of course
> religious criteria—in the criticism of modern literature.[21]

There is also a statement of intent in the book's dust-jacket copy,
which Eliot may well have written, and would certainly have
approved, since it was published by his own firm:

the weakness of modern literature, indicative of the weakness
of the modern world in general, is a religious weakness, and . . .
all our social problems, including those of literature and criticism, begin and end in a religious problem.[22]

And in the lectures themselves he was also anxious to define his
intentions very explicitly: he explained there that he would be
'applying the standard of orthodoxy to contemporary literature',
'illustrating the limiting and crippling effect of a separation from
tradition and orthodoxy upon certain writers', and demonstrating 'the intrusion of the *diabolic* into modern literature'.[23]

The principal difference between these statements and Eliot's
earlier approaches to Christian criticism is in the explicitness of
the connection that he makes between literature and religion;
clearly this book was to be a polemic in a way that none of the
other writings had been. Eliot's previous Christian criticism had
been historical when it dealt with individual writers; it was
about 'the relation of poetry to the spiritual and social life of its
time and other times'. But *After Strange Gods* is concerned with
the immediate situation: it deals only with modern writers, and
addresses itself to contemporary literary questions, though it does
so in a rather surprising way. Eliot calls it 'my illustration of the
dangers of authorship to-day', but the dangers he is referring to
are not those that threaten the author, but those by which the
author threatens society—in short, the 'modern heresies' of
which the book is a 'primer'. It is a book of moral judgement,
and Eliot's tone, usually so mild and urbane, sometimes becomes
angry and denunciatory, the voice less of a literary critic than of
an Old Testament prophet; the final lecture assumes that voice
altogether in the peroration, where Eliot quotes a fiery passage
from *Ezekiel*: 'Woe unto the foolish prophets, that follow their
own spirit . . .'

But though Eliot ends as a prophet, he begins as a modest man
of letters. The first lecture opens with a disarmingly simple statement: Eliot is simply setting out to re-write his important early
essay, 'Tradition and the Individual Talent'. Fifteen years have
passed, and Eliot has changed (he has become a Christian, though
he doesn't mention this crucial factor). Although he does not
repudiate his earlier formulation, he sees that it needs revising:

'the problem, naturally, does not seem to be so simple as it seemed then, nor could I treat it now as a purely literary one.' This is by now familiar behaviour: Eliot revising himself and reaching out from the 'purely literary' to larger issues. He is still against personality and in favour of tradition, but the terms need re-definition and a few new ones must be added (notably *heresy*). *Tradition* in particular has changed; it is no longer a word for a literary inheritance, but rather

> involves all those habitual actions, habits and customs, from the most significant religious rite to our conventional way of greeting a stranger, which represent the blood kinship of 'the same people living in the same place.'[24]

Eliot assumes throughout this first lecture not only that such a traditional society is theoretically desirable, but that it actually exists in the audience that he is addressing. This must be taken as an elaborate pretence—he must surely have known that he was speaking, not to a gathering of Southern Agrarians, but to the heterodox modern world—but it was a pretence that allowed him to make some statements that would otherwise seem intolerably reactionary, to remark that in the good traditional society 'any large number of free-thinking Jews' would be undesirable, and that 'a spirit of excessive tolerance is to be deprecated'. The free-thinking Jews have nothing to do with the argument and it is difficult to see why Eliot inserted such a gratuitously offensive remark, one that stuck to his reputation for the rest of his life; the latter comment is more relevant, for as the later lectures demonstrate it is a statement of the critical attitude that Eliot had assumed.

As literary criticism the first lecture is an empty vessel, and the audience of Virginians must have gone away feeling rather let down; they had come to hear a famous modern poet and had got nothing but tradition and orthodoxy. But one can see what Eliot was doing; he was making the lecture an assertive initial act of integration, proposing the religious, political and social bases on which the following critical judgements would rest. If the 'purely literary' principles of 'Tradition and the Individual Talent' were no longer adequate, *these* were the reasons why.

The two lectures that followed have plenty of critical content, though of an odd kind; one might describe them as Eliot's literary Purgatorio and Inferno (characteristically, there is no Paradiso). In the second lecture, one sees the souls of the distressed—writers whom Eliot admires but whose work has been crippled by their lack of 'a living and central tradition', and in the third, the souls of the damned, the heretics, instruments of the Evil Spirit (D. H. Lawrence, rather puzzlingly, appears in both). It is all very dramatic and surprising—where else would one find the capitalized Evil Spirit in modern literary criticism?—but it is also sometimes grotesque, and suggests that tradition and orthodoxy may have had as limiting and crippling effects on Eliot as he thought their absence had on imaginative writers.

At the heart of the second lecture—and indeed it is the essential centre of the whole critical argument—is a theory of the aesthetics of moral conflict. A perception of Good and Evil, and the eternal struggle between them, is a condition of the spiritual life; but it is also, Eliot argues, a condition of the highest literary life, and one that can scarcely be achieved without the support of a moral tradition. A writer's capacities will be distorted and restricted to the degree that his ideas of Good and Evil are inadequate, private, or non-existent. The assumption here is not simply that belief governs *content*: Eliot is arguing that it also governs the range of a writer's awareness and utimately his capacity for realism and depth of characterization. Hence modern writers are crippled *as artists* by their strange gods:

> It is in fact in moments of moral and spiritual struggle depending upon spiritual sanctions, rather than in those 'bewildering minutes' in which we are all very much alike, that men and women come nearest to being real. If you do away with this struggle, and maintain that by tolerance, benevolence, inoffensiveness and a redistribution or increase of purchasing power, combined with a devotion, on the part of an élite, to Art, the world will be as good as anyone could require, then you must expect human beings to become more and more vaporous.[25]

For this general theory, Eliot offers two sets of examples: a group of stories, and a number of modern poets. The stories are Katherine Mansfield's 'Bliss', Lawrence's 'The Shadow in the

Rose Garden', and Joyce's 'The Dead', and what they provide is a graduated series in terms of moral implications. Mansfield's story has no moral implication at all (but this is all right, apparently because it is brief and 'feminine'); Lawrence's has a negative moral implication (the characters lack any moral or social sense); Joyce's seems to approach positive moral significance (though the only evidence that Eliot offers is a quotation from the final paragraph). In these judgements, Eliot explains,

> we are not concerned with the authors' *beliefs*, but with orthodoxy of sensibility and with the sense of tradition, our degree of approaching 'that region where dwell the vast hosts of the dead' [this is a phrase from the Joyce passage quoted]. And Lawrence is for my purposes, an almost perfect example of the heretic. And the most ethically orthodox of the more eminent writers of my time is Mr. Joyce. I confess that I do not know what to make of a generation which ignores these considerations.[26]

I confess that I do not know how to respond to Eliot's distress, for it is hard to see how his generation ought to behave in order to please him. Apparently by praising Joyce, condemning Lawrence, and patronizing Mansfield; but on what grounds? Eliot's own bases for judgement are not clear, though it seems to include a distinction between Joyce's superior Jesuit education and Lawrence's unfortunate association with an Evangelical mother.

(These stories are offered, Eliot says, because he happened to read them at the same time, while he was at Harvard, but one can't help noticing that they have a common theme—suffering and betrayal in marriage. Not much is known about Eliot's first marriage, but it was clearly a wretched failure, and it was breaking up during the time when Eliot was lecturing in America. I mention this connection not out of a taste for gossip, but to note that even the most determined moralist is never entirely in control of what he will moralize about. Eliot may have gone looking for examples of moral implications, but what he found were examples of sexual cruelty in marriage; and perhaps this element affected his judgements.)

In this second lecture Eliot's principal poetic examples are

Yeats and Pound, two makers of private mythologies who were limited and crippled by their privacy. Eliot is especially good on Pound's *Draft of XXX Cantos*, where he concentrates (as one might expect) on the rendering of Hell. Pound, he says, having no personal belief in either Hell or Heaven, has created a Hell that is perfectly comfortable, because it is a place of punishment for other people, a prison for the people Pound disapproves of; it is a case of a modern mind lacking the support of orthodoxy and tradition, and so trivializing religious concepts. Yeats, treated as another example of the modern mind, is praised largely in negative terms: in his old age he has cast off the private religion of poetry that he had made in his youth (and that had made him guilty, in Eliot's mind, of the crime of Arnoldism—thinking that Poetry can replace Religion), and has settled into a bare but seemly poetic old age.

In Eliot's treatment of these two admired poets there is what seems an essential contradiction. On the one hand he assures us that their difficulties arose through no fault of their own, that they suffered the crippling of talent because they lived in a crippling world. But on the other hand Eliot seems to believe —and indeed the orthodox critic *must* believe—that the option of belief is at all times open to the errant will, and that Yeats and Pound might have made themselves Christian poets if they had tried hard enough; his descriptions of the trifling and eccentric systems that they constructed as alternatives to faith have a touch of impatience about them.

Eliot's own Hell—the domain of his third lecture—is, like Pound's, a place for other people, though it has only two occupants. Thomas Hardy and Lawrence are there as examples of what Eliot calls 'the intrusion of the *diabolic* into modern literature', and his tone when he discusses them is what one might expect of a Christian describing the agents of The Evil One. Which is to say that the criticism in this lecture is so extreme, so indefensible in its extravagant condemnation of heresy, as to be of interest only as a demonstration of the dangers to rational discourse that orthodoxy and moral fervour pose. If this is an example of orthodox criticism, then critics must pray for heterodoxy, for clearly orthodoxy is bad for one's judgement: it leads one to dismiss the wholly unacceptable too quickly, and for the wrong reasons, and to condescend to one's opponents (for to be an opponent is to be one of the Lost).

The quality of Eliot's judgement in these cases is perhaps best shown by quoting a fairly extensive passage from his remarks on Hardy:

> The work of the late Thomas Hardy represents an interesting example of a powerful personality uncurbed by any institutional attachment or by submission to any objective beliefs; unhampered by any ideas, or even by what sometimes acts as a partial restraint upon inferior writers, the desire to please a large public. He seems to me to have written as nearly for the sake of 'self-expression' as a man well can; and the self which he had to express does not strike me as a particularly wholesome or edifying matter of communication. He was indifferent even to the prescripts of good writing: he wrote sometimes overpoweringly well, but always very carelessly; at times his style touches sublimity without ever having passed through the stage of being good.[27]

There is no single clause in this quotation that is defensible as an even possible opinion of Hardy. Hardy *did* hold objective beliefs; he was if anything hampered by too *many* ideas; he *did* desire to please a large audience (if he hadn't, would he have revised his novels for periodical publication?); he *did* write for a public and not for 'self-expression'; he *was* aware of the prescripts of good writing, though he was perhaps naïve in seeking them where he did. As for the final superior thrust, I am at a loss to say what it could possibly mean; how can a style 'pass through' goodness on its way to sublimity, as though style was a passenger on the Northern Line, and goodness was at Golders Green and sublimity at Edgware? Add to this that the example Eliot chooses to judge Hardy by is a minor short story, 'Barbara of the House of Grebe', and one must conclude that what we have here is not so much an act of criticism as a kind of exorcism.

Lawrence is treated less barbarously, because Eliot saw in him a man whose vision was at least spiritual, though it was spiritually sick. Still, the judgements are severe enough: no sense of humour, an incapacity for thought, sexual morbidity. This last point reveals an important, rather Victorian side to

Eliot's critical position. Writing of *Lady Chatterley's Lover*, he says,

> Our old acquaintance, the game-keeper, turns up again: the social obsession which makes his well-born—or almost well-born—ladies offer themselves to—or make use of—plebeians springs from the same morbidity which makes other of his female characters bestow their favours upon savages. The author of that book seems to me to have been a very sick man indeed.[28]

And perhaps he was; but what Eliot is here describing is not a spiritual sickness, or even a morbidity, but simply a violation of the class structure: Lawrence's heresy is a class-heresy, and Eliot's orthodoxy is at this point simply Tory conservatism.

The last of Eliot's Virginia lectures ends with this sentence:

> All that I have been able to do here is to suggest that there are standards of criticism, not ordinarily in use, which we may apply to whatever is offered to us as works of philosophy or of art, which might help to render them safer and more profitable for us.[29]

He had said something similar in the previous lecture, about applying to authors 'critical standards which are almost in desuetude', and we are invited to believe that *After Strange Gods* was composed as a demonstration of what those standards are, and how they should be applied. But in fact it is impossible to discover what Eliot means by standards of criticism here, or even to be sure what the ultimate object of his criticism is. Is he criticizing modern writers for their heresies? Or is he condemning the society that produced them? Some of his individual literary judgements are very sharp, but the general focus of his concern seems social and religious, as when he says, apropos of Hopkins, that 'to be converted . . . is not going to do for a man, as a writer, what his ancestry and his country failed to do'. This is not a judgement of Hopkins, but of what Eliot calls 'a modern environment unfavourable to faith'; and if unfavourable to faith, then unfavourable also to orthodox literature, and the strengths that Eliot finds in such writing. The epigraph that Eliot chose for his book makes much the same point: it is a passage from the German critic Theodor Haecker, on 'Das Chaos in der "Literatur" '. Modern literature is a chaos, and could not be otherwise, given the chaotic state of faith in the world. Literary examples are therefore to be seen only as symptoms of a sickness for which the cure cannot be merely literary: nothing could make Lawrence and Hardy acceptable to Eliot except their conversion to the Church. And even that would not do for them as writers what their spiritual environment had failed to do. The kind of art that Eliot wanted would only come as a consequence of the general restoration of orthodoxy; it could certainly not be a cause of that restoration. And so what we have in *After Strange Gods* is Christian criticism of a kind, but in the voice of the critic-as-prophet, railing against the false gods of men.

Had Eliot arrived, then, at that final state that he described in 'Poetry and Propaganda', where the enjoyment of the arts terminates in a philosophy, and the philosophy in a religion, and where the test of poetry is 'what we ourselves believe'? It would seem that he thought he had, for when he prepared the lectures for publication he added a preface in which he denied the role of literary critic and claimed instead that of moralist. But such a disclaimer won't do, for what is the moral criticism of literature if it is not a form of literary criticism? Perhaps Eliot drew back from the name of critic because he recognized that his moral fervour had led him to take positions that were not critically defensible. Or perhaps he saw, as he apparently had not seen before, that the limitations and deformities that he saw in the writing of his own generation did not have either literary causes or literary cures, that if literature is not, as Arnold and Richards would have it, 'capable of saving us', neither are we capable of saving literature. It may be, as Eliot believed, that men and art can only be saved by a return to orthodox belief; but to put it this way is to put the matter beyond any writer's or critic's control: we cannot will a believing world, nor can we scold one into being. Perhaps it was his awareness of this truth that turned Eliot away from literary criticism, to the larger considerations of his later books, *The Idea of a Christian Society* and *Notes Towards the Definition of Culture*, books in which he could play the role of a Christian Arnold with greater range and freedom. Or perhaps he simply lost interest for a time in literature as a subject for primary concern. For there is a point, for the religious mind, at which literature ceases to matter, or at least takes a subordinate position in the scale of values. Eliot seems to have reached that point in *After Strange Gods*.

Looking back on Eliot's writing between 1927 and 1934, one can see that his whole effort was to integrate his life and thought into one coherent world view based on his Christian faith: to be a Christian in all things. 'I only affirm', he says in *The Use of Poetry*, 'that all human affairs are involved with each other', and that inter-involvement was his subject. But one must conclude that in his critical writing this effort failed. For that failure there are many possible explanations—some theoretical, some historical, some personal. Like many another convert, he was too urgent in his faith, and so wrote polemics when the occasion required criticism. He was never, in any case, at his best in sustained theoretical argument; what he said of Arnold was true of himself: he 'had little gift for consistency or for definition. Nor had he the power of connected reasoning at any length: his flights are either short flights or circular flights'. And he was defending a cause that was directly opposite to the main current of the time, religious and conservative in a political and radical era. While he was lecturing in America, *New Country* and *New Verse* were appearing in England, and it was the conversion experience that those pages expressed that would be influential in the coming years.

But beyond all else, one must conclude that Eliot failed because he misunderstood what success would have been. Auden (who was wiser in these matters) once remarked that there can no more be a Christian art than a Christian science or a Christian diet. There are only Christians who are artists or scientists or cooks; and the same is surely true of criticism. Faith is not a terminology, nor a list of the literary damned, nor even a sound theory of poetry and belief. It does not rest on the surface of a life like oil on a pond, but flows and spreads everywhere—it is the water itself. Eliot would have succeeded as a Christian critic if he had made his Christianity invisible; but he made it visible, and so made his religion seem a way of being reactionary, ungenerous and cold.

We must conclude, then, that Eliot failed as a Christian critic.

But we cannot say that he wasted his strength; for who can say what is waste and what is value in the use that a poet makes of his prose life? The essays that I have been considering were written in the period between the time when Eliot began writing 'Ash-Wednesday' and the time when he began 'Burnt Norton', and the two activities are related. It is difficult to define just what that relationship is, but surely the failed Christian critic played his part in the making of the *Four Quartets*. But even if that were not true it would be necessary to consider this body of Eliot's critical writings; for during these years, this is what he did, and we will not understand his life and work fully until we have mastered it all, the failures as well as the triumphs.

Eliot's Contribution to Criticism of Drama

R. PEACOCK

This essay might be looked on as an experiment to see what happens if we try to isolate a specific dramatic criticism from the general corpus of Eliot's critical writings. The position we can start from is the recognition of two concentrated activities. In his late twenties and early thirties he was formulating, in essays both on poets and on problems, a series of judgements based on general poetic and aesthetic principles; and he was already developing an intense interest, indeed a passion, for verse drama. An ideal of this formed itself gradually in his mind. It came to be expressed partly as a theoretical throw-off from his studiously conducted assessments of Elizabethan dramatists, and partly as a clarification for himself of practical problems which would arise were he to write plays. We feel this dual character in all the criticism of the twenties. Every evaluation is a future precept.

His drama criticism falls into three main parts, each of which is concerned with an aspect of drama and theatre, each is interesting in itself, and each is fruitful in respect of criteria and principles. First, the long series of Elizabethan essays presents itself solidly and importantly; here we find historical assessments, together with a cumulative enumeration of criteria for drama. Secondly, we have an assessment of the situation in the contemporary theatre, and see Eliot clarifying by adverse criticism his practical position. Thirdly, there are more direct statements about his ideal of poetic drama, and the problem of form involved.

The three fields are intricately interwoven because they have a common impulsion from Eliot's desire to write plays and, indeed, to initiate a general revival of verse drama. Thus the critic in Eliot, intellectually excited by a problem of definition, was to be asking the question, throughout thirty-odd years, what *is* dramatic poetry? And the aspiring practitioner asked simultaneously: is it possible today, is there a form it could take, and is there an audience that both wants and needs it?

His writing on the subject is in consequence always two-dimensional, which gives it its exceptional character. His whole approach, writing drama and writing about it, was 'critical', that is, hyperconscious, totally scrupulous; moreover the critical gear in which he propelled his creative vehicle took account of both an author-contemporaries and an author-public relationship. At the very beginning of his essay 'The Possibility of a Poetic Drama' (1920) he says: 'Surely there is some legitimate craving, not restricted to a few persons, which only the verse play can satisfy. And surely the critical attitude is to attempt to analyse the conditions and the other data.'[1] He was really acutely concerned about the revival of a poetic genre, and he instinctively accepted the fact that a genre, as distinct from individual expression, is in part a social creation.

So, turning to the two exploratory essays, the above quoted and 'A Dialogue on Dramatic Poetry' (1928), we see a special kind of criticism. Its essential baseline is the question of starting a revival; its method, however, instead of being, as one might expect, a straight architect's design for the project, is a 'critical' marking-out of the problems arising. His view of the contemporary drama had a negative tone; his study of the Elizabethan drama a more positive direction. The contemporary drama was the enemy, whilst the Elizabethans gave him his evidence, or at least a great deal of it, against the enemy's case. In this connexion the essay of 1924 on 'Four Elizabethan Dramatists' ('Preface to an Unwritten Book') moves naturally into close association with the two more general exercises, being itself, fragmentary introduction that it is, somewhat general in tone. These three essays overlap to some extent, but not in the sense of reshuffling the same ideas; it is in fact difficult to give a logical summary of all they say. But together they focus what became for him a central issue, that of realism versus convention, and the relationship of these two in all poetry, which is both a concern of Eliot and beyond that a perennially interesting problem of aesthetics.

They also make clear a double view of the Elizabethan drama.

Eliot was on the one hand profoundly aware that this body of dramatic poetry represented a great literary movement, the outstanding achievement of drama in England. That it was a verse drama was pertinent, because he believed firmly that verse is necessary to genuine poetic creations. But he does find points for criticism. They have the discipline of verse but are too free and too realistic in other respects. Thus, as his thoughts dwelt on the desirability of a new poetic drama he did not, in spite of his admiration, envisage a revival through simple imitation of their forms. He regarded *Everyman* and Aeschylus more favourably as models.

One feature of this movement, as a movement, apart from intrinsic merits of the plays themselves, impressed him very much. It was the fact that the genre created was subsequently capable of extensive development by many hands. 'The Possibility of a Poetic Drama' is very much dominated by this idea, and an accompanying nostalgia for a situation in which a number of writers are able to take up a genre already available and devote their individual originality to enriching it with variations, thus creating a full cycle of potentiality beyond the powers of single workers.

Comparing the contemporary drama and theatre with the Elizabethan Eliot saw with distaste that it lacked his requirements; he saw no verse, or the wrong kind, no conventions, and an uninspired realism. Certainly it was the time of the nadir of realism. He seems to have had no very high opinion of any of the literature of prose drama, British or Continental, in the earlier part of this century. So much so that, although so interested in the problem, he wasted not a jot of time on the passionately devoted niceties of evaluation he bestowed on the least of the Elizabethans and Jacobeans. He was offended, obviously, by the prosaic style associated with realism, which in the twenties did perhaps need, for the public assertion of standards, some sort of snub from a critic of sufficient authority. He was also contemptuous of the entertainment fringe, which included Coward and Arlen. Since he could not really be required to be interested in these one sees how much trouble he took to be aware of them, and how conscientious his study of the contemporary theatre and its audience was. Many may have shared his feelings. Looking back now we see that he was right to launch his attack; but his basis was very restricted and he did less than justice to some great authors who in the event not only survived in their own work but were a fertile influence on the remarkable drama of the fifties and sixties in Europe.

Eliot was also plagued, in this area of poetry as in others, by his old obsession about poetic works and the philosophy they might too obviously express, not to say advertise. He himself being a philosopher in a professional, academic, sense, his intellectual pride in this respect joined forces with the fact of his adherence to an orthodoxy, one of the Christian positions, to make him impatient of most kinds of lay philosophy or 'philosophy of life'. The modern drama of this century suffered in his eyes from the same weakness as much nineteenth-century Romantic and post-Romantic poetry; it was engaged in formulating or embodying a philosophy as part of its purpose and therefore deviates from the true function of poetry. Goethe, Maeterlinck, Shaw and Ibsen, to name only the most eminent knaves in his perspective, were vulnerable from this point of view. His judgement is logical in relation to a first principle he entertained faithfully, that poetry, fiction and art should eschew the rhetorical statement of feeling, the direct, impassioned, committed profession of beliefs and their emotional aura, and aim instead to organize a set of data, sensuous impressions and images as the equivalent of a feeling-pattern; such a pattern has the eloquence of signature, to set against explicit vocal declamation. But his loyalty to this rigorous principle was so great that it made him insensitive, distressingly obtuse, for critical purposes, to a range of expressive modes and styles that are valid in their own way.

This resulted in a surprising blindness about much modern drama; he tended to throw out both good and bad together, though here and there he retrieves condemnation with grudging half-acknowledgements, as in the cases of Ibsen and Chekhov. To attack aridity and falsity was one thing, to depreciate good prose forms another. However, it may simply have been a deliberate tactical blindness, due to his fixity of purpose over verse. But it would look better in retrospect if the trends embodied in some of the prose drama he deprecated had subsequently proved sterile; in fact they held some of the seeds of later developments in which forms based on theatre imagery and verbal style were to replace with confident effectiveness the poetry of verse.

The 'Dialogue on Dramatic Poetry' is a meandering conversation, with much self-irony. It is not a particularly cogent piece, either as criticism or theory, and a question mark hangs over the use of the dialogue method. Yet it does reflect Eliot rummaging about in a score of possible attitudes and problems, pretending to feel a bit at a loss, scratching or seeming to scratch, his head for once instead of laying down a sharp bit of law, and wondering where the way ahead lies. But he gets his enemies spot-lit: the 'ethical' comedy of ideas (to cite the ageing Pinero in this connexion was prudent); the realism of social drama; the didactic purveyors of philosophies of life, which, like the former, failed to strike to the 'simplified' and 'universal'; the mistaken substitution of literature and drama for religion; and the work of sophisticated but superficial entertainers.

The general drift of argument in the 'Dialogue' is to review the possibility of drama adopting a 'convention' as a basic artistic discipline which would of its nature induce the poetic. Eliot picks up ideas first mooted in 'Four Elizabethan Dramatists', written some four years earlier, but after he had already spent some time on his rigorous, sustained study of the Elizabethans. This essay, cleaner in outline than the 'Dialogue', is organically important in the development, because it shows for the first time in all its clarity the particular motivation of Eliot's criticism:

The statement and explication of a conviction about such an important body of dramatic literature, toward what is in fact the only distinct form of dramatic literature that England has produced, should be something more than an exercise in mental ingenuity or in refinement of taste: it should be something of revolutionary influence on the future of drama. Contemporary literature, like contemporary politics, is confused by the moment-to-moment struggle for existence; but the time arrives when an examination of principles is necessary. I believe that the theatre has reached a point at which a revolution in principles should take place.[2]

The appearance in 1923 of William Archer's The Old Drama and the New was the ideal provocation for Eliot at this point.

It helped him to focus his developing ideas and make a public declaration as a counter-attack. Archer's book defended as progressive theatre much of the prose drama that Eliot himself was up in arms about. In reply, he throws Archer with a subtle insight very unexpectedly together with Swinburne, whom he respected as a critic, pointing out that they both in fact regarded Elizabethan drama as 'literature' primarily and not as effective 'drama'. He takes the line that Archer criticized the Elizabethans for the wrong reasons; he supposed they were not realistic enough and therefore less good than the modern drama. But Eliot sees that they, too, sought realism; by aiming in several directions at once with their plays they failed to act on the first principle of poetic composition, which is to choose your conventions and work within them; of which procedure Aeschylus and the morality *Everyman* are adduced as examples. By convention here Eliot means any convention apparent in subject-matter, in treatment, in verse, in dramatic form, or in generally accepted philosophy. Only by such a device can the material of life be transformed into art.

This is henceforth to be one of his most important principles. He takes up the point in connexion with acting. He finds that actors playing nowadays in Elizabethan plays are either too realistic or too abstract in treatment, and he blames this on the contemporary realistic style which reduced actors' understanding of other methods. He himself would like the job of the actor to be no more than that of a ballet dancer whose general movements are set for him; he is not required to have any 'reality' or personality; he exists only during the dance. In the actor acting in realistic drama the real person of the actor intrudes, and the more realistic the greater the intrusion. The problem is central to the poetics of theatre. It is clearer if we remember that Eliot was basically objecting not only to realistic acting but to plays of realistic content and tendency, which really depend on accurate casting and the consequent identity of the part with the person of the actor. The ideal in Eliot's mind, on the contrary, is of a poetic work, in a formal convention, which requires for its presentation an 'abstract' actor projecting the poet's conception simply and purely.

His own primary criticism of the Elizabethans may be summed

up in the proposition that their art was 'an impure art'. They confused the issue by not deciding in principle what should be their conventions. They suffered from 'artistic greediness', desiring all sorts of effects together, and unwilling to accept limitation.

By virtue of his power of making pregnant distinctions, and of a sort of strategic military eye in the drama area, Eliot appeared to be taking up strong positions in a relatively limited field; but he was in fact attacking the decadence of all the drama and fiction of the realistic, and naturalistic, era. He was fighting a battle in the same campaign as Virginia Woolf in her famous essay on 'Modern Fiction' (*The Common Reader* 1925). His preoccupation with the nature of ballet, and the references to Diaghilev, are neither original nor fortuitous, nor personal problem; the Diaghilev performances in western European capitals were a major revitalizing influence on all the arts. But again the fight was not merely about form. Through not talking much about subject or theme Eliot allows much of his dramatic criticism to appear wholly preoccupied with formal or technical methods. But subject is the determining factor. Virginia Woolf, in the essay referred to, spoke of the distressing lack of 'spiritual' themes and quality in the prevalent materialistic fiction. Eliot, too, was really calling not simply for more 'artistic' surfaces or manner but for themes that transcend mimetic realism and absolutely impose the requirement of formal-poetic symbolism.

The 'Dialogue', running over some of the points raised in the two earlier essays, adds others, the most important being the question of the Mass as a form of ideal drama, and the gradual focusing of the specific dramatic-poetic form, which was to be illustrated from Shakespeare. The former is in a way an ironical red herring, because Eliot uses it to differentiate between actual participation, as a believer, in a religious rite and the purely aesthetic enjoyment of a perfect formal ritual. But it is also relevant in view of the Dionysian origin of Greek tragedy; drama was often closely associated with rituals and their formalization of universal emotions. The phenomenon of the Mass helps him to crystallize out the nature of formal conventions, or 'impersonal' forms, whose expressiveness lies in a bedrock of communal feeling and traditional discipline.

Thus, after passing judgement on the contemporary prose drama, and establishing the prime necessity of formal discipline through conventions, he arrives at the particular problem of the poetic and the dramatic: do they in some way interfere with each other, so that one can only be effective at the expense of the other? Or do they reinforce each other? Whilst this is a question he has to resolve for his own personal reasons it extends far beyond that. Giving, in the scheme of the 'dialogue', a mild Socratic twist to the course of the argument, he lets his participant 'B' put forward the idea that dramatic merit cannot be estimated without reference to poetic merit, and that Shakespeare is a greater dramatist than Ibsen, 'not by being a greater dramatist, but by being a greater poet'. 'For ... what great poetry is not dramatic'; which is, for Eliot, an imprecise remark, not more than a debating point. 'Who is more dramatic than Homer or Dante?' 'If you isolate poetry from drama completely, have you the right to say that Shakespeare was a greater dramatist than Ibsen, or than Shaw?' But in the sequel another voice ('D') corrects and refines:

> If drama tends to poetic drama, not by adding an embellishment and still less by limiting its scale, we should expect a dramatic poet like Shakespeare to write his finest poetry in his most dramatic scenes. And this is just what we do find: what makes it most dramatic is what makes it most poetic ... The same plays are the most poetic and the most dramatic, and this not by a concurrence of two activities, but by the full expansion of one and the same activity.[3]

This passage is of central importance because, virtually transcending criticism, it states a conception that is ideal. It is not mere correct theory, and not necessarily precise about Shakespeare, for whose multiplicity of forms it is a too simplified single principle. It promulgates the ideal condition, almost a Platonic idea, of dramatic poetry, to which Eliot sees Shakespeare approaching nearest, and behind him the nobility of English drama, his Elizabethan contemporaries and successors, in descending ranks. As an absolute conception it has splendour; but it implies an automatic, rather ruthless demoting of any or all prose drama, which finally is too absurd a limitation. Apart from its ideality it can be made a central principle of the poetics of drama, as indeed Eliot does make it in his later essays 'Poetry and Drama' and 'The Three Voices of Poetry'. To support it he needs other principles, which we shall examine together later.

The 'Dialogue' ends its survey of the situation of the twenties on the simple practical note that 'our' desire for a poetic drama should be kept alive, that small interested groups should experiment independently of the commercial theatre, and that a new form of verse should be found that could do for the present what blank verse performed for the Elizabethans.

It would be too simple to regard Eliot's essays on drama as cumulative fragments of a blueprint for his own drama-writing, though in one sense they are so; and too simple to hive off the articles on Elizabethan and Jacobean playwrights as a separate category of historical criticism, though they are indeed a remarkable contribution in that sense alone, inseparable from the corpus of scholarship in that field. For both these currents are directed also by his powerful, insistent interest in the nature of all poetry, and a critical understanding of its variant forms. The sense of many people that the plays are a weaker branch of the Eliot tree, and equally that the critical scholarship is independently valid, tends constantly to obscure the fact that the impulse in Eliot to drama was exceptionally deep and strong; it must remain a central component in his poetic activity, however the plays are assessed. This relates in some respects to the controversial views about Eliot's precise rank. In spite of the resounding adulation of his early lyric work there were moderating voices that saw in him an interesting minor poet rather than a major one. Even granted the quality of his superb innovations of style, and the achievement of the *Four Quartets*, there remains something incongruous in the breadth and incisiveness of his thinking on numerous issues and the relatively small quantity of poetry he wrote. The same discrepancy appears in the contrast between his grand conceptions of classical style, and poetic traditions of Europe established in such achievements as those of Virgil and Dante, and his own implied attempt to contribute to the same tradition. There is a factor missing in this equation. His inveterate preoccupation with drama throws light on this. In his writing and thinking as a whole, as a single activity flowing into diverse channels, there was a greatness of outlook, a powerful radiation of ideas about the fundamental problems of interpreting life, society, the human conflicts, that quite transcends the limits of his lyric poems and cries out for a broader mimesis of life. The poems were a decisive creation, both historically and absolutely. But there was something more comprehensive about his mind and imagination that really did make his total utterance commensurate with poets who wrote much more poetry than he did.

The urge to drama was a profound instinct. He was searching for the canvas, the landscape of manifold human conflict, which would be an adequate representation of human involvement, and which he could impregnate with his interpretations of existence. Eliot, as a poet committed to verse, saw very soon that the drama was the only extended form available to him if he wished, as he did, to move beyond his 'first' voice (meditative) and give a picture of society, of men and women with their actions and conflicts, in situations of suffering and guilt, and in a relation to society as a whole and its values. Such a subject cannot be dealt with in the twentieth century by epic or long narrative, genres which no longer have roots in society or its culture. But Eliot did want to undertake the larger poetic task and portray life, behaviour, and the ethical structure of modern society in relation to beliefs and non-belief. The early criticism and the early poems go together as a keen specialized achievement. The search for a working theory of verse drama, and for dramatic realizations, in a verse and idiom congruent with the social reality of contemporary people, is the link between the specialized performance and the scale of his outlook on the whole of life, literature and ideas.

The forces from this wider outlook and potentiality drove him to plan his drama-writing. It also determined his interest in Elizabethan drama as a corpus of life-material as well as a creation of poetic drama. This was primary. The Elizabethan criticism was not just a superbly cool course in critical anatomy. The contents of this drama, from Kyd to Massinger and Shirley, consist of a mass of essential drama material, social turbulence and moral conflict. There can be no doubt that Eliot's evolving of so concentrated a body of criticism about numerous writers much of whose work is to all practical purposes dead to the theatre was sustained not only by a private wish to write verse plays but by a compelling interest in the moral and social chaos evident in the themes of Elizabethan and Jacobean drama. Eliot after all belonged to a generation that rediscovered evil, desired to feel its reality as part of human reality, however veiled by conscious or unconscious subterfuges. Only such an impulse, operating finally as an obsession, could carry a really living person, as distinct from a curious historian, through the whole mass of this drama, as Eliot was carried. It is noticeable that when he quotes approvingly passages from poets he has strong reservations about it is not only because they are praiseworthy simply for their poetic style; they are vivid expressions of a certain kind of subject-matter, which helps to govern their selection.[4] Thus, however admirable as finely tempered, self-possessed criticism his Elizabethan essays may appear to scholar-critics, they reveal in effect, in the guise of criticism, some of Eliot's obsessional problems. In retrospect they are seen to be every bit as much the co-lateral documentation of the subjective origins of his early poetry, and of his plays, which are all about guilt, as a model piece of criticism on his own principles of analysis and comparison, cool, rational, marvellously poised. His obsession with the subject area, as well as his formal analysis, give these essays, as a group, their committedness, their intensity, their force, their even hallucinatory perspicuity.

In this criticism he was keen not solely to describe the virtues of particular authors, nor to find one or two models to serve his own plans best. He moved steadily towards defining some general principles of poetics. To discover the nerve of dramatic poetry became his persistent aim; this is nearer to aesthetics than criticism. He avoided using technical aesthetics, but constantly expressed aesthetic principles in the language of criticism. His most famous dictum about the objective correlative is of this kind. Most critics stop short of his point of generalized formulation, whilst most philosophers start on the other side, in abstract analysis, of its complex and dense simplicity. He works with great adroitness and concision within a critical idiom, but always on the edge of aesthetics. In historical perspective, moreover, we see that he often started from the aesthetic debates of the period; Croce, Richards, Collingwood are all in the wings. The central 'objective correlative' is related to lines of thought emerging with Cassirer's work on symbolic forms as aspects of consciousness, whilst the role of 'feeling' was to be given elaborate analysis by Susanne Langer.

Because of his position in this general context, together with his practical problem, the criticism of the essays on individual poets constantly overlaps with the more theoretical methods of the essays directly focused on general points. Each of the Elizabethan pieces isolates in turn a principle relevant to the definition, practice, or evaluation of drama; each puts a major problem into special relief. Critics often have a specialized method, or their own group of criteria, and apply them equally to successive authors. It is part of the originality of this large cluster of essays that their author, reading one dramatist after another, evolves gradually, each time from the most informative example, what is virtually a poetics of drama in near-aphoristic form. Certainly Eliot is sensitive to the individual style of his poet-playwrights, but to focus this and also formulate a general principle of all drama is the result of a single insight. At the end of this series of studies of individual writers we can give a set of chapter headings for a poetics of the form. We find the following topics, amongst others, emerging in this way: the material of drama, especially emotions that have to find appropriate expression (*Hamlet*); emotional tone expressed in the total design (Jonson); the problem of types and categories, and inadequate terminology (Jonson); the 'creating' of characters (Massinger, Jonson); realism and the artifice of form ('Four Elizabethan Dramatists'); diction, especially the refinement of plural sensuousness matched in language and imagery (Massinger); poetic verse and dramatic verse (Marston, Heywood); poetry of the surface (Ford); moral conflict central to drama (Middleton); rhetoric and acting ('Rhetoric and Poetic Drama'); dramatic conception and construction (Tourneur); drama and beliefs, or philosophical attitudes ('Shakespeare and the Stoicism of Seneca'); blank verse as dramatic instrument (Marlowe, and passim). In addition these studies aim to establish margins, and a scale; margins on the one side of dramatic rhetoric becoming false hyperbole, and on the other of poetry lapsing into versified prose. Eliot finds along the scale a place for each author according to his robuster or weaker realization of genuine poetry, his 'degree of form' and style. He finds his ideal centre, finally, in the first scene of *Hamlet* and the balcony scene of *Romeo and Juliet*.

It is essential to Eliot's position that dramatic poetry (verse drama) is a type of verse, but not a type of drama; his line is that verse expression, being simply a natural intensification of prose, does not alter drama except to intensify it. Nor is it a mixture of lyric, narrative, and dialogue. He regarded closet drama, in which 'poetry' spreads itself for a private reader, as an untrue form, faulty and misdirected. His basis for poetic values in drama is always the representation of an action, a sequence of human involvement, an indivisible artistic whole; and in no circumstances a frame or grid on which merely to attach poetic divagations. Of the later essays, that on 'The Three Voices of Poetry' (1953) yields, amidst some restatements of simple daily rules of his own, insights of a fruitful kind, capable of wider development, more so than the more directly entitled essay 'Poetry and Drama' (1951). It contains in essence an astute readjustment of classical genre theory, switching from recipient to poet the viewpoint from which lyric, narrative and drama are seen. But his theory of voices could also be said to be influenced by Plato's view of basic poetic forms.[5] Plato distinguished forms according to the 'direct' or 'indirect' address of the poet. The first was realized in the dithyramb, the second in drama, epic being a mixture of the two. This view regarded the indirect (dramatic) form as 'imitation'. Eliot's variant provides for a third mode, in which the poet's address is to himself, neither direct nor indirect, but neutral. In the present state of aesthetics of literature these divisions appear very approximate, no more than scaffolding to help construct more intricate conceptions; but the transference of speech from a narrating poet to fictive dramatic characters, who become the vicarious agents of the poetic statement, is the essential characteristic of dramatic form.

This in itself is not the most difficult problem. The mystery Eliot is always trying to probe is that of characters in a fiction, an action, speaking in verse and enhanced language. A lyric poet, an epic poet, are self-justifying in respect of intensification. They speak as a particular species, poets, and the purpose of their speech is, on the surface itself, to give enhanced meanings, which by their significance, and its incorporation in language, justify the artifice and the raised plane of expression. But drama imitates men, not poets, speaking. So the question arises, what, in drama, justifies, analogous to lyric and epic, the highly incredible artifice of verse and poetic diction?

Eliot takes as a model the poet identifying with the character, speaking in and through the character, so that character and poet have a similar motive for speaking poetry; they are both under a compulsion to 'intensity' of expression, the one by virtue of the emotional pressures from his situation, the other by virtue of his empathy and imagination. But around this character-to-character composition he also has something he calls 'musical design'; and I think we are to understand that there is a kind of music in the speech of characters, and a music in the design of the whole; a point to be elucidated later. Their combined functioning represents his central idea about the poetic-dramatic unison.

The argument from 'intensity' comes out with particular clarity in the following passage:

> But if our verse is to have so wide a range that it can say anything that has to be said, it follows that it will not be poetry all the time. It will only be poetry when the dramatic situation has reached such a point of intensity that poetry becomes the natural utterance, because then it is the only language in which the emotions can be expressed at all.[6]

Eliot is here clearly in line with aesthetic thinking in the twenties and thirties. Although he could speak slightingly of contemporary trends (as, for instance, in the brief references in the 'Dialogue' to what one 'must have read') his views are not unrelated to expressionist aesthetic theory. The idea of representation yields first place to that of expressing feeling. Throughout his criticism Eliot relies on the expression of emotion as the specific, idiosyncratic role of poetry. In the whole argument about belief, about poetry and philosophy, he often has emotion, emotional patterns, in mind; he always arrives back at expression of feeling as the crux of poetry's function. So here, rejecting the realist criterion, he accepts, as the solution of the problem of the unnaturalness of people speaking verse, the naturalness of verse for conveying strong, subtle, or exceptional emotions. In support he can further use his recurrent idea about 'degree of form'; as emotions, including dramatic ones, intensify, you need a higher compression and intricacy of form-making, which the superior organization of verse (rhythm and sound) provides. The emotions he means in this context are of course always emotions arising from the drama in hand, which gives them their particular colouring.

As Eliot applies it the conception becomes an original contribution to poetics of drama. It is made still more persuasive, and more useful, by his careful distinction between the dramatic monologue, as practised by Browning, and true dialogue. The character in a monologue, not being placed opposite other characters in an action, with equal dramatic status, appears simply as a *persona* of the poet himself. It is an intermediate 'voice', positioned somewhere between Eliot's first (meditative) and third (dramatic) voices. He sees it based on mimicry and impersonation, neither of which is involved in either the lyric-meditative voice or the true dramatic character.

But Eliot also keeps his eye on the whole dramatic scheme of a play. The terms he uses are the ordinary ones; a character has to express feelings arising from an action. He has in view, however, without too directly formulating it, the notion that there is a linguistic form that is the natural mimesis of the patterns of the dramatic in the movement of human life; this is what he is aiming to show in his analysis of the first scene of *Hamlet*, in 'Poetry and Drama'; and as a linguistic form it differs from lyric meditation, and narrative. Aesthetically speaking, it is his essential reply to false modes of the poetic in prose plays such as he criticized from this point of view; for example, in Maeterlinck, where the 'poetic' is derived from atmosphere, or the sense of unseen powers. What it does not answer is an adverse implication about prose fiction; if strong feelings need verse for adequate expression it looks as though the novel in principle cannot provide this, which is quite logical but rough on eminent novelists.

Eliot is throughout seeking something he calls 'dramatic poetry'; he explores the Elizabethans in such detail because their production over fifty years was enormously fertile and varied. Deep down, however, he is seeking to combine a metaphor-dominated diction, which ultimately is one aesthetic root of the symbolist aesthetic, with the beauty of formal design in larger patterns that he found more in Continental art and literature than in English, and to which he had access directly from American taste, and not via England; for example, in the classical tradition, in Dante, and in the quintessential formal symbolism, or symbolic formalism, of the Russo-Italian ballet. An acute formal sense is a powerful, un-English trait in his artistic character; he sought, with intellectual and sensuous passion, beauty of composition. English creative activity is additive, agglutinative, tending to patterns of free, capricious organic growth; its emblems are the shrub, the tree, the 'English' garden. We speak, of course, of garden and park design, but mean mostly no more than canalizing nature's own liberty, and camouflaging even this interference. The Eliot counter-taste reaches a long way. It covers his wit and farce, and makes him sensitive to formal beauty and its associated emotional overtones in the comedy of Jonson; in his essay on the latter he clarifies with great insight and sympathy a kind of poetic quality arising from design which is distinct from the poetry of diction or imagery.

This brings us to a component of Eliot's idea of dramatic poetry that extends its scope, going beyond the expressiveness of characters in action on which he bases so much of his argument. In the later phase of his thought, as represented by 'Poetry and Drama', he made an attempt to supplement his general conception with the musical analogy he had previously explored in regard to poetry; it derived, of course, with him as with most, from the symbolist aesthetic. The question to consider is whether this enlargement consolidated his ideas or introduced a new factor more disrupting, or divergent, than synthesizing.

In 'Poetry and Drama' he writes:

It seems to me that beyond the nameable, classifiable emotions and motives of our conscious life when directed towards action —the part of life which prose drama is wholly adequate to express—there is a fringe of indefinite extent, of feeling which we can only detect, so to speak, out of the corner of the eye and can never completely focus; of feeling of which we are only aware in a kind of temporary detachment from action . . . This peculiar range of sensibility can be expressed by dramatic poetry, at its moments of greatest intensity. At such moments, we touch the border of those feelings which only music can express . . . I have before my eyes a kind of mirage of the perfection of verse drama, which would be a design of human action and of words, such as to present at once the two aspects of dramatic and of musical order. It seems to me that Shakespeare achieved this at least in certain scenes . . . and that this was what he was striving towards in his late plays. To go as far in this direction as it is possible to go, without losing that contact with the ordinary everyday world with which drama must come to terms, seems to me the proper aim of dramatic poetry. For it is ultimately the function of art, in imposing a credible order upon ordinary reality, and thereby eliciting some perception of an order *in* reality, to bring us to a condition of serenity, stillness, and reconciliation . . .[7]

It strikes us that Eliot is trying here to bring together a number of things, each far-reaching: his love of drama, his love of an ineffable musical order underlying all poetry, his belief that art's function is to reveal meaning and order in reality, and, finally, his nostalgia for what he calls reconciliation; and bringing these things together he wants them to make a perfect harmony.

He had already spoken, in the essay on Marston, of two 'levels' in poetic drama. The point is interesting because his explanation of 'intensity', and its natural outlet in the hyperbole of verse, could really be quite acceptable as the poetic principle of drama without further help:

It is possible that what distinguishes poetic drama from prosaic drama is a kind of doubleness in the action, as if it took place on two planes at once . . . In poetic drama a certain apparent irrelevance may be the symptom of this doubleness; or the drama has an under-pattern, less manifest than the theatrical one . . . It is not by writing quotable 'poetic' passages, but by giving us the sense of something behind, more real than any of his personages and their action, that Marston established himself among the writers of genius . . . In spite of the tumultuousness of the action, and the ferocity and horror of certain parts of the play [*The Wonder of Women*], there is an underlying serenity; and as we familiarize ourselves with the play we perceive a pattern behind the pattern into

which the characters deliberately involve themselves; the kind
of pattern which we perceive in our own lives only at rare
moments of inattention and detachment, drowsing in sun-
light. It is the pattern drawn by what the ancient world called
Fate; subtilized by Christianity into mazes of delicate theology;
and reduced again by the modern world into crudities of
psychological or economic necessity.[8]

These remarks, written seventeen years previously to 'Poetry and
Drama', contain elements decidedly anticipating the passage
under discussion. But to say that the pattern that underlies is
Fate, or its Christian or modern counterpart, is almost to make it
over-clear, so that it lacks the transcendent quality of the later
passage, created by the ideal musical image.

The later passage is indeed a very remarkable mixture of precise observation and a dream of an ultimate consummation to be
achieved through art. The precision lies in the brief description of
the penumbra of elusive feelings beyond those of specific dramatic action and emotion. Eliot has here added something to his
intensity idea; he has focused therewith an area that is decisive
for the finest effect of poetry but is undoubtedly elusive. In fact
he has here linked up in another way the poet speaking and the
character speaking. His theory of the poetic expression of dramatic characters does not satisfactorily cover the reference between
the poet and the work as a whole, which is something more than
the sum of the characters in it; one has to account for the ultimate unity of vision centred in the author, and embodied in a
unity of style and design. Possibly the opera of Monteverdi, or of
Gluck, would provide a specific analogy for Eliot's order of drama
and order of music created simultaneously. In Monteverdi the
events, the human drama (the life-material), projected in a powerful vocal line, with relatively little choral or orchestral support,
are indeed a simultaneous dramatic and musical order. With
Gluck the analogy would be based on his ideal of powerful
dramatic emotions, apprehended simply in their natural, universal truth, and sublimated into a music of the purest and
noblest classical design, equally natural and universalized.

In many respects, then, Eliot's views on the nature of a perfect
dramatic poetry are a decisive contribution to the poetics of

drama, not covered in this illuminating way by other dramatists or writers on aesthetics, with the exception of Middleton Murry's exploratory chapter ('Imagery and Imagination') in his *Shakespeare*.[9] There are of course signs that it is a very distilled conception. Eliot gives, it is true, a few concrete examples from Shakespeare to persuade us that it has been actually realized; and his quotations from other Elizabethans often tend in this direction, though their exquisite selection is deceptive, making them seem the rule and not the exceptional high points they often are. But the conception has the beauty of an ideal paradigm; it is a poem of theory, almost autonomous; just as his three later plays may be said to cast the shadow, itself beautiful, of this quasi-Platonic form rather than to embody it really forcefully. Nevertheless it focuses as no one else has done the mystery of the poetic 'form' of all drama.

Apart from the aesthetic aspect a further point to notice is how the ideas of the passage tend to overshoot the analysis of dramatic form. After extending the latter, making it as comprehensive as possible, Eliot is in danger of ending with an apotheosis not of drama but of one type of play, the play of ultimate reconciliation, like Shakespeare's later works; and, with *The Elder Statesman* particularly in mind, we feel here that characteristic features of his late phase begin to influence and distort the general idea of poetic drama. In the mixing of critical, aesthetic description of drama with the very all-comprehending image of music, the latter becomes a general symbol of purification, of redemption, whilst the former is assimilated to it as drama-poem-rite. This may mean an induction into serenity and peace, but such terms take meanings from near-religious contexts, and criticism, or poetics, are transcended.

Having concentrated on a few salient points we have not had space to analyse or describe all Eliot's methods and usages in his dramatic criticism. From the many references he makes it is clear that he was extremely knowledgeable about the theatre, playwriting and dramatic literature, many years ahead of his own practical connexion with theatre people. He was not a lyric poet straying lucklessly or mistakenly into drama. He was inwardly attached to it. In an early essay like 'Euripides and Professor Murray' (1920), which is mainly about questionable poetic translation, it is clear that he has a well-aimed grasp of character and the actor's task; he 'conceives' the dramatic personage as such, and not only the problem of versification. It implies an important premiss, a creative liaison with dramatists of the past. In a similar way, without examining tragedy as a category, he is deeply sensitive about this aspect of life. The essay on Middleton bears witness to it. Here he concentrates, in terse, compact phrases, on human character, especially on permanent types of woman. The basis of the essay is moral knowledge of life. It shows Eliot profoundly moved, giving this author his admiration with warmth of feeling, strangely, compulsively generous. He displays everywhere, of course, a special interest in diction and versification, but there are usually hints that he is always aware of the structural features of drama, such as plot, manipulation of stage effects, characterisation, emotional tone, and type of play; his comments on diction and metric can usually be seen to be dependent on a prior consideration of these.

Eliot's position as critic of drama is strange because he chose to write most on a difficult and remote group of dramatists who raise many special, historical questions. What he did is a little bizarre; for urgent contemporary reasons (his desire to have a poetic drama) he went, in order to establish his criteria about poetry and conventions, realism and prose, to a period drama which gave him an extremely oblique view of his real problem, the one that put him in confrontation with his present-day. For most people this means that a series of significant modern dramatists have been pushed into a critical limbo of Eliot's making. It means that he refused, at least as public critic, to face up to a powerful presence in the twentieth century, namely a varied and interesting prose drama that has displaced verse drama, as prose fiction had displaced epic and narrative poetry. This is, of course, easier to see now because we have before us the longer development; we see continuities stretching from Strindberg, late Ibsen, and the social drama of the nineties and after, through both German expressionism and the poetic revivals in France and England, down to a post-war drama completely liberated from the social realism that persisted still in Eliot's earlier years and had become trite and superficial.

In relation to most of this drama Eliot was critically aloof. This meant, however, that he was unable, and unwilling, to apply an enlightening, positive criticism to a large body of reputable work, and displayed his powers in that respect only on the remoter drama. Naturally no one could require him to write about the prose authors if he didn't wish; he was averse anyway to writing criticism about living writers. Nevertheless, with his drama criticism, he was jumping into contemporary waters with arguments and attacks, and so it is inevitable that one should feel a gap of sorts. What we notice, no doubt with hindsight, in the straightening perspective of history—and all this is now historical—is that his vigorous focusing on the twin problem of the nature of poetic drama, and the practical problem of creating it anew, deprived him really of the distanced view that would have let him see more clearly all the forces, literary and social, that had in fact created the situation, and went on reinforcing the trends that were against his dream, insofar as it was the aspiration actually to bring into being a movement of some proportions. Slipping into this position was unfortunate, because, although drama enlarged his own creative effort, as I said above, his intended regenerative criticism was concerned only with a restricted area of the genre and he perhaps underestimated, or did not wish to acknowledge, the major change of direction that was occurring.

As we read his essays on drama in sequence, watching the pattern of criteria developing, we notice that they are wholly tied to the Greek, Renaissance, and French classical tradition. His attempt at a renewal was lucidly calculating and bold but was perhaps a last-ditch stand. The last florescence of the great tradition was the German classical-romantic effort reaching from Goethe to Grillparzer and Hebbel; a movement with which, however, Eliot had little sympathy. It was, moreover, still within earshot of the seventeenth and eighteenth centuries. By Eliot's time the gap had indeed widened.

Another factor in the cultural climate was, by the forties and fifties, the arrival of television and colour-film; in themselves they were not at first felt as threatening until the rapidity of their development took everyone by surprise. Apart from their proving to be a corrosive solvent, preparing the way for the emergence of mass democratic values, they held genuine promise as new media of art, and affected theatre forms inevitably. The large screen film in colour, and television in less forceful degree, have created a dominant form composed of fluid narrative scenes, dialogue, and, above all, visual imagery; in this combination the latter dispossesses enhanced metaphorical speech, a mainstay of verse drama.

Nor did Eliot, nor anyone else, for that matter, amongst the literary, foresee to what an extent the dominant temper would be so unutterably 'conversationalised', in the sense that all elevation of feeling and attitude would be under suspicion. The poetic drama in the Classical and Renaissance tradition did depend not only on a taste for a type of poetry but also on the receptivity for elevated attitudes; that is, genuine ones, not assumed, or rhetorical in a bad sense. Such receptivity has disappeared in the extreme egalitarian temper of the present.

However, Eliot worked out in his drama criticism some valuable central principles of the poetic form he most admired. He produced what is on any count an illuminating set of ideas about permanent features of this form. The two-dimensional interest of the general principle of poetics and the project for an experiment is constantly maintained. It is a distinctive feature. Other dramatists wrote criticism, but as often as not it was a form of justification of their own practice and deviations, under the guise of general principle. In Eliot the principles are not apologia, defensive pleading, but forward projections.

6

The 'Philosophical Critic'

WILLIAM RIGHTER

It has always been supposed that Eliot's life and work, poetry, criticism and social commentary were shaped by at least a degree of that reasoned coherence that one might call philosophical, or reflect a unified and rationalized point of view that one could call a philosophy. Certainly it would seem like folly to take any one aspect of the work in total isolation from the others. Yet insofar as anything called a 'philosophy' enters into any one of those aspects, it will emerge in quite different manners and different degrees. And the ambiguity is the deeper in Eliot the 'philosophical critic', for criticism itself poses this question of wholeness for us in a double sense: to what extent may it be seen as the intentional working out in its appropriate sphere of a principle that pervades the whole? Or to what extent does its practice in the multiplicity of its contexts suggest such a unity that we could inductively derive a clear notion of what 'philosophy' it might imply?

In Eliot's case, his long professional involvement with philosophy is itself one point of departure. Yet the ambiguities are as finely poised as the circumstances are clearly known—the latter in large degree the source of the former. He could have been an academic philosopher and chose not to be. The details of that academic work have been clearly charted by Professor Wollheim, Dr Bolgan and others. The process of its abandonment remains obscure. Late in life, perhaps with some persuasion, he came to publish his doctoral dissertation on Bradley, and may have come to take his early philosophical studies more seriously. Yet many scattered remarks, perhaps more emphatically in his later essays, treat his philosophical work with a diffidence that approaches the dismissive.

How heavily do such remarks—or at least those which point

to that particular and isolatable intellectual episode—weigh upon our sense of the whole? Its duration of five or six years would alone give us pause. Yet if we invoke some such fiction as 'Eliot's philosophy' it is not necessarily that period or work of that kind which come to mind. The dimensions suggested may be much more closely attached to the defender of classicism, tradition, religious orthodoxy and political conservatism, a coherence of a broader and vaguer and more pervasive kind than that of a precise conceptual frame derived from an academic discipline, a coherence closer to that which distinguished Dante from Shakespeare. And as such, one which defines the series of active stances which mark the course of Eliot's life—in the confrontation of modern chaos with traditional order, of the fragmentation of sensibility and thought characteristic of the present age with a rationalized recension of traditional wisdom. If the poetry may in the more vertiginous of its juxtapositions have suggested otherwise, it was a misunderstanding of the relation of a technique of dazzling novelty to the reasoned purpose of an ultimate aim. And the criticism, especially in its earlier and more creative phase, asserts the presence and importance of some level of rigour, of appeal to a demonstrable ground of discrimination which might be thought to imply a philosophical basis of choice. It is an activity requiring standards which one must assume to have some, however unspoken, source of justification, and in which the feel for more rigorous, astringent and severe critical stances cannot be unrelated to the values which inform them.

This is, of course, not merely a fiction, but a simplistic one. Yet it may have the useful purpose of providing a rough frame for the way in which the various aspects of the *oeuvre* seem to ask to be considered. After all, Eliot could hardly have said that his poetry, criticism and other discursive or argumentative prose proceeded from wholly different assumptions about the world, or wished to say conflicting things about it, even if they are quite different languages and the use of those languages argues a radically different sort of activity. It is as process, and as forms of the imagination that they are different. And as forms of claim upon us they differ as well, in the impingement of whatever truth they hope to contain. But the first of these differences is much more susceptible to schematization, however opaque some of the implications may be.

One can see the working of such a dubious neatness in a recent interview with Sartre, in which Sartre explains the difference between two of his intellectual forms, or imaginative selves, in the language that characterises his philosophical and his literary work:

> What distinguishes literature from scientific communication, for example, is that it is not unambiguous; the artist of language arranges words in such a way that, depending on how he emphasises or gives weight to them, they will have one meaning, and another, and yet another, each time at different levels . . . in philosophy, every sentence should have only one meaning. The work I did on *Les Mots*, for example, attempting to give multiple and superimposed meanings to each sentence, would be bad work in philosophy. If I have to explain, for example, the concepts of 'for-itself' and 'in-itself', that can be difficult; I can use different comparisons, different demonstrations, to make it clear, but it is necessary to stay with ideas that are self-contained: it is not on this level that the complete meaning is found—which can and must be multiple so far as the complete work is concerned. I do not mean to say, in effect, that philosophy, like scientific communication, is unambiguous.[1]

The mind moves between singularity and plurality, between surfaces and depths, simplicity and complexity. But one could hardly call this an evolved or refined working out, and it certainly gives a further ambiguity to the philosophical passages in *La Nausée* or to the elaborate and fictionalized examples of moral action in *L'Etre et le Néant*. There seems to be some curious law by which the greater the precision with which such distinctions are made, or the greater the literalism with which they are expressed, the more ambiguities multiply. And the clear division between uses of language, so reminiscent of I. A. Richards's distinction between scientific and emotive, is too crude to be useful, while his dangling admission that there is ambiguity in philosophical language as well may point rather unreflectively at the 'different comparisons, different demonstrations' required to 'make it clear'. And the emphasis falls too deadeningly on dis-similarity, on the mutual exclusivity of two forms of activity.

An oddity of this interview was the selection of *Situations* as one of the works Sartre most commended to the future, without any concern for the place of critical language, or that not-wholly-philosophical language of commentary on social and political matters that compose so much of that series of volumes. But clearly he placed a value on particularity that both literary occasion and historical event or moment could provide. In avoiding an enquiry into such language he may also have avoided the embarrassing elusiveness of those forms whose appropriate development is tied up with the things on which they are parasitic.

For Eliot the approach to one's literary activity at the level of relations between the forms of language employed is one that has virtually no systematic exposition. Philosophy itself is seldom mentioned except in terms of fragmentary asides. But through the criticism there is a rough effort to separate out the literariness of the critical involvement, and to define it in terms of an almost unintended overspill from the creative interests of the writer. Rather than describing and relating alternative modes of dis-course, there seems a double impulse: to point to the special nature and apartness of poetry, and to regard one's other uses of language as ancillary. And the result is not to distinguish alternative forms of the imagination, but to focus on one's own creative process as the ground on which one sees the extending out of subsidiary and wholly dependent comment. 'It is a by-product of my private poetry-workshop; or a prolongation of the thinking that went into the formation of my own verse. In retrospect, I see that I wrote best about poets whose work had influenced my own . . .'[2]

The interesting word here is 'prolongation' as if it were not a difference of kind in the two modes of thought. But surely this is not what can be intended. It is perhaps rather that the by-product is afterthought, which surfaces in relatively casual and occasional ways when the main process has been arrested. There is no doubt of course about the totality of subordination or of relative levels of importance. And this is consonant with Eliot's tendency to elevate the studies of particular writers above the 'phrases of generalisation' which have been such a source of embarrassment. When the latter surface it is as utterances the 'force [of which] comes from the fact that they are attempts to summarize, in conceptual form, direct and intense experience of the poetry that I have found most congenial.'[3]

This would beg the question of the bases of congeniality, if it were not that we have a great deal to go on, and it certainly begs that of the relation between 'conceptual form' and 'direct and intense experience'. It almost implies that the summary by way of conceptual form could convey the same experience in all its intensity. But again this is unlikely to be intended, although some remarks about the *Paradiso* hint at the possible powers of conceptual language. It is rather that generalization is another level at which the derivation takes place—at a further degree of remove from the creative process. Perhaps the closest level of contact with this process is represented by talk about technique. Yet one 'cannot say at what point "technique" begins or where it ends'.[4] Just as generalization can be treated as a form of subordination, so can the emphasis on the apartness of the literary— although that too, like technique, seems to have no distinct beginnings and ends since 'it is impossible to fence off *literary* criticism from criticism on other grounds, and . . . moral, religious and social judgements cannot be wholly excluded . . .'[5] for after all, does not '. . . poetry as certainly [have] something to do with morals, and with religion, and even politics perhaps, though we cannot say what'?[6] On the other hand there are occasions when 'the "historical" and the "philosophical" critics had better be called historians and philosophers quite simply'[7]—although to be fair this last comment seems to refer more to method than to area of interest.

Now my aim in this is not so much to dramatize the muddle artificially by using quotations from diverse sources, but to suggest that in spite of some remarks to the contrary there is a reticence before the problem of criticism that is essentially permissive. I don't mean simply that it admits of inconsistency, something impossible to avoid when dealing with multiple contexts and purposes, but that it is relatively unconcerned with this multiplicity of pull. I also hope I do not seem to take all that wholly at face value some of the remarks in the late criticism which I have quoted. These essays seem to me to be of little critical interest, but to be sketchy fragments of intellectual auto-biography. There are useful observations, qualifications and cor-rections with respect to what one once thought. And while marked trends and perspectives can be seen in this, there is seldom as much of a conceptual map as in the Sartre interview.

These late essays perhaps suggest, with their mixture of caveat and retrospective consistency, the strength of a lifetime's habit of working with certain presuppositions, ones which were widely shared, and accepted without a great deal of *arrière pensée*. There is a basic common ground assumed, often implicitly, by many Anglo-Saxon critics, that there are orders of language that have rough identities and are exercised by the appropriate per-sons:

(1) philosophers, who argue conceptually about abstract mat-ters;

(2) poets, who make images and arrange words into verbal structures which while not exactly logical are largely within the rules, grammatical and otherwise, which govern the use of a natural language. (Or if they break away from such rules the very break is intelligible because such rules exist);

(3) critics, who discuss the works created by poets in a language which in some ways resembles that of (1) but may, especially perhaps for Eliot and other poets, be the spin-off of their own language and therefore have some affinities with it.

Anyone who would assume such an ordering would qualify it in a variety of ways. But I mean it less as a highly controlled scheme than as a collection of habits. And one of the corollary habits is that of taking 'poetry' to stand for literature as a whole, in its essential and special features. Then too, the distinction between abstract and concrete, between conceptual and image-based verbal constructions may be more a convenient rule of thumb than a set of water-tight compartments. Yet if one accepts that this rough distinction runs through our critical thinking, it is still criticism itself that is the anomalous thing, and its principal interest lies in its being so. In practice the ambiguity lies in the fact that the language which interprets or explains must seem to be intelligible in a way in which the thing explained is not, to have a clarity, an accessibility and general import in which the subject of explanation is linked with larger and more immediately intelligible worlds of discourse. And even the avoidance of generality in explanation by the continual reference back to the particular only doubles the ambiguity.

For Eliot the implications of this are largely avoided, partly perhaps because there is little extended interpretation in his critical work. Philosopher perhaps, poet with a totality of commitment, critic by accident of circumstance, the third role seemed posed in terms of occasion until time's passage suggested a retrospective and diffident assessment. And this thinking hardly focuses seriously on the nature of the critical mode itself. Yet there are at least two major attempts to rationalize the anomaly: one his extended argument in *The Use of Poetry and the Use of Criticism,* with his own chosen model of 'philosophical critic', and another, his 'Charybde et Scylla', an attempt to use critical language as a mediation between his philosophic and poetic selves, and to act the 'philosophical critic' himself.

Yet I am treating the term as if it had a single sense, or as if its multiple senses are clear, and it is as well to spell out the possibilities of a sense, partly because Eliot's own interpreters have clearly employed it in different ways, partly to map the scope of the problem which has confronted us from the beginning, the relation of the whole to the part, of the overriding principle to the specialized activity or at least the concentrated moment when particular and general meet. I shall begin by means of caricatures, with five senses of the 'philosophical critic'.

(1) To criticize precisely in terms of an evolved philosophical system, providing all of the appropriate pigeon-holes where criticism would have its distinctive place among other intellectual activities. 'System' also implies that the map of the pigeon-holes would be a sequence of ordered relationships all intelligible in terms of each other. Such a philosophy might be that of Hegel and his descendants, or of Aquinas. Eliot sometimes speaks of Dante as if he had such a systematic and rationalized world-picture, and a number of scattered remarks seem to suggest that he found an overall sense of order of this kind desirable. Yet with respect to the value of Dante's own work for him, Eliot has distinguished sharply between the necessity of believing Dante (which as Graham Hough has recently said,[8] neither Eliot nor

any of the rest of us are in a position to do) and *assent* to his poem as a poem.[9] I say sharply rather than clearly because the implications are not clear, least of all what force is to be given to 'assent'. Whatever it means, it does not imply acceptance of a system. Various remarks about Maritain may flirt with the notion of a modern adaptation of Dante's form of order, but this is not taken very far. (And elsewhere Eliot even suggests that Dante himself '*qua* poet' need not have believed or disbelieved the Thomist doctrine that his work embodied.)[10]

(2) A critic might be called 'philosophical' in the sense that his language of critical discourse was shaped, and consciously, by certain philosophical concepts, or that it employed terms which had far-reaching philosophical implications and which connected particular observations about literature with those implications. Dr Bolgan may have something like this in mind when she says that '. . . Bradley's philosophy may very readily be seen as pro- viding the metaphysical system from which all of Eliot's major critical concepts derive, and by which their meanings are con- sequently everywhere controlled . . .'[11] Unfortunately she gives almost no examples of how this might work in critical practice. The use of 'entelechy' to point the difference between under- standing and explanation might seem promising, but the term is not specifically Bradley's and the matter is introduced with immense diffidence and not followed up. If there are shadows of the notion of 'internal relations' in the criticism, they weigh no more heavily than any other source of formal unity. As for the impersonality of the poet there is clearly some background in Bradley, although the relationship between the doctrine and its background seems open to query. Wollheim has put the matter as generously as one might reasonably wish. And as for the famous 'objective correlative' Wollheim is surely right that '. . . there is some obscurity how this critical theory is to be con- nected with those parts of the philosophy which it seems to parallel'.[12] Finally, the famous dialectical movement discerned by Dr Bolgan and Dr Lu seems little more than Eliot's habit of can- vassing one or two alternatives before settling on a third. It may well be that long study of idealist philosophy gave shape to a mental tendency, and this might relate obliquely to what Eliot says about Bradley's influence on his style. But to show that there

is a consistent pattern, and that the final term represents a synthesis or resolution requires a demonstration that has not been given. There may be other hints or vague analogies, but nothing which shows how the meanings of critical concepts are 'everywhere controlled'.

(3) There is also a sense in which the practice of criticism may have through its own particular character certain philosophical consequences without necessarily having its source in a particular theory. It is too easy to talk as if 'philosophy' has some primary character as informing principle, to which critical practice adapted. But the alternative may be held, that features of critical practice, developed from the observation and comparison of particulars, define an area of activity whose very existence has philosophical significance. Insofar as we account for the human condition, literature and the comment on it are part of that accounting. This may seem to be pitching the matter at a fairly low common denominator level, and the sort of philosophical activity implied is closer to concern with the working of language in analytical philosophy than it is to metaphysical system construction. Our interest here in any critic's contribution will lie in our assessment of his innovative power with respect to critical concepts, language or technique. Here Eliot's work has been more taken for granted than examined, although it has often been assumed that Eliot was the predecessor or founder of the 'new criticism'—an attribution which seemed rather to bemuse him: '... I fail to see any critical movement which can be said to derive from myself ...'[13] But insofar as that elastic collective has a method or created a body of concepts or a critical language, it derives much more from I. A. Richards, and develops in terms of close reading and interpretative skills. These are things in which Eliot hardly seems interested: there is little close reading in his work and something of an aversion to interpretation and explanation. He put his own aims in terms of understanding and enjoyment, with the insistence that understanding was not to be confused with explanation. And enjoyment is clearly tied up with education, taste and other psychological or cultural imponderables. Of them later.

(4) One may criticize in accordance with a set of attitudes, a personal 'philosophy' or group of presuppositions which might

be held at any of a variety of levels of consistency and intensity. These attitudes reflect the claims of one's culture as a whole and of particular institutions within it. Between ideological commitment and academic neutrality, between the strong and the vague, there are multiple levels of coherence, and the measure of them is much of the order of that in which persons may be said to cohere. It is clearly better to have unified than dissociated sensibility. (The marginal relation of the latter concept to its philosophical origins is noted by Wollheim.) The relation of social stability and order to the non-dissociated self seems to rely on some equation linking literature, sensibility and society. But this is to a large degree merely assumed, and the intangibility of the elements often seems to suit both an elusiveness in Eliot's own reasoning, and the commonsense assumption that connections must be there however one would choose to spell them out. One may get a picture of sorts from works like *The Idea of a Christian Society* without applying it directly to literary judgements.

(5) Beyond this there is something more intangible still in a kind of philosophical manner or style—a deliberateness, a cultivated irony or gravity—a stance. This may be what Herbert Howarth means by saying that Eliot's '... prose writing impresses, and one might even say subdues, the reader with its philosophical order'.[14] The appeal to a sense of reasoned order may be through a kind of rhetoric in which one feels the 'philosophical' and measured presence. Kenner remarks on the deliberate parodic stance in Eliot's critical language and its ironic and distancing aspect. Yet Eliot seems to have felt that one flaw in his earlier critical language lay precisely in the implications of stance, in the authority of a manner which seemed neither substantial nor attractive. Such a quality too much isolated might parallel his own remark about Arnold, 'He had no real serenity, only an impeccable demeanour'.

Needless to say this categorization is not intended to be the kind of sorting out that Eliot himself might have done. And even had he made such distinctions it would have been at another level of finesse, a characteristic and cautious chiaroscuro. But even such brutalities show that at a variety of levels, and with different strengths and weaknesses of claim, Eliot's involvement

with philosophy is a double one, with the use of a concept can-
celled or qualified by incompleteness, irony, disclaimer, or simply
unwillingness to carry the implications through. He often seems
to reach, then put aside. Yet on two or three occasions he uses
the expression 'philosophical critic' as if the person in question,
Richards (to whom on one occasion he links William Empson)
gave a proper sense to the term. Certainly one of the most
sustained and systematic series of general arguments in his work
is that directed against Richards in The Use of Poetry and the
Use of Criticism. The volume itself has a development and
extendedness totally atypical of Eliot's critical writing, while
its mixture of diffuseness and polemic contains a range of observation and reference that has a centrifugal effect on the overall
design. Nevertheless, it is in such sustained development that the
consequences of observation, or the lack of them, can be worked
out, and where the fuller characteristics of the language that
works them out may be seen. For this the very selection of
Richards as antagonist goes some way to giving the argument a
form.

But the 'philosophical critic' is curiously balanced, in the person of Maritain, with the philosopher concerned with the arts.
They are both concerned to 'determine the position of poetry'
the one in a pagan, the other in a Christian world. There is,
however, a clear difference between the practising critic trying
to work out the function of literature in a particular historical
moment, and the theoretical aesthetician adjusting the terminology of a comprehensive system to his awareness of the vitality
of modern art. The parallel is uneasy, as the latter is concerned
with accommodating the radical and creative with a traditional
body of belief, the very act of accommodation which occupied
such an important place in Eliot's whole intellectual life.
Richards, on the other hand, has chosen in The Waste Land the
most important poetic monument of that intellectual life as the
model of the 'severance between poetry and all beliefs' and
the intolerable misconception arises exactly through his modern
version of Arnold's heresy of salvation through poetry, in which
the psychological and cultural function of poetry comes to
replace the belief it might have conveyed. Maritain needless to
say knows better: '. . . religion saves poetry from the absurdity

of believing itself destined to transform ethics and life: saves it
from overweening arrogance.'[15] So the truth of poetry lies outside of poetry, and the religious thinker is concerned with a
truth to which the poem is only a vehicle.

In much of Eliot's writing this is exactly what it would seem
logical to expect, and it can be outlined with a severe dogmatism:

> It is our business, as readers of literature, to know what we
> like. It is our business, as Christians, *as well as* readers of liter-
> ature, to know what we ought to like. It is our business as
> honest men not to assume that whatever we like is what we
> ought to like; and it is our business as honest Christians not
> to assume that we do like what we ought to like. And the last
> thing I would wish for would be the existence of two litera-
> tures, one for Christian consumption and the other for the
> pagan world. What I believe to be incumbent upon all Christ-
> ians is the duty of maintaining consciously certain standards
> and criteria of criticism over and above those applied by the
> rest of the world; and that by these criteria and standards
> everything that we read must be tested.[16]

Put in this way however the criteria of the 'ought' ring with
a false certainty, which is made easier by a lack of the need to
justify their grounds. And when dealing with another belief as
absolute—if of another sort—he is capable of praising Trotsky
for his recognition of the distinction between beliefs as *held* and
beliefs as felt, which seems to bring us back to the same type of
uncertainties as 'assent' to the poem.[17] But in both of these contexts, all is stated, nothing is argued—no reasons are adduced.
Richards and Maritain (and Trotsky for that matter) are like
actors, stating a point of view, and we see them not so much as
givers of reasons as figures occupying stances, to be described in
terms of attitudes. Richards does not so much have a philosophical position which one might refute, as a 'modern emotional
attitude' which one 'cannot share'. As indeed Dante had a
'saner attitude towards the mysteries of life' than Shakespeare,
and Trotsky gave in *Literature and Revolution* 'the most sensible statement of a Communist attitude'. Has the word been
carefully selected to contrast with the logically schematised, and
to suggest those psychological dimensions where sympathies

may be engaged and exposure to polemic readily opened? The psychological force is important, but it does not look as if the matter has been nicely weighed.

Consider the variables in the description of Richards and the forms of difference with him: Richards is a 'serious moralist' with a 'theory of value' that one 'cannot accept'; he has 'philosophical conclusions' with which one may be 'dissatisfied', yet discriminating taste in which one can 'believe'. Does the discrimination in his taste depend upon his theory of value? One might have thought from certain passages in *The Principles of Literary Criticism* that there was a clear theoretical connection. And the consequence might seem to follow that believing in discriminations made on the basis of a value theory which one cannot accept is distinctly odd. But Eliot is not interested in consequence or connection.

He turns to questions of experience and enjoyment, to the possible ground of their authenticity, and hence to observations about literary education, changes in taste and those historical and psychological conditioning factors which play upon the evolution of taste. In doing so there is a blurring of the intellectual and experiential ground of our discrimination. We are escorted by stages which move from 'intensity of feeling' to 'appreciation' which brings a more intellectual 'addition', to an 'organising' which goes beyond our elementary selection and rejection, to a 'reorganising' in which the evolved pattern of taste readjusts to the introduction of some new element which threatens its equilibrium. There is no harm in this rather casual sketch of levels of development but it does beg the question of the criteria by which the 'organisings' and 'reorganisings' should take place. If we are to take seriously the implications of Eliot's whole intellectual outlook the education of taste could hardly be a random process of growth, but a directed activity according to certain principles, which one presumes would not be those of 'the modern emotional attitude'. We might turn to Christianity in the sort of terms seen in 'Religion and Literature' but that passage almost uses the force of 'ought' as an inhibition to any growth process and might suggest too total a subordination to the extra-literary in its most negative forms. In any case, Eliot does not bring process and informing principle together—something perhaps more characteristic than not of his work as a whole. In this case the description of a process has been substituted for a justification of what should go into it.

There can be no objection to the fusion of feeling, thought, attitude and belief as interdependent in any sensible talk about poetry, but the difficulty with Eliot's handling of the multiple aspects of his subject is an uncertainty as to what he will light upon as the explanatory element in a particular case. Most pervasive perhaps are those references to feeling and enjoyment, somewhat accentuated in the later criticism, and expressive perhaps of some, at least, not wholly rationalized presuppositions that have a philosophical colouration. There is however a sense in which the enjoyment that poetry produces seems introduced as an unanalysable end term in explanation, which does not allow of further distinctions and descriptions, certainly unlike the analysis it might receive from Richards in terms of psychological components and quantities. Opposed to a science of feeling, there seems to be a mystique of feeling, which is useful largely because of its resistance to analysis, its explanatory opacity. This must be examined in other contexts.

What I have tried to give here is of course not an account of Richards's theory of poetry and Eliot's alternative to it. It is rather a consideration of a moment's encounter, where the language Eliot uses in stating his understanding of Richards and the character of the arguments he thought appropriate in setting out his criticism reflect the character of his work as a whole. This has hardly been a 'philosophical' response, but has dissolved the argument into a variety of disconnected, or at least logically unrelated elements. The multiplicity of appeal to differing frames of reference, standards, levels of psychological commitment, alternative principles of coherence, may partly indicate a lack of any interest in the working of critical language itself. The final suggestion that 'critical speculation, like philosophical speculation and scientific research must be free to follow its own course . . .'[18] seems more a permissive gesture than an indication that there is any particular configuration to the 'course', especially when its consummation is seen in the tendency to enhance our own enjoyment. At every stage one has looked at a different guideline because a different aspect of a problem has been in the foreground.

While I have been emphasizing the discontinuities within what presents itself as a synoptic rationalization, it is worth mentioning the special problem of relating particular and general, considering especially the self-consciousness which inheres in the very sense of belonging to the tradition one is describing. So Eliot is in effect using an historical frame for a conceptual argument, and his imaginative involvement with particular moments of critical history seems to move counter to the overall explanatory impulse which goes into his own confrontation with his historical moment. So even the latter breaks down into such oddly sorted examples as Trotsky and the Abbé Bremond. The whole rationalization seems to have posed the kind of conditions, in attempting to relate intellectual coherence to historical sensibility, that made it unsympathetic to his particular talent.

An analogous case is shorter and more retrospective, as if the effect of historical distancing that enables him to treat his own work as belonging to the past, and the rapprochement between the disciplines that have shaped his life, may gain in clarity through distance. The 'Charybde et Scylla' of his lecture in Nice in 1952[19] represent the claims of philosophy and poetry. The relevance to criticism may be oblique but the separation out of the languages of concept and imagination may help to give criticism its necessary frame. Two senses of 'philosophy' are distinguished: one which identifies the general outlook and beliefs of a poet, and another which is an intrinsic property of the poem itself 'et qui ne peut être traduit en concepts'. Eliot is of course perfectly aware of the strength of normal claims for the first sense and that the latter poses special conditions for the use of the word. What we seem to find in some poems is an intellectual pleasure which corresponds to the philosophy of the poem. Take Mallarmé, whose poems may not in the usual and literal way make sense, or at least when literally interpreted manage to elude us, whom one does not read with the awareness of a Dantesque intellectual substance. Yet neither does it cause a pleasure which is that of the senses: 'Il m'a donné un exercise intellectuel et un plaisir intellectuel . . .', a pleasure which is a

direct effect of the 'philosophy of the poem'. I shall return to
the problem of the two kinds of pleasure. But the passage which
follows is sufficiently revealing of a way in which Eliot had
come to see his own poetry to be worth quoting at length:

> Evidemment, cette formule 'la philosophie du poème' ne
> s'applique pas également à toutes sortes de poèmes. Elle s'
> applique au mieux aux poèmes de ces poètes qui, s'ils n'avai-
> ent pas été poètes, auraient pu être philosophes. Elle com-
> prend des poètes qui, s'ils avaient fait de la philosophie au lieu
> de faire de la poésie n'auraient peut-être atteint qu'une très
> modeste place en tant que philosophes. Et parmi ceux-là, je
> ne vous cacherai pas que je me compte moi-même. (Car il me
> semble que c'est inévitable quand un poète fait des théories
> sur la poésie, le genre de poésie sur lequel il concentre son
> attention, c'est son propre genre de poésie. Comme Valéry l'a
> dit 'il n'est pas de théorie qui ne soit un fragment, soigneuse-
> ment préparé, de quelque autobiographie'). Quand je parle de
> 'philosophie d'un poème' j'ai dans l'esprit, avant tout, un
> poème écrit par un poète qui a fait des études philosophiques
> et qui a peut-être même construit des théories philosophiques
> originales. Ces théories ont joué un rôle important dans sa for-
> mation, et donc paraîtront dans sa poésie, mais dans une
> forme dans laquelle elles ne sont plus proposées en tant que
> théorie mais présentées comme des faits d'expérience, des
> éléments qui composent, avec toute son expérience de la vie
> sous ses différentes formes, les matériaux, la substance de ses
> poèmes. Des philosophies différentes, des opinions philoso-
> phiques opposées qui ne peuvent pas dans le domaine de la
> discussion philosophique être maintenues simultanément,
> peuvent être ainsi unies et réconciliées sur le plan poétique. Je
> dirai de plus que dans cette opération, il y a un travail intel-
> lectuel d'organisation qui est analogue au travail conceptuel
> du philosophe. Et je dirai aussi que les sentiments d'un lec-
> teur délicat, en s'assimilant un poème de ce genre, sont ana-
> logues à ses sentiments lorsqu'il s'assimile l'ouvrage d'un
> philosophe. Seulement, la *compréhension* d'un ouvrage philo-
> sophique et la compréhension d'un poème sont deux choses
> très différentes. C'est parce qu'on ne comprend pas ce fait

qu'il y a différentes façons de *comprendre*, qu'on nous a infligé tant de fausses explications de la poésie philosophique: toutes ces explications qui réduisent en fait la philosophie d'un poème à des termes abstraits: soit des maîtres de philosophie du poète, soit des concepts venant de sa propre pensée lorsqu'il faisait de la philosophie et non de la poésie.[20]

The autobiographical point should be taken, and this passage clearly represents an attempt to account for a relationship which had long given him an awareness of oppositions to be resolved. But such self-reference almost erects the framework for a category of one or two and creates its intelligibility from the cases of himself and Valéry, or those rare persons whose thought is founded in philosophy, but whose actual literary works do not convey this except indirectly. This suggests some curious chemistry which converts the abstractions of philosophical thought into something lived, and thus material for a further transformation in which their particular features as philosophic argument, especially the principle of contradiction itself, are so sublimated that contradictories, or at least 'opinions philosophiques opposées', can co-exist on the 'plan poétique'. But the very existence of this 'plan' may pose an evasion of the problem it sets out to solve. For if the co-existence of opposites in an alternative form of intellectual organization means the difference between contradiction and resolution, the poetic level has in some degree become at the same time the antithesis of the philosophic, and a means of transposing the awkwardnesses into an area where there is simply a formal blessing on their incompatibilities.

Yet the movement of thought into experience, into that experience transmuted by words, might indicate that the 'plan' defines itself less as an area of implication than as an order of words. And would not such a view move us back towards Richards's notion of *The Waste Land* as effecting a severance between poetry and what it is supposed to be about? And would it not as well dull the registers of experience itself? For one thing, the casual sequence in which the experience in question becomes transmuted and is valued for that transmutability may indicate a self-conscious selective process, as may even the creation of original philosophical theories—all directed towards the poem itself and its 'philosophy'. One is reminded of what Pound said of Eliot in September 1914: 'He is the only American I know of who has made what I can call adequate preparation for writing. He has actually trained himself *and* modernized himself *on his own*.' One grasps an image of enormous self-assuredness and self-containment, with a conscious and controlled development subsuming all of its elements, including the Bradley phase, singlemindedly into the final product. That Eliot had had some such subordination and development in mind is something he later spells out quite literally. The ideas drawn from philosophy are important insofar as they have formed the poet's mind and have been 'assimilées (comme un fertilisant, pourrait-on dire) dans cette *couche* profonde de l'expérience qui constitue le sol même dans lequel les germes de la poésie se nourrissent'.[21] That is, they do not even belong to the substance of the product, but are an ancillary device for bringing it into being.

The formula by which conceptual thought moves into experience to help bring about the poem has a counterpart in what Professor Donald Davie has recently written of Pound: when 'sense-perceptions conceptualized in language can . . . be experienced as if they are immediate, may not concepts be substantialized in language so they can be experienced immediately, as if they were perceptions?'[22] Hence a reversal of what seems the normal process by which things become intelligible, with perceptions and images receiving conceptual expansion, and where they are considered in conceptual terms. The concept as immediately experienced must, like the 'plan poétique', substitute the immediate and experienced (words which for Eliot might well have an echo of Bradley) for what would be the normal expectations in a conceptual language. And whatever intelligibility adhered to this would be found as the concrete realization of the language of the poem, directly perceived, the 'philosophie d'un poème' itself.

Perhaps Davie's suggestion might as corollary require the abolition of criticism as it is now practised. It is normally supposed that what is explained is in some way opaque and difficult, and that interpretation works by rendering into a more accessible and common language of agreed meanings. What

would result from reversing this and translating our concepts
into more directly felt and therefore immediately intelligible
percepts? Would this mean an end to steps that move from one's
understanding back to the concrete occasion in which it rests?
Or would we find some retranslation process a necessary step?
Certainly Eliot allows for two different forms of understanding,
for philosophical works and for poems. And it is because we
have failed to grasp the difference in these forms of understanding that we have had inflicted on us the false and reductive
explanations of the 'philosophie du poème'. Yet what force do
we give to the analogy between two forms of intellectual organization? There are several puzzles: does the 'travail intellectuel
d'organisation' refer to the process by which philosophical and
poetic works are created, or to some innate characteristic of
their structure—to process or to order? And what of the 'sentiments' of the 'lecteur délicat' in taking in these two distinctive
forms of discourse? Is this process of assimilation a rough description of the reading process which is in some way contrasted
with the end product of understanding? If so, what value have
the 'sentiments'?

The answer to such queries will not be found in Eliot and
any construction is quite conjectural. For one thing the difficulty in the term 'analogy' is that of allowing for either strong
or weak resemblances, and the usual temptation in accepting
weak senses is that stronger ones are easier to spell out. If one
wishes—and here the elusiveness of Eliot's thinking is felt. The
move from the analogous assimilation to the separate understanding is probably the movement from similarity in coming to
grips with two complex orders of words to a realization of the
difference in their kind of import. But here again the difficulty is
little more than pushed away and the meaning is far from clear.
What is clear is the intention of securing the protection of
poetry from the vulgar error that poems can, for the purposes of
explanation, be reduced to the ideas they contain. Eliot had
obviously suffered much from that kind of literalness of mind
which, by asking one to say exactly what one means, confirms
one in the belief that it cannot be said in that way, and that if
it could it would no longer be the same thing—or even the same
sort of thing. So the impulse is understandable to separate out

the 'kinds' of thing, yet point out the close relationship that existed between them in his own working out of the 'philosophy of the poem'.

As a personal testimony this is more satisfactory than it is as a theoretical statement, and any general conclusion would require further elaboration to give a sense of what its import might be. The resolution of the double concern—as philosopher, as poet—with his immediate experience and double invention of a language appropriate to conveying it seems to succeed best in terms of a lifetime's development, and have its analogy, with different force in different cases, only in the work of other poets who felt a similar duality. The example which develops an essentially confessional moment is characteristically not from his own work but from Valéry, and the argument turns on the comparison of the commonplace in Gray's *Elegy* and the special originality of *Le Cimetière Marin*. Most of the actual comments on the poem are concerned with its language. But two points may illuminate the distinctions made above. One is the remark that whatever we might derive from the poem of a philosophical kind would be less than the poem. Would such a remark apply to Dante too, and qualify the distinction between categories made earlier in the lecture, when discussing the transmutation of a passage from *De Anima* into poetry, in which the poem seems to belong to the same mode of thought as Aristotle's? And there is a comment on the '... structure philosophique, une organisation non pas seulement de réactions successives à une situation donnée, mais de réactions à ses premières réactions'.[23] This seems to suggest a notion of levels of generality, or some kind of dialectical movement which might have Idealist ancestry, although the philosophical structure might appear to have a psychological instantiation. Whether or not this is so is not made clear.

This brings us back by a circuitous route, by way perhaps of a certain deviousness in Eliot's own thought, to the most persistent ambiguity in the notion of the 'philosophical critic', which runs unevenly through the five caricatures that I suggested earlier. One who criticises according to some philosophical principle may not instantiate that principle in the act of criticism itself. Yet in establishing a relationship between the conceptual and creative aspects of his work, Eliot paradoxically became a kind of philosophical critic—without wishing to apply such a discipline or the fuller consequences of his observations to the order or language in which they are made. To what extent would one wish to require that the 'philosophical critic' should be concerned with the nature of the activity involved in the moment of commentary? Eliot is hardly so concerned in any direct way, and the few approaches to such considerations are retrospective. The criticism has no sense of a life in its own right.[24] The 'phrases of generalisation' are fitful sparks. And the terms that point most deeply to philosophical presuppositions are those that lie in what on the surface seems the most easily used, least examined and least explained part of his vocabulary.

I mean by this what I have already described as his use as an end term in explanation of the terms 'feeling', 'pleasure' and 'enjoyment'. The persistence of these suggests a point beyond which Eliot feels justification need not take us, and may also indicate an area of philosophical commitment which is not wholly articulated and which plays a larger part in his thought about literature than he himself acknowledged. Or at least chose to see in terms of their consequences.

One or two remarks set out with a deceptive casualness the historical circumstances in which, for Eliot, the dominance of explanatory criticism must be rebalanced by the rediscovery of enjoyment. The extensive passage in 'The Frontiers of Criticism' which sets out some appropriate senses of 'enjoyment' also places it in the centre of his critical thinking. The earlier formulation 'the elucidation of works of art and the correction of taste' is translated, for advantage of tone, into 'promote the understanding and enjoyment of literature'. And these do not stand in any form of opposition as separate activities of the mind, for 'to understand a poem comes to the same thing as to enjoy it for the right reasons'. He is quite aware of the danger of question-begging in 'right reasons' but the expansion given by 'to the right degree and in the right way' hardly adds more than a hint of measure and scale. The addition of 'relative to other poems' may tighten the context (a problem in itself) but the remarks about not taking pleasure in bad poetry convey some notion of a scale of excellence which corresponds to a scale of pleasures, with nothing connecting beyond the assumption that the two really ought to match.

Eliot recognizes the further difficulties in 'enjoy', but the discussion of the relation of 'enjoy' to 'get enjoyment from' and to the connection with 'joy' does not really help with the nature of the pleasure we get from poetry and how it connects with understanding.[25] It is one thing to say that we cannot enjoy without understanding, but if you then say that understanding is the right sort of enjoyment the circularity takes much of the explanatory force out of it. One may see the use of the connection to refute the sort of arid explicator who makes no place for pleasure in his form of understanding. Yet the two demands which seem to be made on understanding—that it should conform to some notion of correctness and involve immediate enjoyment—may not account for the gap between the requirement for public explanation of the criteria of correctness and the subjective grounds of enjoyment. The one has features that can be stated and pointed to while the other is part of a personal tangle more difficult to inspect.

However, an important corrolary of this version of understanding founded in enjoyment is that it is essential to recognize that one is understanding a poem as a poem. Hence Eliot's lack of interest in the enormous literature which may inform us about poems and be quite interesting in its own way, but which does not contribute to our understanding of the poem as poem. This might seem to apply not only to works of a background or informational kind (the case he gives is The Road to Xanadu) but to those analyses which consider the poem as linguistic object, but one which is not, simply because it is a poem, different from other complex linguistic objects. (Something analogous is true of the Jakobson and Lévi-Strauss analysis of Baudelaire's Les Chats.) Certainly in such analyses the fact of being concerned with poems is something that can be recorded in terms of the description. But this does not seem to touch on what Eliot means by 'as a poem'. For the features described may be those of any closely-wrought but non-poetic verbal structure, or if there are features which might be thought to apply to poetry specifically they might also apply to bad poems or to mere verse, or anything using verbal characteristics usually attached to poetry. And I take it that this is something that Eliot does not mean—the pleasure and understanding that go with 'as a poem' clearly exclude bad poems and versification. The effect is that for Eliot there is an aesthetic mystique which is essential to the idea of the poem. And this mystique is served by words like 'pleasure' or 'feeling' which have in turn their own form of opacity. 'Pleasure' could hardly be directed too easily outward to the usual range of meanings which attach to hedonism of whatever kind, to anything beyond a restricted and rather genteel range of its connotations, yet it is absolutely primary to Eliot's thinking about poetry.

'Feeling' has a special ambiguity because of the supposition that Eliot's theory of impersonality and the classicizing elements in his criticism showed a hostility to emotional excess and the kind of personal indulgence in feeling which is associated with Romantic and Post-Romantic poetry. But clearly this particular stance, which combined with a marked desire to distance himself from whatever might be interpreted as a personal utterance, does not prevent his use of 'poetry as felt' as opposed to 'poetry as statement'. In fact the notion of feeling as realized in the poem itself may serve to distance one from any notion of the poem as reporting literally on the feelings of the author. In any case, what poetry acts upon is the 'sentiments' of the 'lecteur délicat', and 'it may make us from time to time a little more aware of the deeper, unnamed feelings which form the substratum of our being, to which we rarely penetrate; for our lives are mostly a constant evasion of ourselves, and an evasion of the visible and sensible world. But to say all this is only to say what you know already, if you have felt poetry and thought about your feelings'.[26]

Beyond this and behind it Eliot does not tell us where to go. One effect of the covert adoption mentioned earlier of something like Richards's 'two uses of language' is that of helping to set poetry apart from the claims and erosions of everyday life. These are feelings and pleasures of a special kind. Yet there is no point, I think, in extending the implications of Eliot's use of feeling as a critical tool (the extrapolations of a precise Bradleian theory of feeling and perception from the actual critical uses of the term seems wholly special pleading), for the intention is not to develop a concept for any kind of explanatory purpose, but to present the primary, essential, and essentially unanalysable element of our lives upon which poetry works.

Notions of pleasure and feeling are however combined in that of 'taste' which, if not always and necessarily to be corrected, is the subject of a process of changes sometimes called education, and which brings those psychological sources of our response to poetry into some kind of rapport with the best that has been, if not known and thought, turned into the verbal complexes we call poems. And because taste is something that is subject to this evolution it must link this best in the cultural tradition with the sense of being immersed in the present. Eliot is careful to balance tradition with the inevitability of change, with revolutions in sensibility, with the necessity in every generation to re-read, reinterpret and revalue. The importance of this lies in his recognition of process, of something quite at variance with the notion of a fixed, stratified, unchanging hierarchy of preserved values. It suggests a highly historicized imagination, and a commonsense acceptance of the necessity by which our reading is conditioned by the circumstances of our lives. 'Taste' works as a concept linking self and history, and always comprises both the elements of the inheritance and the contingencies which play upon them.

I do not mean to understate the degree to which Eliot turns away from the movement of his own society, or the degree to which the social criticism has a 'périssons en résistant' ring to it. This is especially striking in several remarks about the modern reader's inability not only to conceive of the role of the supernatural in the world, but even to conceive of anyone else seriously doing so. But this does not exclude his acute awareness that the very fact of poetry in culture, and of culture in society, and of society in the natural history of mankind is subject to a mixture of contingency and natural law. With this, there is a sensitivity to the modifications that process makes of tradition which is not merely a turning of one's back. And while I would not go so far as to suggest that a reputedly conservative, hier-archical, theocentric notion of literature and culture is shot through with relativist, positivist and hedonist elements, there is nevertheless in Eliot's notion of taste and the historical awareness that goes with it a placement of the ground of judgement in an evolving self whose development is open-ended. And the essential role of pleasure is one guarantee of that openness.

Certainly the notion of the education of taste consists in multiple adjustments to our increasing awareness of the order of world literature, to which the writer belongs through the act of writing and which the reader apprehends more fully and accurately as his knowledge increases. And certainly that growth and that education involve working out an appropriateness in the scale of appreciations which cannot be done in a freely subjective or permissive way, and which must accept the objective character of the order in which the word one writes is a part, and the word one reads finds its place. However, there are complications. One is that in the insistence on the subordination of the individual to the collective and established order, the importance of the collective is more vivid than the nature of the principles which the collective embodies. (This is perhaps especially true of 'The Function of Criticism'.) Eliot's conviction, which probably owes something to Royce, that an individual cannot fully realize himself either as a man or as an artist without submitting to the disciplines and standards of his own tradition and culture, is something which could as easily be true of many other traditions and cultures. And Eliot often seems caught between the notion that the modern writer (and reader) is the inheritor of all the great artistic and intellectual traditions of the past, and the necessity of determining the relevant features of a central tradition appropriate to his own life.

So what at some moments looks as if it tends to the absolute, towards system and fixed standards, is from another point of view ready to accept a cultural relativism and the ambiguity of our position in the face of it. And the explanations that the experienced critic might be tempted to give the young about the differences of rank, position and degree among poets are probably to be avoided, as the necessary ground of the understanding of 'degree' is experience of life: 'The perception of *why* Shakespeare or Dante or Sophocles holds the place he has is something that comes only slowly in the course of living'.[27] So it is hardly a matter of applying measures or rules. Nor is education a matter of heeding what you have been told. And 'place' has the splendid ambiguity of suggesting simultaneously an abstract, an historical and a psychological location.

The result is an eclecticism in which the use of taste, at whatever stage in its evolution, as an organizing principle is subjected to many purposes, and the process of deciding about relevance is subject to weak and variable forms of control. Yet, of course, this eclecticism and openness has its necessity for a writer who is constantly adjusting the implications of his own modernity to a deeply felt inner need to identify himself with the distinctive features of an at least partly alien society. The American Eliot, in constructing the European, felt conflicting pressures behind his need for a coherent point of view. And he was deeply aware that, however fully one absorbed a cultural tradition, taste is founded in personality—however disagreeable the word—with all of the psychological and circumstantial variables which act upon it. (Yet the account of this in *The Use of Poetry and the Use of Criticism* refuses to be drawn into 'any discussion of the definitions of "personality" and "character" '.)[28]

Such a recognition reveals another and equally unresolved conflict between the synthesizing instinct and the desire to give a separate shape to the study of literature. A concomitant of thinking of a poem 'as a poem' and accepting the complexities of the ground of taste is Eliot's emphasis on the uniqueness of literature—the separation of the literary from other criticism is brought out in the later essays. This in effect moves counter to integration of a 'point of view'. Looking through the critical work as a whole one notices a quite characteristic shift from seeing in context and emphasizing local relatedness, to seeing in terms of whatever unity one's 'point of view' might possess, to an assertion of the uniqueness of literature, requiring separate consideration of its particular problems. This three-way movement both contains a reaching out to grasp the multiple aspects of a work, and yet has a distinctive splintering effect which leaves one without a final sense of any conceptual whole.

The realization of this should alone, through the very lack of anything reasonably resembling a synthesis, cast some doubt on the claims made concerning Eliot's dialectic. The recent flourishing of this word, hardly uttered in Eliot's lifetime, conveys largely the need for some conceptual tidying up which the work itself does not supply. The movement of Eliot's mind, as I have said, is more that of the careful sifting of alternatives than a dialectical path to an ultimate fusion. And throughout his work words like 'coherence', 'unity', or 'order' may be used in a variety of contexts without their implying a precisely employed method. Perhaps we might view in sympathetic terms a related notion of such precision when Dr Lu remarks that 'The whole of Eliot's criticism is a calculus of the conditions of unification . . .'[29] without being able to find any procedures in a calculus which could be methodically employed, or any sense in the word beyond the figurative, or that of a principle underlying the unity. What seems to be fulfilled is an emotional necessity.

There are dangers verging on absurdity in any attempt to give a picture of the kind of unity which would destroy the complexity of the 'eclectic' Eliot, to smooth over the inner conflict to show that there is a consistent development which is directed by some original philosophical form. There is no way to avoid the shifting frames of reference, the multiplicity of mind, the individuated attention, to turn it into some neat conceptual package without vitality or interest. Of course, the form limited the design, and the diverse and particularized reflect the occasional character of so much of his critical work, shaped by an immediacy that is not a philosophical term, but the individual piece in its situation and moment. Some occasions may arouse the generalizing impulse—as unavoidable as it is distrusted— but they do not give it the freedom to speculate at developed length. Theoretical remarks are scattered through the occasional pieces like tempting but misleading *obiter dicta*. And the few stretches of sustained argument—on which I have had to concentrate in my search for the 'philosophical critic'—are far from typical of the whole. More often there is a touch of evasiveness before the necessity of elaboration and the drawing out of consequences. It is as if the 'philosophical critic' underwent some kind of imaginative failure, and deferred to the sense of the immediate—a Bradleian word no doubt, but one representing the unity of theory far less than the pressure behind it. The fragments of philosophical language add up to little more than a distant evocation of what they might have meant.

Does the case of such a philosophical refusal tell us only about the character of Eliot's own conflict, or does it pose something of the contradiction in the notion of the 'philosophical critic'? If we take it as a reflection of Eliot's gradual movement away from the philosophical thinking of his early years (which to Wollheim suggests a genuine decline in his intellectual powers) we can only do so by putting his critical work and thought about literature closer to the centre of his concern than it really was. If literature mattered, the thinking about it was still secondary, and the conflict within his thought between schematic ordering and centrifugal pressures had many sources and took many forms. Yet it is possible that the necessity to situate himself as a critic in a workable point of view brings out this conflict in an especially vivid way.

Our query remains open and still before us. Does the failure of the 'philosophical critic' reflect an impossibility in Eliot's own situation, an enquiry cut off by the terms of its own circumstances? We can see how Eliot was caught between two languages and two traditions. His education, piecemeal as it may have been, drove him towards a continental tradition, derived from Hegel, by way of Royce and Bradley, where all is rational, which values unity, wholeness, non-dissociated sensibilities, and where art is of central importance in the formation and economy of the human mind. On the other hand he assimilated the Anglo-Saxon respect for the individual case viewed empirically as simply another object of attention, the charm of the discrete particular, and the rather special English diffidence before great ideas, promoting a deflationary, ironical, even whimsical ('rhythmical grumbling') view of oneself and one's work. The American Eliot was a natural eclectic who had neither to hand nor undertook his his own form of resolution.

Or does the problem lie beyond himself in the nature of talk about literature? One can at least see a weak analogy between his situation and our own, where Anglo-Saxon critical thinking seems at the limits of the empirical and toys, however uncertainly, with the thought of methodologies derived from an alien philosophical tradition. But the implications of the analogy would require their own study. And insofar as we may be asking if the notion of the 'philosophical critic' contains its own contradiction, the question would lead us beyond Eliot's example.

7

A Poet's Notebook:
The Use of Poetry and the Use of Criticism
W. W. ROBSON

In one respect T. S. Eliot is unusual among critics of eminence: he left on record (in 'To Criticize the Critic', 1961) an extensive and severe commentary on his own criticism. Opinions about this depend on one's view of Eliot. Those who dislike him will see it as a characteristically slippery action, a cunning bid to steal his opponents' thunder. Those who admire him will feel gratitude for his candour, and may reflect on how greatly we should have valued such an apologia—and *mea culpa*—on the part of Samuel Johnson or Matthew Arnold. Whatever view we take, Eliot's remarks on the scope, limitations and shortcomings of what he wrote on other authors are so penetrating that there seems little for anyone else to add or subtract. Of course a man is not usually a good judge in his own cause; but in this case the task of judgement has been performed so well that one might think inquiry into Eliot's prose writings should now be left to those whose chief interest is in his accomplishment in the 'other harmony', or in material relevant to the study of his poems and plays. Or perhaps it should be left to those interested in appraising —nowadays often in a hostile spirit—his religious, social or political point of view; or searching, with the F. R. Leavis of recent years, for evidence of impure motives and unworthy moral and emotional attitudes. The effect of Eliot's remarks on his own criticism has been to push into the background the question, how *true*—true for others, as well as true for him— is this or that judgement on this or that writer, and this or that injunction on points of literary principle. Eliot himself has become our main guide in helping us to see the extent to which his criticism can be 'placed' and 'dated'. As a writer of critical prose he had the great advantage, over some more recent pundits who invoke his name, of the ability to write interestingly. Yet it is he himself who tempts us to find in his criticism what Professor Raleigh found in *Paradise Lost*: a monument to dead ideas.

There is, however, one of Eliot's books, dealing with matters of literary criticism, which he does urge us to take account of for its intrinsic and not merely its documentary value. This is *The Use of Poetry and the Use of Criticism* (1933), based on the lectures he gave in 1932–3 on the Charles Eliot Norton foundation at Harvard. Eliot changed his mind about these lectures. In the preface to the first edition he spoke of 'another unnecessary book', which he had been obliged to publish by the terms of the Foundation. But re-reading them many years later he found to his surprise that he was 'still prepared to accept them as a statement of [his] critical position'. 'The lectures', he declared in the 1963 preface to the second edition (1964), 'seem to me still valid . . . I am ashamed neither of the style nor of the matter.' Although he '[did] not repudiate "Tradition and the Individual Talent"', he reprinted *The Use of Poetry* 'in the faint hope that one of these lectures may be taken instead of "Tradition and the Individual Talent" by some anthologist of the future.' So we have Eliot's own sanction for inquiring, in the spirit of the book itself, what is the *use* of what he offers us; how far he helps us to cope with the hard questions he raises about criticism and poetry.

But to play down the book's biographical interest is not to deny that this is considerable. Indeed, *The Use of Poetry* may be remembered now chiefly for that interest. It is to this book we turn to find what Eliot has to say about his intentions (or lack of them) in writing *Ash-Wednesday* (p. 30), the history of the development of his own taste in poetry (p. 33), Evelyn Waugh's father's attack on him and Ezra Pound as 'drunken helots' (p. 71), his partiality for the Scots (p. 72), his own experience in composing poetry (p. 144), his struggle, up to 1932, with the problems of writing poetic drama, and what he aimed at in the dramatic fragments he entitled *Sweeney Agonistes* (p. 153). Memorable, too, are the vivid glimpses we are given of the Eliot of the personal poetry. Writers on Eliot often quote the passage, doubtless autobiographical, about a child finding a sea-anemone for the first time (p. 78), placing it beside the lines on the 'old crab' in the early 'Rhapsody on a Windy Night'. Another passage is often related to 'Journey of the Magi'; it reveals also an affinity between Eliot's sensibility and Virginia Woolf's.

> Why, for all of us, out of all that we have heard, seen, felt, in a lifetime, do certain images recur, charged with emotion, rather than others? The song of one bird, the leap of one fish, at a particular place and time, the scent of one flower, an old woman on a German mountain path, six ruffians seen through an open window playing cards at night at a small French railway junction where there was a water-mill: such memories may have symbolic value, but of what we cannot tell, for they come to represent the depths of feeling into which we cannot peer. We might just as well ask why, when we try to recall visually some period in the past, we find in our memory just the few, meagre, arbitrarily chosen set of snapshots that we do find there, the faded poor souvenirs of passionate moments. (p. 148)

Here the lecturer's dais and the prose framework seem to vanish, and we are alone with the poet.

There is another way also in which the lectures sound personal —a rather disconcerting way. Towards the end, when Eliot cumbrously descends from the lecturing tone and endeavours to meet his fellow-men on equal terms, there are sudden lapses from that prim prose.

> As things are, and as fundamentally they must always be, poetry is not a career, but *a mug's game*. No honest poet can ever feel quite sure of the permanent value of what he has written: he may have wasted his time and *messed up his life* for nothing (p. 154: italics mine).

Eliot's friend Frank Morley has plausibly suggested that in *The Use of Poetry* the figure of Coleridge is a *persona* or symbol of Eliot himself. This is the Coleridge whom he sees as a haunted and a ruined man, doomed to live with the knowledge that he could never again reach the level he had once reached in a few great poems. Here Eliot was in fact, as he came later to realize, unjust to Coleridge; he did not evidently know at that time how much the earlier poet managed to achieve in the long years after his *annus mirabilis*. But there is no doubt that Eliot himself, at the beginning of the nineteen-thirties, had grave doubts whether he would be able to write any more poetry. He thought of himself not as a 'poet' but as a man who occasionally wrote poems. It is natural that his thoughts should turn to this classic example of the poet from whom the Muse has withdrawn; however unaware he may have been of Coleridge's second career, not only as a compulsive talker, but as a writer on criticism, metaphysics, psychology, political economy, and religious thought. And so he chose to end the lectures with the sad ghost of Coleridge beckoning from the shadows. (We may also remember, as Eliot himself perhaps did, the tragedy of Coleridge's broken marriage.) All this is sympathetic. Yet the final reference to Coleridge seems tasteless. Certainly Eliot had the right to suggest a parallel between himself and Coleridge. He was at least as great a poet and critic. But he should have left it for others to do so.

Finally, the occasion of the lectures should be remembered. Eliot had been brought back to the United States, after seventeen years' absence, to deliver them. Before him was to stretch the 'low dishonest decade' of the nineteen-thirties. Time has not lessened the force of those words which Eliot quotes from a letter of 1869 in Charles Eliot Norton's *Life and Letters* (Norton is speaking of the years after the American Civil War):

> . . . I wonder . . . whether we are not to have another period of decline, fall, and ruin and revival, like that of the first thirteen hundred years of our era. It would not grieve me much to know that this were to be the case. No man who knows what society at the present day really is but must agree that it is not worth preserving on its present basis. (p. 15)

A minatory tone comes into the lectures whenever political and social problems loom into view. For *The Use of Poetry* marks the beginning of Eliot's major concern with public questions in the age of Hitler, Franklin Roosevelt, and Stalin. Eliot's social and political views are to-day unpopular. He is seen as the militant issuer of reactionary 'calls to order'. It might be fairer to remember him as a detached—though far from dispassionate—observer of the post-Christian world. As a Christian theorist he had, of course, his confession, his 'commitment'. But he was enabled by his philosophy, as some of today's ideologues may not be by theirs, to allow for the contingent, contradictory, unpredictable way things happen, and value is distributed, in art and literature and life generally. Eliot's philosophical responsibility overlapped with his duty as a poet: to maintain the contact between language and reality which so many forces in the modern world collaborate to destroy. It seems that he felt more in common with people who manage to believe *anything*—such as sincere Communists—than with half-believers, lost in a mist of words. A remark about Wordsworth in *The Use of Poetry* may be applied to Eliot himself.

> ... when a man takes politics and social affairs seriously the difference between revolution and reaction may be by the breadth of a hair ... Wordsworth may possibly have been no renegade but a man who thought, so far as he thought at all, for himself. (p. 73)

Some of that tone in Eliot's writing which readers today find disagreeable may be due to his feeling of frustration at having to contend, not with the opposition of the intellectual community, but with its indifference. It is this indifferentism that, with damaging consequences for his later reputation, he calls Liberalism. Acerbity and increasing despair accompanied his efforts to explain to Liberals that Christianity is not a sentiment but a hypothesis about the world. On the other hand, Eliot did not feel happy among the zealots. For them too he speaks words to ponder, in the appendix to *The Idea of a Christian Society* (1939).

> So far as a man sees the need for converting *himself* as well as the World, he is approximating to the religious point of view. But for most people, to be able to simplify issues so as to see only the definite external enemy, is extremely exhilarating, and brings about the bright eye and the springy step that go so well with the political uniform. This is an exhilaration that the Christian must deny himself. (pp. 95–6)

W. B. Yeats, writing to Lady Gerald Wellesley (6 July 1935), struck a similar note; but his alternative to zealotry was different.

When there is despair, public or private, when settled order seems lost, people look for strength within and without. Auden and Spender, all that seem the new movement, look for strength in Marxian socialism, or in Major Douglas; they want marching feet. The lasting expression of our time is not in this obvious choice but in a sense of something steel-like and cold within the will, something passionate and cold.

Eliot's humility may be more attractive.

This sombre contemporary background is always present in *The Use of Poetry*. But for the most part the book is concerned only with literary criticism. As such, it has sometimes been judged inferior to Eliot's earlier essays. This judgement may be right: but some of the things that have been said to support it seem unfair. Thus more than one writer thinks Eliot mistaken in adopting a chronological approach, which did not suit him. But Eliot had good reason to seek for a place in that line of poet-critics who adorn English literature: Sidney, Ben Jonson, Dryden, Addison, Johnson, Wordsworth, Coleridge, Shelley, Keats (of the letters), and Arnold. All these poets are discussed in *The Use of Poetry*, and to discuss them in their historical succession seems right and natural. Furthermore, over and above his personal authority as a distinguished poet, Eliot was qualified as an expert in at least some of the literary periods that his undertaking required him to traverse. His connoisseurship of the drama of Shakespeare's time is well known from *Elizabethan Essays*, and it is put to good use in the second lecture. His examination of Dryden's critical terminology shows keen historical awareness, and does something to atone for his irritable cavilling, in the sixth lecture, at some of Arnold's phrases. Similarly he may be forgiven for his inadequate and petulant remarks on Addison because of his admirable comments afterwards on Johnson. (It is interesting to see how in his later lectures on 'Johnson as Critic and Poet' (1944) some of the ideas he tried out in *The Use of Poetry* are developed in a more mature style.) Here and there, it is true, the scholarship of *The Use of Poetry* is faulty, and Eliot did nothing to correct it in the second edition. We still read there, for example, that Coleridge did not 'acclaim' Donne (p. 72), though by 1963 Eliot knew that Coleridge did indeed acclaim

Donne, and repeatedly. The hasty composition of the lectures is no doubt responsible for such blemishes. (In the preface to the second edition Eliot says that they were written during the course.) They do not invalidate *The Use of Poetry* as a contribution to literary history at least as valuable as anything by the academic writers Eliot mentions with respect, such as Ker and Saintsbury.

But the main concern of the book is not with literary history but with matters of critical principle, and it is into these that we should now look. Early on, in the first lecture, Eliot makes an often quoted pronouncement.

> The rudiment of criticism is the ability to select a good poem and reject a bad poem; and its most severe test is of its ability to select a good *new* poem, to respond properly to a new situation. (p. 18)

This pronouncement, like other dicta of Eliot's, can be paralleled in Sainte-Beuve, who remarks, in his book on Chateaubriand and his literary group, that the sagacity of the judge and the perspicacity of the critic are tested by works not yet tried by the public. 'To judge at first sight—that is the critical gift; how few possess it!' *Combien peu le possèdent*, says Sainte-Beuve, and our first reaction is to wonder whether Sainte-Beuve possessed it himself. Proust thought that Sainte-Beuve failed to appreciate *all* the great writers of his time, and contrasts him with Anatole France, who laid no claim to the *magisterium* of the judge, and offered solely his personal impressions; and yet in spite (or because) of this, was far more generous and perceptive about his rivals than Sainte-Beuve ever was. Could one make a similar *ad hominem* retort to Eliot? Into the field of contemporary literature Eliot rarely ventured; and when he did, he seems not to have come out with any valuable recommendations. At any rate, I have never met anyone who concurred in his grave praise for the poems of Harry Crosby. It would seem that few of those who have been recognized by posterity as important critics—and no academic critics whatsoever—have been good talent-spotters. We might conclude, on practical grounds, that the test Eliot proposes is too severe. A more reasonable demand of critics *de carrière* would be that they write informatively about works other readers have discovered for them. (Even in this, some fail.)

A more theoretical kind of objection might be made to Eliot's seeming assumption that the goodness of a poem is an essence or quality, which it either has or has not. This way of looking at poetry is only plausible if we confine our attention to poems which are universally recognized as good, and to poems which are by-words for failure. But these two categories exclude the bulk of poems that have been written. Tastes notoriously vary, and most of us would agree that there is a vast range of poetry in which variations of judgement are perfectly legitimate. In any case, is goodness (or badness) an essence or quality at all? One might take the view that to call a poem good or bad is to do no more than give or refuse endorsement to the judgement that it possesses or lacks certain properties which happen to be held in esteem by the individual critic, or by readers in a particular literary period. And the course of literary history makes it clear that such properties vary greatly from time to time, and from reader to reader. The test of a critic's ability might then be whether he can recognize the properties that a given poem possesses; not whether he arrives at a judgement of merit or demerit which many of his contemporaries assume to be automatically supervenient or consequential upon them. The test of his quality is his descriptions, not his evaluations. The trouble with this, as with all other efforts to find objective literary criteria, is that the properties of poems, as of other works of art, seem actually to undergo change. They appear to possess certain properties at one time and not at another. Some improve with the years, some deteriorate, some vanish. The poetry of Edward Young, and perhaps the poetry of Boileau, glowed brilliantly for about a hundred years; then the light went out. Perhaps the painful search by academic critics for stable and enduring material—'literary artefacts'—on which to base their judgements is as delusory as the similar belief, common among philosophers, in the supra-historical persistence of 'concepts'.

All the same, Eliot's dictum—that new poems are the test—retains some value. But it should be regarded as a counsel of perfection, or word of caution, to those who attempt criticism, a reminder of the long history of their failure to anticipate the verdict of posterity. The next critical principle he proceeds to

lay down is a revival, in modified form, of the old doctrine of
the dramatic Unities. Clearly there is something in this doctrine.
An audience grows restless, without necessarily knowing why,
when the parts of a play do not pull together. A modern discussion would have to take into account the expectations of theatrical
audiences in particular historical circumstances ('conventions').
The possible influence of films would also have to be considered.
In its Renaissance form the doctrine of the Unities is perhaps
not very interesting. It is historically important as regards the
French stage; but on its invalidity as an account of the practice
of ancient Greek drama A. W. Verrall pronounced incisively.
It is, he says, 'a mere piece of confusion, arising from a false
attempt to justify practices which, *so far as they existed* [Verrall's
italics] had a totally different origin' (*Lectures on Dryden*, 1914).
One's first reaction, in reading of the wrangles of the sixteenth
and seventeenth centuries on this topic, might well be one of
wonder. How could intelligent men have for so long been spell-
bound by so arbitrary a prescription? (After that, it is sobering
to speculate on what future literary historians will see as a comparable dogmatism of our own time.) But the exposure of the
fallacies involved can be interesting. We can read with pleasure
a classic piece of common sense on this subject, the remarks of
Johnson in his *Preface to Shakespeare* (1765). And for a more
subtle discussion we may go to Johnson's contemporary Lessing,
who in his *Laokoön* (1766) draws the distinction between 'delu-
sion' and 'illusion' that is indispensable for a proper treatment of
the problem. Then, as a paradoxical defence of the doctrine of
the Unities, we might consider the peculiar pleasure we feel
when they are violated to good purpose. This may be part of the
pleasure we take in the treatment of Place in Barrie's *The
Admirable Crichton*, or of Time in Bennett and Knoblock's
Milestones. Is it part of the pleasure we take in *The Winter's
Tale*? When I last saw that play the dramatizing of the change
of generations, between the beginning and the end, had a most
moving effect. F. R. Leavis has a fine suggestion in an essay in
The Common Pursuit (1952), when he puts forward as a possible
superiority of *The Winter's Tale* over *The Tempest*—a play that
has often been praised on account of Shakespeare's ingenious
elimination of the time-gap—the 'depth and richness of signifi-

cance given, in *The Winter's Tale*, by the concrete presence
of time in its rhythmic processes, and by the association of
human growth, decay and rebirth with the vital rhythms of
nature at large'.

No critic was better qualified than Eliot to add something of
real value to this durable debate. His own increasing struggle
with the problems of playwriting should have been enough to
ensure that. But what he says is brief and disappointing. He
endorses Sir Philip Sidney's strictures on the drama of his day,
without arousing our interest in the conventional pedantry
which is all Sidney has to offer on the topic of the Unities. Nor is
the attitude Eliot strikes as a defender of neo-classicism, invoking
the name of Aristotle, strengthened by his appearing to realize
only belatedly (p. 47, footnote) that 'the Unities' can claim no
support from the *Poetics*. Aristotle says nothing about the Unity
of Place, and his reference to the Unity of Time is casual; he
merely remarks that the usual practice of tragedy was to confine
itself, as far as possible, to the action of twenty-four hours. There
is nothing prescriptive about it. Nor is Eliot's case improved by
his citing, as a case of triumphant faithfulness to the Unities, of
Joyce's *Ulysses*. (No doubt he did so with a twinkle, since Joyce
was not yet a respectable author in the Harvard of 1932.) It is
true that the action of *Ulysses*—and of *Mrs Dalloway*—like that
of *Oedipus Rex*, takes place in one day. But the reason is different
in each of these works. In any case, no one has ever thought the
Unities had to do with anything but plays.

The conclusion Eliot soon comes to is that the Unities of Time
and Place are merely special cases of what he calls Unity of
Action. And this in its turn proves to be a special case of Unity
of Sentiment, ignored to their detriment, Eliot thinks, by some
Elizabethan plays, for example *The Changeling*. (Eliot was
writing before the appearance of William Empson's ingenious
defence of the double plot of that play in *Some Versions of
Pastoral*, 1935.) The Unity of Sentiment is, then, to use Eliot's
own terms, a law, not a rule. And it is this law that the defenders
of the traditional Unities were really—and legitimately—up-
holding. This may be so. But the trouble with the updated
doctrine Eliot offers us is that it has no teeth. The traditional
Unities may be arbitrary, but at least we are in a position to

decide whether a particular play observes them or not. Mr Curdle in *Nicholas Nickleby* could have found plenty of plays which answer to his demand for 'a kind of universal dovetailedness with regard to place and time'. Perhaps the same could be said of the Unity of Action, though when Eliot mentions Shakespeare's *Henry IV* plays as an example it is not clear what he is thinking of: if *Henry IV, Part II* exhibits Unity of Action it is hard to imagine any play that could be fairly said to lack it. But the final overriding prescription of Unity of Sentiment is very vague. Does *The Dynasts* show it? does *Cavalcade*? Does it amount to more than asking that a play should have unity of *some* kind? to requiring, with Mr Curdle, 'a sort of general oneness, if I may be allowed to use so strong an expression'? It has always been the trouble with neo-classicism that the more reasonable its propositions, the more they slide towards analyticity.

But Eliot's stance as the stern neo-classicist seems to disappear in the course of the argument. Was it anything more than a pose? Perhaps he felt that his appearance in this rôle was something he owed to his old teacher Irving Babbitt, or to the twentieth-century French neo-classicists he so admired. If so, he compares unfavourably, when he adopts it, with some of the French critics. He does not show the willingness of Julien Benda, for example, to see merits in his opponents' position. The neo-classicism for which Eliot became famous in the nineteen-twenties seems to bring out the least alluring quality of his writing: that frosty, self-important tone which mars *The Use of Poetry.*

> The majority of critics can be expected only to parrot the opinions of the last master of criticism. . . (p. 109).

> What I *call* the 'auditory imagination'. . . (p. 118)
> (italics mine)

This tone is insufferable. Eliot says of Matthew Arnold that 'he is most at ease in a master's gown', but this does not seem to be true of Eliot himself. *At ease* is what he never sounds. These lectures lack the quality that charms us in Addison (to whom he is so harsh). I am thinking of things like Addison's discussion of true and false wit in the *Spectator* for 7 May 1711:

I intend to lay aside a whole week for this undertaking, that the scheme of my thoughts may not be broken and interrupted; and I dare promise myself, if readers will give me a week's attention, that this great city will be very much changed for the better by next Saturday night.

In *The Use of Poetry* it seems that Eliot cannot smile.

But the important objection to Eliot's neo-classicism is not that it is chilly, but that it is half-hearted. It is interesting to learn from Quentin Bell's *Virginia Woolf* (1972) that in September 1933 Eliot told Mrs Woolf he was no longer sure there could be a 'science of criticism'. This is ironic, coming from T. S. Eliot, the last of the great literary pundits, the idol of the academies, more responsible than any other single individual for this very influential conception of criticism. His loss of faith in it may account for a bored, perfunctory element we sense in *The Use of Poetry*. It may also be the reason why those *enquêtes* into Shaw, Wells, Kipling, and other modern 'heretics', now and then promised in the *Criterion*, never appeared. Perhaps Eliot had come to recognize that his own interest as a critic was in what he *liked* in another writer's work. He was also coming to have forebodings about his own influence on criticism. These are suggested here by his deprecatory reference to a 'criticism which seems to demand of poetry, not that it shall be well written, but that it shall be "representative of its time"'. While agreeing with this, we might agree also with Yvor Winters, a more full-blooded literary conservative than Eliot, when he tartly retorts that it was Eliot and Pound and their disciples who had always been demanding that poetry should be 'representative of its time'. Nowhere is the relation in Eliot between the innovating poet and the literary traditionalist more uneasy than in *The Use of Poetry*.

But as the lectures proceed the self-conscious neo-classicism becomes merely a notional basis for the development of ideas which belong to Eliot's mature thinking. This remark about 'communication', for instance, is a better phrasing of his thought on this topic than any he had found before.

If poetry is a form of 'communication', yet that which is to be communicated is the poem itself, and only incidentally the experience and the thought which have gone into it. (p. 30)

We think here of his later remark in 'The Frontiers of Criticism' (1956), when he is deprecating the claims of Herbert Read and F. W. Bateson to have illuminated some of Wordsworth's poems by reference to his biography and purported psychology.

> When the poem has been made, something new has happened, something that cannot be wholly explained by *anything that went before*. (Eliot's italics)

And to strengthen the force of this warning to the practitioners of *Quellenforschung* (of all kinds) we can subjoin a remark by a later author writing from a very different point of view—Sartre in *What is Literature?* (1947): 'The appearance of the work is a new event which cannot be *explained* by anterior data.' Eliot's discussion of this subject shows a maturity of thought and clarity of expression lacking in passages more often quoted, such as the famous pronouncement on the 'objective correlative' in the essay on *Hamlet*, or the lofty sentence on the 'auditory imagination' in *The Use of Poetry* itself. Such passages offer portable phrases for our notebooks; but they bring an arrest to thought rather than an advancement, and they are not free from the suspicion of attitudinizing.

The question of poetic greatness, or, as he calls it, of differences of degree among poets, is one to which Eliot recurs in the lectures. He observes in the appendix to the first lecture, where he is considering the place of the study of literature in the educational process, that it is not a matter which is easy to clarify for schoolchildren or undergraduates. It seems to have puzzled Eliot himself, and for good reasons. He was anxious to retain judgements of scale in the criticism of poetry. Yet he wanted to reject the ethical criteria proposed for them by Matthew Arnold. His solution here, in so far as he finds one, is to emphasize the *historical* constituent in judgements of greatness. In the course of some sensible comments on Herbert Read's too eccentric post-Eliot map of the history of English poetry he remarks that

> ... the great poet is, among other things, one who not merely restores a tradition which has been in abeyance, but one who in his poetry re-twines as many straying strands of tradition as possible. (p. 85)

And, while praising Landor, for whom Pound had a cult, Eliot draws a useful distinction between him and Wordsworth, who was 'an essential part of history', while Landor was 'only a magnificent by-product'. Here Eliot generalizes: 'in estimating for ourselves the greatness of a poet we have to take into account also the *history* of his greatness.' This generalization could be used as a caveat against Winters's cult of Greville, as well as Pound's cult of Landor. The development of English poetry might well have been much the same if they had not lived; they were not influences. But though Eliot's suggestion seems acceptable so long as we are thinking of a Landor or a Greville, it seems less persuasive when we think of Blake. Blake is in such critical favour to-day—and, I believe, on the whole justly—that there is some discomfort in denying him greatness. Yet it cannot be denied that he had little or no influence on later poets. This is a case in which we see the value of distinguishing, as Eliot does, between a poet's place in literature and his place in its history. It is the *relation* between these two placings which is mysterious. Matters would be simpler if we could regard 'greatness' as purely—or primarily— a historical term. But it is difficult to use the word like that, and Eliot himself does not so use it, for he speaks of 'estimating *for ourselves* (my italics) the greatness of a poet'. And I imagine that those who consider a Blake or a Greville or a Landor great would reply that he is a great poet for them, whatever his influence or lack of it. Eliot's discussion has the merit of crisply re-stating the problem rather than suggesting a plausible solution.

This may also be said of a more controversial part of the lectures, which deals with a subject much canvassed in the nineteen-thirties, the so-called 'problem of beliefs'. Eliot's discussion of it, though tentative, is of value. But the issue is clouded by his decision to make it the occasion for disparaging the poetry and personality of Shelley. In some ways Eliot's frankness is commendable. I wish all literary eminences had been equally frank about their predecessors. And he makes it plain that he is reporting his personal reaction to Shelley; he lays no claim to judicial impartiality. But to make these remarks in a context of such solemnity gave them, for many of his followers, the force of a papal edict. And we cannot banish the suspicion—in view of his repeated sniping at Shelley in previous essays—that Eliot uses the occasion for one of those carefully planned and executed literary assassinations which Conrad Aiken recalls from the early days of the *Criterion*. However that may be, Eliot's remarks were very influential. (They were to be reinforced a few years later by Leavis's chapter on Shelley in *Revaluation*.) As a result, Shelley has become the least known of the major English poets. Younger school and university teachers took their cue from Eliot and Leavis, and their pupils did not properly get to know a poet who might have become one of their greatest friends. The oracle had spoken: Shelley the man was 'almost a blackguard', and Shelley the poet 'almost unreadable'. To this day Shelley has not recovered the fame he enjoyed in the nineteenth century. A writer in *Essays in Criticism* (October 1975) notes that 'in Britain at least he is still out of favour'.

But the problem Eliot raises can be discussed without considering the justice or otherwise of his remarks on Shelley (or his references to Goethe, which are much more outrageous). This is the problem of how far, if at all, it is possible not only to enjoy, and rate highly, but even fully to *understand*, a poet who propagates or assumes a point of view from which the reader seriously dissents. There is no agreed solution to this problem among literary critics, theoretical or practical, at the present day, and the revival in the West of Marxist criticism has made it again a live issue. Eliot's contribution is to divide poets' 'beliefs' into three categories. First, there are beliefs which the reader finds 'acceptable', which he may actually share with the poet. Second, there are beliefs which Eliot describes as 'tenable'. These are beliefs which the reader does not share, but can imagine himself sharing, which can be respected as worthy of credence by a sane and intelligent person. Finally, there are beliefs which the reader can neither share nor imagine himself sharing; and it is these which, Eliot thinks, animate Shelley's major poems and prevent Eliot's enjoyment and real comprehension of them.

An objection might be made to Eliot's position, that he draws the distinction between poetry and philosophy too sharply. He approves of Lucretius and Dante because they did not philo-

sophize on their own, but got on with the poet's job. But even
if we grant (as some would not) the thoroughgoing Epicurean-
ism of Lucretius and the thoroughgoing Thomism of Dante, we
do not have to admit that they are in this respect typical of
great poets. It might rather be thought that their alleged subordination to an external system of beliefs makes them
untypical. There have been poets who thought for themselves,
and some of them have even influenced philosophers, as in the
case of Goethe. But at the time of *The Use of Poetry* Eliot despised Goethe, and one of his major aims in this book is to dis-
credit the notion of poets as independent thinkers.

What seems to be the really crucial issue Eliot evades. This
is the difference between ideas which can safely be relegated to
the *musée imaginaire*, which may require intellectual understanding but are no longer a serious challenge, and, on the other
hand, ideas which are still alive and kicking. It is surely these
which constitute the 'problem of beliefs', for those for whom
there is one. For this reason we might judge that Eliot only
skirmishes with it here. But his distinction between acceptable,
tenable and untenable points of view seems good common sense.
It should, however, be supplemented by the practical conclusion, which Eliot himself was to come to later (though not in the
nineteen-thirties), that when a critic finds a writer's point of
view utterly unsympathetic he should refrain from writing
about him at all. It is true that sometimes a sincere attempt to
understand a difficult author may result in unexpected insights.
As Eliot remarks, with a Yeats-like flourish:

> . . . a critic may choose an author to criticise, a role to assume,
> as far as possible the antithesis to himself, a personality which
> has actualised all that has been suppressed in himself; we can
> sometimes arrive at a very satisfactory intimacy with our anti-
> masks. (p. 112)

(He says something like this about his state of mind in writing
his critique of Kipling, published in 1941.) But the sense of a
moral obligation to be fair is not usually enough to sustain the
imaginative effort of entering a point of view one finds odious.
One should leave such authors alone.

Eliot's entanglement in the difficulty about 'beliefs' is noticeable throughout the later part of *The Use of Poetry*, which is concerned chiefly with Matthew Arnold and his modern successors. The treatment of Arnold has been the object of some adverse comment, and rightly. In some ways it shows Eliot at his worst. He seems to write in a mood of peevish irritation. He is unjust to Arnold's lasting achievement in propagating a humane conception of culture, and sometimes descends to mere gibes, as in his reference to Arnold's school-inspecting (p. 110). And his tone in general is unpleasantly reminiscent of the animosity shown towards Arnold by Walter Raleigh and Lytton Strachey in their essays. The irritation may be due in part to his dislike of Arnold's habit of presenting a Low Church point of view in a High Church manner. But his deeper objection is evidently not to Arnold's style, but to something else, something that Eliot seems to have felt as a challenge to his own existence as a poet, an attempt to block the sources from which his poetry came. This comes out in his often quoted demur to Arnold's saying, apropos of Burns, that 'no one can deny that it is of advantage to a poet to deal with a beautiful world'.

> ... the essential advantage for a poet is not, to have a beautiful world with which to deal: it is to be able to see beneath both beauty and ugliness; to see the boredom, and the horror, and the glory. (p. 106)

Similarly, taking his turn in the long series of castigators of Arnold's famous dictum: 'Poetry is at bottom a criticism of life', Eliot comments:

> At bottom: that is a great way down; the bottom is the bottom. At the bottom of the abyss is what few ever see, and what those cannot bear to look at for long; and it is not a 'criticism of life.' If we mean life as a whole—not that Arnold ever saw life as a whole—from top to bottom, can anything that we say ultimately, of that awful mystery, be called criticism? We bring back very little from our rare descents, and that is not criticism. (p. 111)

These retorts have often been quoted. But they have been admired for what they tell us about Eliot himself, not about Arnold. To me they show a trace of attitudinizing—Eliot's worst fault as a critic. And to concentrate on them is to ignore the merits of Eliot's discussion, his ability to take further the questions that Arnold had raised. Many of the points he makes are fair comment, and show a deep knowledge of his subject. His brief critique of Arnold's poetry may be too severe, and it contains one or two judgements which sound odd, as when he calls 'The Forsaken Merman' a charade—has one really to suppose, in reading that poem, that the speaker has a tail? But a judicious admirer is likely to find that Eliot, while dwelling on Arnold's faults as a poet, does also mention the things that make us like Arnold's poetry, and describes them as well as any critic has done. And his closing reference to Arnold's essay 'The Study of Poetry' is the best summary ever made of Arnold's distinction as a literary critic.

> . . . to be able to quote as Arnold could is the best evidence of taste. The essay is a classic in English criticism: so much is said in so little space, with such economy and with such authority. (p. 118)

This is something that could be said of Eliot himself when he is at his best; and I would add that when he is at his best he is an even better quoter than Arnold.

When he comes to Arnold's modern successors the heated tone disappears from Eliot's writing. He sounds more troubled and more tentative, an inquirer rather than an inquisitor. The position of I. A. Richards, then the most influential modern critic (apart from Eliot himself), Eliot regards as essentially the same as Arnold's; but his objections to it are made with a courtesy and a sympathy he denies to Richards's Victorian predecessor. He puts forward reasonable, if somewhat laborious, strictures on Richards's 'ritual for heightening sincerity'—the recommendation that we should meditate on the immensity of the universe, and other portentous subjects, as a preparation for reading poems. (Curiously enough, Eliot does not make the point—perhaps he thought it too obvious—that there are many poems to which so solemn an approach is plainly unsuited: The Rape of the Lock, for example.) Eliot's real target here is modern secularist religiosity—Russell's 'bad prose' in the Conrad-like 'Free Man's Worship', the sentimental verbiage issuing from the twentieth-century equivalents of Arnold's attempts to 'mediate between Newman and Huxley'. Later attempts in this vein only serve to strengthen the conviction that Eliot was right. 'Culture' in the honorific sense has become an irritatingly vague word, conducive to complacency and woolly thinking.

It seems even possible to defend Eliot's reference, taken from Jacques Maritain, to the influence of the devil on modern literature (p. 137). This was much ridiculed at the time, and Eliot may have been unwise in his wording, which made him sound like Peacock's Mr Toobad ('He said, fifty times over, the devil was come among us'). Belief in the devil is optional for Christians: he is not mentioned in the Creeds. In the second edition Eliot dropped the footnote promising further treatment of this subject—which looks forward to *After Strange Gods*—and he came to regret the later book and, in effect, to expunge it from his canon. Yet since Eliot wrote these words a growing proportion of the serious literature of the Western world has been perverse and abnormal. Only a reader totally at one with the sceptical-permissive climate of our time would deny that; and if many do, the continuity of humanity would appear to be in peril. Fear of the 'stock response' seems to have led some writers and readers into a state of mind in which any recognizably human reaction is stigmatized as sentimentality. How far this disturbing trend actually affects the lives of most people is not certain. But we may reflect that in the cinema the pornography of the sixties is yielding to the sadism of the seventies, while the proponents of the new enlightenment are distinguished by their insistence—shades of Peter Quint and Miss Jessel!—on their right to deprave children. So Eliot does not seem to have been tilting at windmills. That the evil trend he discerns has something to do with the decline of Christianity there is no doubt; and the questions he asks in the closing pages of *The Use of Poetry* remain very pertinent—even, or especially, for agnostics.

But in the end the book may be remembered, not for its treatment of this or any other problem, but for its *obiter dicta*. It is a poet's notebook, especially memorable when concerned with a subject on which Eliot is always interesting: the responsibility of the poet. This, of course, is a theme which has occasioned much frenzied insincerity, and one of the attractive aspects of Eliot is that he is quite free from that frantic insistence, so common in bad artists and critics, so rare in good ones, that we are all madly concerned with art and poetry at every moment of our lives. Equally sympathetic, and as salutary now as when he wrote, is his effort to divert attention from the poet to the poetry. He disagrees with Bremond over the relation between poetry and divine inspiration; and surely Eliot is right here, and Cowley right when he addresses the departed Crashaw:

> Poet and Saint! to thee alone are given
> The two most sacred names of Earth and Heaven.
> The hard and rarest union which can be
> Next that of Godhead with Humanity.

And Eliot already foresaw the exaltation of personality which in our times has produced such phenomena as Norman Mailer, or the intense curiosity about the sex-lives of minor Bloomsbury figures. His own personal restraint and sobriety makes the seriousness of his claims for poetry the more impressive.

> The people which ceases to care for its literary inheritance becomes barbaric; the people which ceases to produce literature ceases to move in thought and sensibility. The poetry of a people takes its life from a people's speech and in turn gives life to it; and represents its highest point of consciousness, its greatest power and its most delicate sensibility.
>
> (p. 15)

And in another of these dicta we have an example of something familiar to readers of Eliot's poems, a point at which a characteristic self-observation turns into a statement of general truth.

> [Poetry] may make us from time to time a little more aware of the deeper, unnamed feelings which form the substratum of our being, to which we rarely penetrate; for our lives are mostly a constant evasion of ourselves, and an evasion of the visible and sensible world. (p. 155)

For the rest, when the neo-classical trappings are laid aside, what Eliot really appeals for is a catholic taste in poetry. His virtue is that he is always reminding us how hard it is to acquire this: most critics' statements about 'poetry' only apply to a limited range of it, the poetry they themselves can appreciate. The moral he draws can be found in what he said in writing of Dryden some years before.

> Our valuation of poetry, in short, depends upon several considerations, upon the permanent and upon the mutable and transitory. When we try to isolate the essentially poetic, we bring our pursuit in the end to something insignificant; our standards vary with every poet whom we consider. All we can hope to do, in the attempt to introduce some order into our preferences, is to clarify our reasons for finding pleasure in the poetry that we like. (*Selected Essays*, 1932, p. 309)

At a time when in the literary world 'fashionable madmen raise/Their pedantic boring cry', we should be grateful for what Eliot gives us in the best parts of *The Use of Poetry*: that memorably expressed good sense which we honour with the name of wisdom. He does not offer new things, but enables us to see familiar things anew. 'But to say this is only to say what you know already, if you have felt poetry and thought about your feelings' (p. 155).

8

Eliot's 'Tone'

ROGER SHARROCK

Much of the significant vocabulary of post-Romantic literary criticism reveals the attempt to take over terms originally belonging to the plastic and musical arts and apply them to literary structures. Form, texture, atmosphere, rhythm, harmony, tone, supersede in the age after Coleridge the older descriptive tools, fable or plot, manners, diction and sentiments; literary analysis abandoned the rhetorical mode in favour of an aesthetic approach enabling the critic to see all the arts as constituting a universal expressive language, poetry being distinct from the other arts only in its use of human speech or written characters to achieve the common end—the creation of artistic objects.

In approaching the elusive question of tone[1] in any writer, and certainly in one as complex and evasive as Eliot, it seems best to avoid any too premature involvement with theory and to let my preliminary remarks stand as a bald and no doubt oversimplified account of what is an historical fact. Yet it might as well be admitted that there is a prime difficulty and distortion in applying to literary works terms suggestive of extension in space, physical surface, plastic harmony or totality: this is because the poem is a sequence of words existing in the time of reading it or hearing it recited; because of this time-character it can never in the strict sense be regarded as an 'aesthetic object' at all. Lessing pointed this out in the eighteenth century before German unified aesthetics had been incubated by German idealist philosophy. The crucial passage in *Laokoön* is that in which he demonstrates that the account in Homer of the shield of Achilles is primarily a description of the stages in the forging of the shield, not a picture in words, because of the time-character of the poetic art.[2] Once this discrimination has been

made, it becomes necessary to exercise extreme caution in
employing visual metaphors for the functioning of poetry, and
the same applies to metaphors from music, implying pure sound
as distinct from verbal meaning, though here the necessary discrimination is a different one, lying as it does between two arts
existing in time. But caution over terms need not involve the
wholesale dismissal of the aesthetic conception of the art-object,
whether the necessary metaphors be visual or musical.

There are of course those who would reject any general
aesthetic theory as a mere figment of idealist metaphysics, meaningless when separated in twentieth-century popular usage from
the other tenets of absolute idealism. Aestheticians like R. G.
Collingwood have presented easy targets for these total critics
who have drawn attention to their ignoring of particular works,
their claim that neither the representational in art, nor religious
art, nor the element of craft in artefacts, has anything to do
with art proper in its disinterested purity.[3] It must be recognized, though, and here I suppose I am proposing a mediation
between the historical and the normative aspects of the question,
that if a coherent body of ideas, however little related in its origins to artistic practice, has been allowed for a period of time to
affect practice, new styles of art will emerge. This indeed is what
happened from Coleridge and Novalis to Rimbaud and Yeats,
from Rimbaud to the Surrealists, from Picasso to Jackson Pollock.
If 'the excellence of every art is its intensity', in Keats's phrase,
then the artist will tend to stretch technique to the limits in
order to attain a heightened and transcended self-consciousness,
whether he is deliberately aspiring after the Absolute or not.
Once intensity of performance becomes the chief aim, the
imaginative writer is like a modern athlete for whom constantly
researched training techniques are always taking fresh seconds
off the mile.

In any case, the critics of Romantic and expressionist aesthetics who base their rejection on the link between such aesthetic
theories and subjective idealist philosophy must abide by the
logic of their argument: fashion is one thing, and the thing it is
may be said to be that you actually see very clearly and with a
certain appreciation of a number of the rational grounds why A
(in) may be right and B (out) may be wrong. A majority of

English academic philosophers may still prefer to float in the
warm currents of the British empirical Gulf Stream. But the
questions are open. It may be that in approaching the 'reality'
of works of art a merely empirical or psychological approach
through signals and stimuli is not adequate and may only
sweep the true problems under the carpet. The exploration of
the stream of consciousness in the great masters of early
twentieth-century literature, in Eliot and Yeats as well as in the
novelists Conrad, Joyce, Virginia Woolf, Proust, and Lawrence,
was conducted in a manner closer to that of the absolute ideal-
ists than to that of their philosophical rivals; these writers
present a many-levelled conception of consciousness and of the
relation between the perceiver and his world:

> The fact that we can think only in terms of things does not
> compel us to the conclusion that reality consists of things. We
> have found from the first that the thing is thoroughly rela-
> tive, that it exists only in a context of experience, of experi-
> ence with which it is continuous. From first to last reality is
> experience, but experience would not (so far as we know) be
> possible without attention and the moment of objectivity.[4]

That is the young Eliot on Bradley. And to maintain that attention and render that moment of objectivity remained the major
goals of Eliot's poetry. The ghost of the author of *Appearance
and Reality* advances through the Cimmerian empirical darkness—*ibant obscuri sola sub nocte per umbras*—'Mr. Bain
believes that the mind is a collection, but if this is so, who col-
lects Mr. Bain?' But if the ghost of Bradley is invoked it is time
to come to Eliot who wrote his thesis on him and to tone, which
is a way of trying to define the indefinable addition in what each
said, as philosopher and critic respectively.

Eliot thought Bradley had an indubitable claim to permanence on account of his gift of style; this is perhaps an unusual
judgement for someone trained as a professional philosopher, as
Eliot was, to make on behalf of another philosopher. In his essay
on Bradley he compares him to Arnold, his own predecessor as
literary critic and schoolmaster to those to be saved from the
Philistines. He sets side by side Arnold's famous apostrophe to
an Oxford bathed in the last enchantments of the middle age

and an extract from *The Principles of Logic* on how appearances
may be felt to hide 'some fuller splendour':

> ... the sensuous curtain is a deception and a cheat, if it hides
> some colourless movement of atoms, some spectral woof of
> impalpable abstractions, or unearthly ballet of bloodless cate-
> gories. Though dragged to such conclusions, we cannot
> embrace them.

Eliot comments that the Bradley passage may well be superior
to that by Arnold: Arnold's effort to glamourize in phrases like
'ineffable charm' has not worn at all well; but he adds: 'Any one
who is at all sensitive to style will recognize the similarity of
tone and tension and beat'.[5]

What is remarkable in Eliot's comment is that he effectively
fuses, or perhaps confuses, the two most available meanings of
tone: the indication of scale or tonality in music and the ordinary social meaning—social style, 'I don't like your tone' (perhaps merging with 'of voice' and thus moving back to music by
way of tone of voice). 'Tension and beat' draw the hidden metaphor towards the musical. The comment on that touch of emotional self-indulgence in Arnold which has made his style wear
less well balances this with the ordinary meaning of social tone.
Eliot is here speaking of the critical or philosophic prose which
he most admired, and, to some extent, imitated. This is prose
which offers a grave rhythmic beauty and a play of images
without the opulence and the sheer naïve self-assertiveness of
Ruskin or Swinburne in their critical writings. Eliot's own manner
has subdued the rhythms and suppressed the metaphors (or
transformed them in the early criticism to harsh pseudo-
scientific ones) but the essence of the style, the Harvard-
Oxonian dying fall, is still there: '[The poet] is not likely to
know what is to be done unless he lives in what is not merely
the present, but the present moment of the past, unless he
is conscious, not of what is dead, but of what is already
living'; 'The sad ghost of Coleridge beckons to me from the
shadows'.

Rhythms, the balance of units of meaning in units of clauses,
dying cadences, are indeed present in Eliot's prose, but it is probably not profitable to pursue this aspect of tone at the expense

of the other, the ordinary or social one. It is the latter I am mainly concerned with. But the two senses cannot be entirely separated and it may be sufficient to say in passing that for such a musical poet (in the structural sense, as he would have understood 'musical'), apart from the obvious relation of the parts and themes of *Four Quartets* to sonata form, the relation of works like *The Waste Land* or 'Gerontion' to the tone poem has not received as much attention as it deserves from the critics. Hugh Kenner and others have rightly stressed the operatic-dramatic aspect of *The Waste Land;* but as Eliot says in his lecture, 'The Three Voices of Poetry', 'in every poem, from the private meditation to the epic or the drama, there is more than one voice to be heard'.[6] The character parts, Mr Eugenides and the ladies in the pub, are subdued to the 'voice of the poet addressing an audience', and even to the 'voice of the poet talking to himself'. The tone poem from Liszt to Strauss was music's tribute to the supremacy of Romantic literary aesthetics, but as music became literary and descriptive, poetry in its turn began to practise the rendering of mood and atmosphere achieved by the tone poem, Debussy's *L'Après-midi d'un Faune,* say.[7] The closest analogue for 'Gerontion', much closer than Browning's or Pound's dramatic monologues, is Elgar's *Falstaff Overture* where there is to be found a similar evocation of encounters in the past all directed to the creation of a single atmosphere and character. *De la musique avant toute chose*, and I suppose the link between musical tonality, or the method of the tone poem transferred to verse, and tone in the social-literary sense, my main concern, is that in the former the impossible attempt to approximate utterance to music leaves a verbal meaning deliberately blurred, vaguely suggestive, or multiple, while in the latter the very notion of 'tone' is undefined, a *je ne sais quoi*, a modernist version of the late Augustan principle of taste employed as an escape-clause from the neo-classical rules. Let us, though, think of Eliot and the tone poem, not digressively, but in terms of the close connection between the music of mood of Debussy and others and the poetry of vague, yearning, half-defined mood of Mallarmé and others, their Symbolist contemporaries. There need be no artistic vagueness in the precise, musical rendering of a vague, half-defined mood; though the artist is presented with a problem similar to that of the novelist who has to make a bore amusing, not directly boring to the reader. This world of pure mood in which the world of getting and spending is suspended or rejected is the world of Mallarmé and Laforgue, of Corbière and Debussy; it is also the world of Prufrock and of the *persona* of 'Portrait of a Lady'.

To reject the everyday world is a luxury, though if the will and the intelligence are there it need not be a too expensive one. After the direct, violent attacks of the early Romantics, and the spectacular withdrawal of their successors into Bohemia, narcotics, and private worlds (Poe, Gérard de Nerval), the later nineteenth-century dissociation of the artist from the *bourgeoisie* takes on a new form. The attitude now, as we encounter it in Laforgue and to some extent in the early Eliot, is to express disenchantment while maintaining a surface of polite, ironic conformity. The artist now becomes the dandy who wears a correct uniform and appears to make the best thing possible out of a life essentially tragic and meaningless by playing along its surface. Another aspect of this conformity or deliberate disguise is the pressure on the artist or writer of the growing cities; he can no longer pretend not to be influenced by the new society of the street and the crowd and the urban cliché. So Laforgue and Eliot-Prufrock celebrate Paris and London even while they cultivate Hamlet and Pierrot. The new dandy often plays the role of the *flâneur* who moves in the crowd but not of it, observing the stream of life as it flows:

> Mais, lainages, caoutchoucs, pharmacie, rêve,
> Rideaux écartés du haut des balcons des grèves
> Devant l'océan de toitures des faubourgs,
> Lampes, estampes, thé, petits-fours,
> Serez-vous pas mes seules amours! . . .
> (Oh! et puis, est-ce que tu connais, outre les pianos,
> Le sobre et vespéral mystère hebdomadaire
> Des statistiques sanitaires
> Dans les journaux?)
> (*Oeuvres de Jules Laforgue* (Paris, 1947), ii, 146)

For Eliot, too, the yellow fog that rubs the window-panes, the men in shirt-sleeves leaning out of windows, the short square

fingers stuffing pipes, are as much constituents of consciousness
as the nostalgia at its centre.[8]

What I have loosely called the suspension or rejection of the
accepted everyday world operates at three levels, all connected.
The most familiar of these is represented by the alienation of
the writer from the prevailing assumptions of bourgeois society.
However, at a deeper level this denial of social and moral conventions is matched by a metaphysical denial of the 'reality' of
the extended, objective world, the same for everybody and still
there when we turn the corner of the street, belief in which is
a prerequisite for living the life of ordinary bourgeois activity.
Life is a series, an infinite regress, of finite centres of consciousness; 'thinking of the key, each confirms a prison': the limited
point-of-view of the individual consciousness and the complexity
of the series inhibit true knowledge and permit only guesses
about any God or Absolute in whom all the finite centres or
monads are reconciled. Both Laforgue and the early Eliot ironic-
ally invoke the Absolute. How one believes affects the way one
sees and every sane man has his own mode of hallucination
depending on his theory of knowledge. The beautiful dead stillness of a loaf or a cup by Chardin reflects the observed otherness
of a Cartesian world. So at a third level the dandy or flâneur who
has dissolved the hard, objective world sees a luminous, shim-
mering universe of points of light and points of view, the world
of Impressionism and of pointillisme, the transparent envelope
of Virginia Woolf's famous rebuke to Arnold Bennett. For the
modernist writers of the early twentieth century the prelude to
'making it new' was to see it new, through the employment of
fragmented urban experience, or the sharp juxtaposition of
imagist verse, echoing the dissociated perspectives of cubism.

We have come from the musical tone of symbolist poetry
aspiring to become pure art and to transcend the social meaning
of words, to find correspondances in the vowels as well as in
nature. The need to dispense with social meaning and participation causes the poet, in the wake of Baudelaire's great example,
to strike the pose of the dandy and flâneur. Thus we come to
that other kind of 'tone', the subtler means by which a speaker
or writer establishes an attitude to his audience.

Nine years after the publication of The Sacred Wood and

three years before that of *Selected Essays* there appeared I. A. Richards's *Practical Criticism* (1929). In that book Richards discusses tone as one of the four kinds of meaning to be found in all articulate speech. The speaker 'chooses or arranges his words differently as his audience varies, in automatic or deliberate *recognition of his relation to them'*.[9] As might be expected Richards finds tone more elusive than the other aspects of meaning (sense, feeling, and intention) and less easy to discuss. He simply draws attention to the manner in which in certain Augustan writers, for instance, an exquisitely adjusted tone may raise to a high rank a poem commonplace in thought (his example, about which not everyone would agree, is Gray's *Elegy*). For Richards tone is literary good manners, and he uses it as a stick with which to beat the over-insistence or condescension of much nineteenth-century poetry.

The first extraordinary thing about the success of Eliot's literary essays is that their appeal depends so much on a marked personal tone, and yet their plea for impersonal, objective methods in literary study effected a critical revolution.[10] Two generations of critics and teachers have been influenced by that revolution, and even after Northrop Frye and the Structuralists it is still a main element, if not the main element, in the schools of literature which grew up in the universities after the second world war. The second extraordinary thing is that Eliot should have established this assured relation with his readers when his personality is so remote and reserved; he remains the invisible poet, 'Old Possum', as Pound liked to call him, playing possum and lying low. I shall try to investigate these two paradoxes of the success of Eliot's criticism.

The tone of Eliot's mind as revealed in the early essays (up to, say, *The Use of Poetry and the Use of Criticism* in 1933) is fastidious and sceptical, avoiding premature dogmatic formulations. He disarmingly admits inconsistencies, but, in not subscribing to any general aesthetic theory, holds that such self-denial is a prerequisite for any honest literary perception, since 'a system almost inevitably requires slight distortions and omissions'.

'In my end is my beginning': it is necessary to go back to the germinal work, the essays collected in *The Sacred Wood* (1920),[11] to find in a pure form the relation between what is said in his criticism and the authoritative personal tone. The general method of each essay is that 'revaluation' within an accepted English and European pattern of literary reputations which has since become the stock form of critical activity here and in America, proliferating in thousands of articles. The opinions advanced in the revaluation may be novel or even revolutionary, but the terms in which they are offered are those of public persuasion within a recognized system. Thus there is a shock effect: trenchant orthodoxy rubs shoulders with striking unorthodoxy. Aristotle is praised as 'a man of not only remarkable but universal intelligence; and universal intelligence means that he could apply his intelligence to anything'. If the middle-aged, conventional reader of the *Times Literary Supplement* in 1919 had not begun to doze off he was jerked up two pages later by: 'Of all modern critics, perhaps Remy de Gourmont had most of the general intelligence of Aristotle'. An acceptance of the traditional pre-eminence of Homer and Virgil is found alongside the oblique disparagement of Milton. Each type of statement is made in the same way, with complete confidence, without qualification, and usually with extreme brevity: '. . . after the erection of the Chinese Wall of Milton, blank verse has suffered not only arrest but retrogression'. There is a rhetoric of these early essays and it is the rhetoric of the dandy, sober and correct, more sober and correct than the crowd, and now turned from being a symbolist poet to being a perfect critic. The quiet, firm, precise tone is the exact embodiment of the thought, and a closer examination of it can lead us to look more closely at the thought.

In *The Sacred Wood* the ideas and style are already fully formed and the sense of speaking from an assured position is in the young Eliot quite dauntingly middle-aged. Some critics, Coleridge, for instance, give the sense of having begun an inquiry which has still a long way to run; the impression left by a reading of *The Sacred Wood* is that a completely honest and rigorous intellectual survey of the highest order has been carried out as it were off stage, and that what one is getting is not even a full report of the results, but simply the application of a few of those results, devastatingly and accurately, to certain current problems of literary value that have come in Eliot's way.

It is a mistake to think that the dandy is flamboyant. He
stands out by the very perfection and restraint of his correctness. All is in place and he is never caught with a loose
cravat:

> My morning coat, my collar mounting firmly to the chin,
> My necktie rich and modest, but asserted by a simple pin—

But Prufrock failed to maintain the dandy stance. Brummell's
dress was dark and restrained and never varied much. In the
later essays the dandy restraint, the mystery of withheld knowledge, is absent; the stylistic impact is blurred rather than
sharpened; certain features of the original approach are
explained and developed as Eliot moves further towards explicitly theological and sociological attitudes to literature. But the
dandy does not explain his elegance. He leaves us to wonder
how he does it.

Some of the sleight of hand of the younger Eliot is to be attributed to his using critical reviews and essays as propaganda for
his own poetry and that of Pound; there is also some subterfuge
about the favourable presentation of other new writers felt to be
importantly connected with Eliot's creative work (significantly,
Joyce). One can generalize and say that all the great English
critics have been poets seeking to justify their own practice in
poetry (F. R. Leavis is the outstanding exception). Eliot
resembles Sidney, Dryden, Johnson, and Wordsworth in this
respect. But his criticism is by no means simply a programme for
the poems he was writing in this period. The relation between
the critic and the poet in Eliot is a more intimate and subtle one
than that between theorem and demonstration. It lies in his
conception of the disinterested intelligence, that rare gift of
mind possessed by Aristotle and Remy de Gourmont. This
intelligence has the capacity to possess and digest the past and
make it comprehensible to the present. The point is made at the
end of the spirited onslaught on Gilbert Murray, 'Euripides and
Professor Murray':

> We need a digestion which can assimilate both Homer and
> Flaubert. We need a careful study of Renaissance Humanists
> and Translators, such as Mr. Pound has begun. We need an

eye which can see the past in its place with its definite differences from the present, and yet so lively that it shall be as present to us as the present. This is the creative eye; and it is because Professor Murray has no creative instinct that he leaves Euripides quite dead. (p. 70)

This comes at the end of three concluding paragraphs into which are packed a compendious sketch of recent and contemporary classical studies and their employment of psychological and anthropological methods, what Eliot terms 'the heavy food of historical and scientific knowledge that we have eaten'.

The process of digestion by the disinterested critical intelligence is analogous to the way in which the impersonal poet in the essay 'Tradition and the Individual Talent' is described as absorbing a variety of different experiences and converting them to 'a new art-emotion'. The poet too must master the past and make it present, for

... he is not likely to know what is to be done unless he lives in what is not merely the present, but the present moment of the past, unless he is conscious, not of what is dead, but of what is already living. (p. 53)

Both poet and critic use intelligence; the difference between them is that for the poet it is largely a negative instrument enabling him to avoid unnecessary cerebration and let the unconscious process of absorption of experience take its course.

In passages like those quoted there is an urgency of tone which communicates its peculiar excitement to the reader. Something is necessary; certain measures must be put into action immediately. 'This is really a point of capital importance': '... these are not faults of infinitesimal insignificance'. The reader is treated seriously as one fitted to be trusted with serious matters. This is one reason for the lasting appeal of the book to any one genuinely interested in literature and particularly the young reader. Does this business-like seriousness conflict with the image of Eliot as critical dandy which I have presented? I think not. The dandy is serious but not solemn; he is concerned about what is to him important, though not to the crowd. He speaks in the rebuke to the solemn scholarship candi-

date in Cyril Connolly's *sottise* who said he had not read Ray-
mond Radiguet because he was not in his period: 'On the contrary, he is very much in our period!'[12] He maintains the
surface, the texture (or the quality of the language) because he
knows that is the only way to hold in the chaos that lies
beneath the surface of the human animal and its transience.

With the possible exception of the ambitious 'Tradition and
the Individual Talent' no clearly defined principles emerge from
these essays. The prevailing tone is dry, ironic and cagey, as if
full-blown theorizing is for fools; just as the touches of urgency
flatter and excite the reader, so does the air of something being
held in reserve, unspoken: it is as if there are certain understood things between cultivated people, not to mention a formid-
able apparatus of reading in all the principal European languages, which need not be paraded or expounded and can
simply be taken for granted.

There are no large gestures and a good deal of banter at the
expense of the large gesture. 'Poetry is a superior amusement: I
do not mean an amusement for superior people. I call it an
amusement ... because if you call it anything else you are
likely to call it something still more false'; 'the only cure for
Romanticism is to analyse it'. 'Immature poets imitate; mature
poets steal; bad poets deface what they take, and good poets
make it into something better, or at least something different.'
This splendid epigrammatic sentence may be thought to embody
almost all of what Harold Bloom had to say over fifty years later,
with a great deal of posturing and neologism, in *The Anxiety of
Influence*. It comes from the long review of Cruickshank's study
of Massinger. This is perhaps the least satisfactory of the essays
in *The Sacred Wood* because it is difficult to see what side Eliot
is on; is he praising, blaming or excusing Massinger? The fact
is that the discussion of Massinger is merely a peg for insights
like the one quoted and wider observations on the development
and decline of Jacobean and Caroline tragedy. This is a case
where the oblique justification of Eliot's own poetic practice and
that of Ezra Pound blurs the focus of the essay; in a really successful essay like that on Ben Jonson, the focus is clear, and Eliot
manages effortlessly to combine a revaluation of Jonsonian
comedy and its two-dimensional treatment of character, step by

step with the oblique advocacy of the sort of formal non-
naturalistic design he was following in his poems and already
beginning to aspire to in the drama:

> Of all the dramatists of his time, Jonson is probably the one
> whom the present age would find the most sympathetic, if it
> knew him. There is a brutality, a lack of sentiment, a polished
> surface, a handling of large bold designs in brilliant colours,
> which ought to attract about three thousand people in Lon-
> don and elsewhere. (pp. 110–11)

What is remarkable is that this brilliantly clever and knowing puff for Jonson succeeded, and two generations on the thirty
thousand successors of the three thousand (or whatever consti-
tutes the core audience of the Royal Shakespeare Company) no
longer need conversion; or rather, Eliot prophetically read the
mind of the age; though one suspects that nowadays lack of
sentiment and the enjoyment of brutality are the main ingredients of appreciation and that the pleasure in the handling of
large bold designs comes a poor third.

The absence of theoretical statement, unless it is backed by
something like scientific proof or experimental reference, means
that there are no key phrases enshrining a dogma like Wordsworth's 'the real language of men', no wooing slogans like
Arnold's 'the best that is known and thought in the world'. The
manner is dry and reticent, and yet it is stimulating because of
a reserve of intellectual passion all the more impressive because
of the sense of its being held in check. And we feel that what is
being held back is not so much a body of undeclared principles
as a bitterly acquired knowledge of the business of living, passion as well as intellect. It comes out in these words near the
end of 'Tradition and the Individual Talent':

> Poetry is not a turning loose of emotion, but an escape from
> emotion; it is not the expression of personality, but an escape
> from personality. But, of course, only those who have per-
> sonality and emotions know what it means to want to escape
> from these things.

This is a significant variation on Villiers de L'Isle Adam's
'Living—our servants can do that for us!' It substitutes for an

aristocracy of taste and art an aristocracy of suffering, marked off from ordinary men by its ability to transform the suffering personality into art. The note of dandy arrogance is sustained, but for a brief moment it looks as if Eliot is lifting a curtain to reveal his attitude towards a topic about which in these early essays he generally remains exasperatingly silent, the relation of poetry to the moral life. But the glimpse is tantalizingly brief, and the escape from personality is presented as the privilege of the poet, not something possible to the reader or critic who is not a poet. As so often in *The Sacred Wood* the argument is sustained at vital points by what are in the nature of confidential reports on the attitude of the creative writer; these reports serve to sweep aside any opposition on account of their air of authenticity.

Since at least the outline of the story of Eliot's unhappy first marriage has been made public, it is impossible not to associate passages like that on the escape from emotion and personality with suppressed personal experience. Indeed the whole theory of poetic impersonality is, one suspects, fertilized by the strains of personal unhappiness.[13] Eliot classes *Hamlet* as a failure because Shakespeare did not find a suitable 'objective correlative' for the sexual disgust that is the play's poetic raw material; he himself took more care to achieve personal invisibility when two years later in *The Waste Land* he assembled its myths and dramatic *collages* into an impenetrable disguise for his 'prolonged grouse'. This is yet another aspect of the critical essays which reflects the preoccupations of his poetry. We have seen the absorbing, transforming intelligence at work both in the critic and the poet, exercizing itself on the literary tradition in the former, in the latter on the accumulation of experience and emotion. Now the critic, speaking for the poet, makes a kind of mystery of the personal emotion to be overcome; so does the poet in the original epigraph to *The Waste Land*: 'The horror, the horror.' There is a shadow line in the essays as in the poems. Finally, the strategic display of learning in the essays corresponds to the parade of the mind of Europe in *The Waste Land*, belatedly summarized in the notes added to the poem at the last moment: 'These fragments I have shored against my ruins'. It will be noticed that it is not the *Poems* of 1920, with the

exception of 'Gerontion', but *The Waste Land*, a poem still to
be written, which most closely reflects the interests and methods
of *The Sacred Wood*. The conclusion is that the poem was
slowly incubating in Eliot's creative mind at the time when the
essays were written.

The qualities of impersonality, mystery, and authority, in
combination with the display of reason and learning, are the
ingredients of success. *The Sacred Wood* is essentially a book
that spoke to the individual who was weary of emotive uplift in
criticism, tired of the detritus of the Nineties, and flattered to
be treated as a member of an ideal civilized public. The impression effected by the tone is predominant because in his handling
of ideas Eliot is habitually cautious and evasive. In this he is
the successor of Matthew Arnold, however temperamentally
opposed to Arnold he may be on other grounds. He describes
Arnold as more a propagandist for criticism than a critic; to
both of them the critical intelligence is not merely worthwhile
but indispensable. They share a common aim: the defence of the
rigorous intellectual analysis of artistic works in an England
which is felt to be potentially hostile to such an approach. In
1920, sixty years after Arnold's fulminations, all his work was
to do again; today, at almost the same distance of time, Philistinism in England is quite dead and the cultural danger is the quite
different one represented by the media and still more by a media-
governed attitude of mind: skilful vulgarization with an eye to
the market. As Arnold had done, so Eliot in his later work
moved towards a broader interest in the problems of culture and
society. Arnold had taken the strain of the new learning of
Europe in the early nineteenth century, German philosophy
after Hegel and French positivism; he had made his pilgrimage
to Paris. So had Eliot, and where Arnold tended to beatify
Sainte-Beuve, Eliot did the same for Remy de Gourmont. As a
Europeanized American, a Jamesian expatriate more European
than the Europeans, he prepares with his friend Ezra Pound to
lay siege to the literary capitals of the real Europe for the cause
of an ideal Europe, a Europe of the mind.

The Sacred Wood establishes a critical bridgehead in the face
of possible opposition from the prevailing literary world; heterodox views had been aired in such sacrosanct places as the

review columns of the *Times Literary Supplement.* To use the title of one of the volumes of Mr Leon Edel's life of Henry James, Eliot and Pound laid deliberate siege to London, and London fell in the end, and after it the whole Anglo-Saxon literary and academic establishment. There were of course pockets of indignant resistance which remained to be mopped up at a late stage of the campaign: Gavin Bone's donnish sneer at 'an American critic, a Mr Eliot' was published as late as 1943.[14] The essays of *The Sacred Wood* as they were published in the *Egoist,* the *Athenaeum,* and the *TLS* between 1917 and 1920 represent a deliberate seizure of power by a minority using infiltration rather than direct attack somewhat in the manner that Lenin and the Bolshevik leaders seized power in the same years. Pound has a remark in a letter which illustrates this sense of conspiracy; he is criticizing a rare failure of tone in a review where Eliot had abandoned his habitual insinuation for a bludgeoning approach: 'That's not your style at all. You let *me* throw the bricks through the front window. You go in at the back door and take out the swag.'[15]

The characteristic insinuating tone can be seen in the careful dropping of certain names in the margin of the main arguments of the essays. The references to Milton and the Chinese Wall of his blank verse have of course become notorious. The favourable references to Stendhal and the extremely hostile ones to Meredith are also worth mentioning:

> How astonishing it would be, if a man like Arnold had concerned himself with the art of the novel ... had shown his contemporaries exactly why the author of *Amos Barton* is a more *serious* writer than Dickens, and why the author of *La Chartreuse de Parme* is more serious than either. (p. xi)

'The few people who talk intelligently about Stendhal and Flaubert and James ...', 'the suspicion is in our breast that Mr Whibley might admire George Meredith'; 'The Charles Louis Philippes of English Literature are never done with, because there is no one to kill their reputations; we still hear that George Meredith is a master of prose, or even a profound philosopher'. These allusions are peripheral to the discussions of poetry which are the concern in the forefront of the essays, as are the allusions

to innovation in the novel by Conrad and Joyce. Faults and
virtues are hinted at, but not even the suggestion of a critical
case is made out; yet the allusions occur in the course of carefully reasoned arguments; they therefore draw to themselves
from the main argument some of its logical persuasiveness and
weight of judgement. Arnold had made the mistake, in England
a fatal one, of arguing with his countrymen about religion
before he had convinced them that his literary views were worth
listening to; also, he generalized too much. Eliot made neither
of these mistakes. Instead he carried out a series of small-scale
reassessments of particular writers so well that the reader could
fill in the gaps between these new landmarks for himself, as one
joins up the dots in a child's drawing-book, so that a whole new
orientation of English literary tradition began to appear. It was
even possible to deduce what was wrong with George Meredith
(I take it to be the double crime of fine writing and home-made
philosophizing) and why the Stendhal novel named should be
La Chartreuse and not Le Rouge et le Noir.

The stock assumptions which these reassessments were to
undermine need not be described at length. They have been
lucidly analysed by Mr C. K. Stead in The New Poetic. Briefly,
Eliot's polemic is directed against three presuppositions of late
nineteenth-century poetic mythology: first, the idea that only
the genius, the great man matters, and that he is solitary, owing
nothing to the community of his fellows. Eliot calls this 'the
perpetual heresy of English culture'. Arnold had written in the
same way of the folly of despising criticism as an activity of a
lower order and of neglecting the need for a free current of ideas
to refresh the creative writer. Eliot follows Arnold's very phrasing closely, speaking of 'the rapid circulation of ideas'. He argues
the need for second-order minds which are not the same as
second-rate minds. The great man may be greater for a current of
fresh ideas which only the second-order minds can maintain,
while the poet who is less than great will certainly profit from
that current. Here again in another sixty years the revolution
has been accomplished, not of course entirely owing to the
influence of Eliot's writings, but through impersonal pressures
in our society and the advent of mass education. There is no
lack now of second-order minds and, at any rate until recently,

our public arrangements have been geared to the production of a great many more.

The second assumption, clearly linked to the first, is that the quality of a work of art is dependent on an unanalysable personal emotion which lies beyond intellectual discourse and which the beholder or audience shares with the artist. The third assumption is that poetry offers some form of uplift, consolation or philosophy or beautiful thoughts. For if the poem as poem cannot be analysed, the ideas and moral attitudes that are taken up into it are at least detachable, and give the critic something to talk about.

Eliot's criticism of all these presuppositions is that they draw the reader's attention away from the poetry to something else, the pleasant emotions generated in him by the poem, the interest of the personality he feels is being revealed to him, or some kind of ennobling statement about life which might range in value from a world-view to a Christmas cracker motto. 'Honest criticism and sensitive appreciation is directed not upon the poet but upon the poetry.' All views are false which try to substitute something else for the poem. In arguing for the substantiality and integrity of poetry as itself and not another thing Eliot is returning to the chief Romantic doctrine of poetic uniqueness in order to criticize later aberrations of that doctrine. Thus over what I have called the second assumption, of an unanalysable poetic emotion, his attitude is ambiguous: his treatment of the poem as imaginative fusion achieving a unique emotion through manipulating the associations and lexical meanings of words puts him with Coleridge and the Symbolists:

> For this ordinary emotional person, experiencing a work of art, has a mixed critical and creative reaction. It is made up of comment and opinion, and also new emotions which are vaguely applied to his own life. The sentimental person, in whom a work of art arouses all sorts of emotions which have nothing to do with that work of art whatever, but are accidents of personal association, is an incomplete artist. For in an artist these suggestions . . . become fused with a multitude of other suggestions . . . and result in the production of a new object which is no longer purely personal . . . (p. 6)

Here is a view of the self-sufficiency of the art work which echoes symbolist theory and yet is used to demolish the reliance on indefinable personal emotion derived from the same source.

This statement appears in the first essay of *The Sacred Wood*, 'The Perfect Critic', which, with 'Tradition and the Individual Talent', comes nearest to laying down a programme to be carried out in the reappraisals of particular poets that follow. After 'The Perfect Critic' come sketches of various contemporary or recent 'Imperfect Critics'. All the latter are interested in something other than the poem as unique and independent object. Swinburne has taste and enthusiasm but stops short of analysing the special qualities which attract him. George Wyndham is a romantic aristocrat and his intelligence therefore is not sufficiently disinterested. In Paul Elmer More and Irving Babbitt the moralist precedes the critic of poetry. Only Aristotle and Remy de Gourmont are allowed to approach perfection.

The key words used in the paragraph describing the perfect critic are 'intelligence', 'feeling' and 'feelings', 'emotion', and 'sensibility' (the latter used less frequently than the other words). Combinations of these terms occur throughout the essays. They suggest that Eliot's hidden theory of poetry is based on a theory of human perception, more precisely on a scepticism learned from Bradley about the extent of the degrees of human knowledge: 'Human kind cannot bear very much reality'. In experience from moment to moment, feeling (sensation) and thought, or reflection on the feeling, come together in the continuous stream of consciousness, so that the poet looking faithfully at his experience can never satisfactorily separate sensation-in-itself and feeling that is already on its way to becoming an object of attention. Abstract thought comes later, after both the original experience and the fused thought resulting from it; so does emotion, for in Eliot's usage emotion is something that develops around an experience at a later stage, not a part of it like the immediate feelings—it is both a luxury product and a step on the road towards increasing indefiniteness. The followers of Hegel, for instance (like Professor Eucken who banged the table and said '*Was ist Geist? Geist ist*. . .'), 'have as a rule taken for granted that words have definite meanings, overlooking the tendency of words to become indefinite emotions'.

The classical severity of this, the austere intellectual tone, is aimed at getting the critic away from emotions and personalities and abstract systems to the hard facts of real moments of perception. There is a paradox here. Eliot's intellectualism, his approval of the hard definite outline, as in the comedies of Ben Jonson or the novels of Stendhal, his distrust of the blurred emotion hovering between creation and the outpouring of personality which he shrank from in Meredith and later in Lawrence[16]—all these are directed to a conception of literature which is not intellectualist, but envisages a 'whole man' in whom thought, feeling, and even muscular sensation are blended. Also, the final end of the creative process is not completely under the control of the will. As in his poems, 'Human kind cannot bear very much reality', or, 'You know and do not know, what it is to act or suffer'.

The primacy of sensation, the poverty of abstract thought, and the idea of involuntary participation in a higher reality— these suggest the influence of Bradley. Eliot had finished his doctoral dissertation on Bradley in 1916, four years before the publication of *The Sacred Wood*. Hugh Kenner and Kristian Smidt have drawn attention to Bradley as a more continuous influence upon Eliot than any poet he was studying in this period. In Bradley we meet a stress comparable to Eliot's on the concentration and transformation of sensuous experience:

> feeling and will must also be transmuted in this whole, into which thought has entered. Such a whole state would possess in a superior form that immediacy which we find (more or less) in feeling; and in this whole all divisions would be healed up. It would be experience entire, containing all elements in harmony.[17]

Eliot, like Bradley, is elegantly dismissive of facile solutions; he too combines scepticism about the possibility of our knowledge of reality with metaphysical depth in recognizing an ideal system behind appearances. Before he embraced Christian belief and practice Eliot indicated his adherence to some ultimate level of understanding experience—'the notion of some infinitely gentle Infinitely suffering thing.' The notion of understanding is transferred from the human reason to the creative perception of the artist. It was a liberal illusion, condemned at Harvard by Irving Babbitt, in Paris by Charles Maurras and Jules Lasserre, that man with his discontinuous nature could hope to understand himself; thus the artist must cultivate impersonality to maintain the gap between 'the man who suffers and the mind which creates', for through the latter only can understanding come.

The assimilation of Bradley is an important element in Eliot's thought but it is not the whole story. There is elegance, but none of the dandy in Bradley; the arrogance, the occasional swagger, the drawing of the idea of impersonality to extremes of abnegation and destruction of personality—these elements in Eliot's early manner he made all his own, but I suspect that Remy de Gourmont was the master who taught him how to practise them.[18] When Eliot says things like 'The progress of an artist is a continual self-sacrifice, a continual extinction of personality', the accent of de Gourmont's logical anti-intellectualism is there. Eliot quotes in the essay on Massinger from *Le problème du style*:

> La vie est un dépouillement. Le but de l'activité propre de l'homme est de nettoyer sa personnalité, de la laver de toutes les souillures qu'y déposa l'éducation, de la dégager de toutes les empreintes qu'y laissèrent nos admirations adolescentes.

As well as the tone of paradox there is in de Gourmont's principal critical writings an eloquent plea for the union of mind and body, for thinking with the body:

> Nous écrivons, comme nous sentons, comme nous pensons, avec notre corps tout entier. L'intelligence n'est qu'une des manières d'être de la sensibilité... Car tout se tient et l'aisance intellectuelle est certainement liée à la liberté des sensations.

As in *The Sacred Wood*, in *La culture des idées*, *Le chemin de velours*, and *Le problème du style*, intellectual precision is placed at the service of the primitive, the involuntary, the discontinuous and the immediate.

Thus the only good lines in the 'dreary sequence' of Drayton's sonnets in *Idea's Mirror* are said to be those in which he writes in terms of concrete actuality:

> Lastly, mine eyes amazedly have seen
> Essex' great fall; Tyrone his peace to gain;
> The quiet end of that long-living queen;
> The king's fair entry, and our peace with Spain.

Salvation may be found through immediacy, through that 'bewildering minute', the contingent moment. Intelligence is not an abstract function set over against the senses and emotions, but the effort of a sensibility to know itself. The passages in *The Sacred Wood* where the dry logic is relieved by a more emotive phrase are those that signal the poet's power to look into the dark places of human life; such a phrase is 'looking into the Shadow' which evokes the difficulty of the life of reason. In that phrase there is mingled reminiscence of the titles and themes of two stories by Conrad—another explorer of the dimension of human life lying beyond the control of reason— *The Shadow-Line* and *Heart of Darkness*. The latter provides an outstanding case of the split between conscious, personal, civilized intention, and that assertion of the dark side of his nature which teaches man more about himself—'Mistah Kurtz, he dead'.

This discussion of Eliot's tone in his early essays has dwelt on its urgency, its dandy's assurance and poise, its scepticism as to principle, its frequent deviousness and occasional mystery. These qualities compound a style of remarkable fascination, uniting as they do critical precision and bold suggestiveness, the appeal to the intellect and an appeal to the pre-logical sources of human life more effective than that of Lawrence because less strident. The impulse that drives these qualities has two principal sources: what I have called the veritable campaign conducted by Eliot and Pound to establish new objective canons of literary taste, and the deep need to work out a personal creative problem. After *The Sacred Wood* it must be admitted that the excitement goes out of Eliot's literary criticism. There are a number of reasons for this, and it would be unfair to demand from the distinguished elderly lecturer on an invited occasion the special freshness of a young man's book. Something may be

attributed to the change from the form of the book review to the
form of the lecture, the change from the exploratory to the *ex
cathedra*; Eliot's platform manner is dull and hedged round with
qualification:

> All I have affirmed is, that a work which consists of a number
> of short poems, even of poems which, taken individually, may
> appear rather slight, may, if it has a unity of underlying
> pattern, be the equivalent of a first-rate long poem in estab-
> lishing an author's claim to be a 'major' poet.
>
> ('What is Minor Poetry?', 1944)

There are many sentences like this one in the lectures collected
in *On Poetry and Poets* (1957). But more important reasons for
the change are surely to be found in the fact that the impulses
behind the earlier criticism had worked themselves out. The
campaign had been successful and the ardour of propaganda was
no longer required. One of the most explicit of the hints thrown
out in *The Sacred Wood*, that concerning a revaluation of the
English poetic tradition based on the line of wit, was followed up
by Eliot himself in *The Use of Poetry and the Use of Criticism*
(1933) and more laboriously by F. R. Leavis and the writers in
Scrutiny. As for the creative and personal problem, which I
would baldly describe as the creation of meaning out of suffering while preserving truth to experience, it was fully worked
 out in *The Waste Land*, *Ash-Wednesday*, and *Four Quartets*.

Thus the early hints and observations on style and metre,
valid as some of them still seem, and the basis of much of our
thinking about poetry, may be traced to an extremely personal
and special epistemology. Great poems are complex and impersonal because they correspond to those isolated moments of
which contingent experience is composed; both poem and
moment of experience are complex structures of feelings in
which perceiving subject and objective outer world merge. In
saluting the author of *The Sacred Wood* one has to add another
name, Eliot's own, to his list of imperfect critics, another
creative writer *manqué*, but one who was to realize himself fully
in the medium of verse over the next twenty years.

Apart from the way in which they illuminate his mind, the
most lasting achievement of these essays, in spite of the imper-

sonal programme, is, by the close examination of language and
metre, to catch for us Marlowe, or Jonson, or Massinger, and
render the 'feel' of their work. It is by a scrupulous regard for
the actual words with which poetry is made that Eliot, though
writing in the symbolist tradition, avoids those extreme illusions
about the poem as art-object or pure music to which I referred
at the beginning of this essay:

> The end is where we start from. And every phrase
> The sentence that is right (where every word is at home,
> Taking its place to support the others,
> The word neither diffident nor ostentatious,
> An easy commerce of the old and the new,
> The common word exact without vulgarity,
> The formal word precise but not pedantic,
> The complete consort dancing together)
> Every phrase and every sentence is an end and a beginning,
> Every poem an epitaph.

9

Eliot, Arnold, and the English Poetic Tradition

C. K. STEAD

The important critic is the person who is absorbed in the present problems of art, and who wishes to bring the forces of the past to bear upon the solution of these problems.

The Sacred Wood

Every renewal of the sense of possibility within an art depends on a corresponding reappraisal of its history. Such a reappraisal was offered by T. S. Eliot in his essays written during the second and third decades of this century. Eliot in effect changed our perspective on English literary history, and the influence of his essays was so strong and so widespread that by 1950 it was scarcely possible for a critic to embark on any aspect of English poetry from 1600 to the modern period without at some point touching on, being influenced by, or at least dissenting from, something that stemmed from Eliot.

The critical orthodoxy which Eliot replaced was that of Matthew Arnold—the late Arnold of *Essays in Criticism Second Series*, which was in its turn very largely an orderly reassertion of the basic principles of English Romanticism. Arnold had begun as something of a rebel against the great figures of the early years of his century; at least he had wanted to mark out for himself as a poet a space where he would not be overshadowed by them; and perhaps more particularly (like Eliot after him) to distinguish himself from their degenerate heirs, his now forgotten contemporaries. Hence the elements of 'classicism' in his early criticism. But Arnold was to find his place finally, not as a rebel against the great Romantics, but as the most persuasive latterday spokesman for their poetry and for the tradition they had invoked to support it. The reputations of Wordsworth and Byron in particular, and also of Gray and Milton, were given new support by Arnold, while the obloquy into which Dryden and Pope had fallen since 1798 was confirmed.

Arnold's influence was long lasting. In 1933 Eliot wrote: 'Examination of the criticism of our time leads me to believe that we are still in the Arnold period.'[1] In 1941 Allen Tate wrote: 'Arnold is still the great critical influence in the universities, and it is perhaps not an exaggeration of his influence to say that debased Arnold is still the main stream of popular appreciation of poetry.'[2] To this I can add my own testimony, for what it is worth. In the fifth and sixth forms in New Zealand in the late 1940s—a time when some little literary history was still taught in New Zealand schools—I learned that Pope and Dryden were classics of our prose and that Wordsworth was the third great English poet after Shakespeare and Milton. I did not hear much about Arnold, but the judgements were couched in terms I now recognize as his. When I enrolled at Auckland University College in 1951 I learned an entirely new version of English literary history, and I learned that it was Eliot's.

These versions of history are at times so overpowering, so all-pervasive, and so bound up not only with the criticism of poetry but with the practice of it as well, that it can be difficult to see them with any degree of detachment. My purpose here is to try to see afresh the historical orthodoxy Eliot established, which means in part to see it against the background of the orthodoxy it replaced.

The most famous sentences which fixed in the minds of his contemporaries and of several generations succeeding him at least the negative aspect of Arnold's view of the literary history of England are those about 'Dryden, Pope, and all their school', whose poetry was 'conceived and composed in their wits' whereas 'genuine poetry is conceived and composed in the soul'. Theirs was the language of prose, not of poetry, and it was Gray's misfortune, and the explanation of why 'he never spoke out', that he was 'a born poet' who 'fell upon an age of prose'.[3]

There are some sentences Arnold wrote in 1881 which fix this view in a broader historical frame:

We had far better than the poetry of the eighteenth century before that century arrived, we have had better since it departed . . . We do well to place our pride in the Elizabethan age and Shakespeare, as the Greeks placed theirs in Homer. We did well to return in the present century to the poetry of that older age for illumination and inspiration, and to put aside, in great measure, the poetry and poets intervening between Milton and Wordsworth. Milton, in whom our great poetic age expired, was the last of the immortals . . . The glory of English literature is in poetry, and in poetry the strength of the eighteenth century does not lie.[4]

Arnold had a hierarchical mind and his English hierarchy was headed by Shakespeare, Milton and Wordsworth in that order. Milton, though second to Shakespeare, was superior to him in 'sureness of perfect style'. He was 'the one artist of the highest rank in the great style whom we have'.[5] Wordsworth lacked style, but he had 'fidelity', he had '*life*' (the italics are Arnold's, and not once but many times), and he taught us 'joy'.[6] To these three poets may be added the others to whom Arnold assigned their various and relative places; and the hierarchy is expanded to include European as well as English poets.

One structure of Arnold's criticism, therefore, might be represented as a simple tennis-club ladder. But another (and here he resembles Eliot in the structure if not in the details of interpretation) is the historical curve, representing a high point in Shakespeare, only a very slight drop to Milton, a sharp dip into the eighteenth century, and an upward curve with the arrival of Wordsworth. The downward curve in poetry, however, is accompanied by an upward one in the quality of prose.

This is the view we have learned at least to reject, if not positively to despise. For my purposes at this point, however, it should be considered neither right nor wrong but simply one way of seeing, which Eliot replaced by another.

Eliot's principal statements on this subject occur in his essay on the Metaphysical Poets and put forward a theory which explains literary developments in terms of what might be called a piece of historical psychology. In the seventeenth century 'something . . . happened to the mind of England', a 'dissociation of sensibility ... from which we have never recovered'. The result was a decline in the quality of poetry, for while 'the language became more refined, the feeling became more crude'. Whereas in the best of the Metaphysical poets and Jacobean dramatists we find 'a direct sensuous apprehension of thought or recreation of thought into feeling', in the poets who succeed them feeling and thought are progressively more and more dissociated. By the time we get to the nineteenth century we find poets think and feel 'by fits'. One or two passages in Shelley and Keats reveal 'traces of a struggle towards unification of sensibility. But Keats and Shelley died and Tennyson and Browning ruminated'.[7]

This 'dissociation of sensibility' was in the first version of the essay in question said to be 'due to', in the later version 'aggravated by',[8] the influence of Milton and Dryden. 'Each of these men performed certain poetic functions so magnificently well that the magnitude of the effect concealed the absence of others' —and by turning to the essay 'Andrew Marvell', published in the same year, we may find what functions each performed.

Early in the Marvell essay Eliot writes: 'Out of that high style developed from Marlowe through Jonson ... the seventeenth century separated two qualities: wit and magniloquence.'[9] 'Wit' here suggests Dryden, 'magniloquence' Milton —and this is confirmed eight pages on: 'Dryden was great in wit, as Milton in magniloquence'; but Dryden by isolating wit and Milton by dispensing with it, 'may perhaps have injured the language'.[10]

Eliot's history, then, is like Arnold's in representing a decline in English poetry after a high point reached in the late sixteenth–early seventeenth centuries. But for Eliot the decline begins a little earlier (in Milton) and continues longer into the Romantics and beyond. If there is recovery at all (and there are clear hints of this) it is in the poetry Eliot himself and Pound were writing in the years following the First World War. The nature of the decline, or its causes, are also differently described. Whereas Arnold sees a decline in eighteenth-century poetry caused by poets composing in their 'wits' instead of in their 'soul', Eliot sees an unfortunate separation of the faculties we may suppose 'wits' and 'soul' to represent—a separation of

'intellect' and 'feeling'; but he adds that where such a separation occurred, the greater damage to the poetic tradition was
done by the poetry of 'soul' (Milton's 'magniloquence') than by
the poetry of the 'wits' (Dryden's 'wit').

Some years after he first set forth this view Eliot reiterated
it, emphasizing again the superiority of Dryden over Milton as
an influence on the poetry that followed:

> I have said elsewhere that the living English which was Shakes-
> peare's became split up into two components one of which
> was exploited by Milton and the other by Dryden. Of the
> two, I still think Dryden's development the healthier, because
> it was Dryden who preserved, so far as it was preserved at all,
> the tradition of conversational language in poetry: and I
> might add that it seems to me easier to get back to healthy
> language from Dryden than it is to get back to it from
> Milton.[11]

In 1920 *The Sacred Wood* appeared, establishing Eliot as an
important new critical voice. A year later he wrote the three
essays enunciating the view of literary history which was to
become *our* view—'The Metaphysical Poets', 'Andrew Marvell'
and 'John Dryden'. The three essays appeared together under
the title *Homage to John Dryden* in 1924, and it is surely their
influence in succeeding decades which put the Metaphysical
poets and Jacobean dramatists at the centre of academic studies
of English literature, made the study of Dryden (and by extension of Pope) respectable, and set up at least some barriers to the
appreciation of Milton and of what Eliot called 'the popular
and pretentious verse of the Romantic Poets and their successors'.[12] 'The line of wit', as F. R. Leavis calls it, is essentially
Eliot's line; and Leavis, like every other major modern critic,
could trace his development back to a source in Eliot's early
criticism, and in particular to those three essays.

Yet the essays contain their own half-concealed uncertainties
and disclaimers. Though they appear finally to bury Arnold,
Arnold still speaks in them; and it is this point I wish now to
turn my attention to.

The essay on Marvell defines more clearly the 'wit' of poetry
that has not suffered the 'dissociation of sensibility'; and at the

same time, because the comparison is in part with Dryden, it shows how the beginnings of that 'dissociation' place limits on Dryden's achievements. Marvell is not a great poet, as Milton and Dryden are, but he is a 'classic'. 'There is . . . an equipoise, a balance and proportion of tones, which, while it cannot raise Marvell to the level of Dryden or Milton, extorts an approval which these poets do not receive from us.'[13] His wit is 'an alliance of levity with seriousness (whereby seriousness is intensified)';[14] whereas in Dryden 'wit becomes almost fun, and thereby loses some contact with reality'.[15]

What troubles Eliot is a lack of 'seriousness' ('high seriousness' Arnold would have called it) in Dryden—and he makes the same point a few years later when he says that Dryden's satire is 'in the modern sense humourous and witty' but that it lacks 'the proper wit of poetry'.[16]

In the essay on Dryden Eliot quotes (misquotes, in fact) Arnold saying that the poetry of Dryden and Pope 'is conceived and composed in their wits, genuine poetry is conceived in the soul' and rebukes him for it.[17] 'Dryden', Eliot insists, 'is one of the tests of a catholic appreciation of poetry'[18]—and he goes on to try to correct the view of Dryden that had been fashionable in the nineteenth century and was, no doubt, still current in 1921. But late in the essay Eliot concedes two points against Dryden: first, that he had 'a commonplace mind'; second, that although Dryden's words 'state immensely', 'their suggestiveness is often nothing'. Eliot goes on: 'The question, which has certainly been waiting, may justly be asked: whether, without this which Dryden lacks, verse can be poetry?'[19]

Having put the question, however, Eliot retreats from it and does not answer. 'What is man to decide what poetry is?' he asks. He proceeds to quote and to praise Dryden's elegy on Oldham. And he concludes: '[Dryden] remains one of those who have set standards for English verse which it is desperate to ignore'—verse, not poetry, and it is Eliot himself who has made the distinction.

Dryden had 'a commonplace mind', he 'lacked . . . a large and unique view of life; he lacked insight, he lacked profundity';[20] his poetry lacked verbal 'suggestiveness': it is, on close inspection, strange 'homage' that is offered to Dryden in the book of that title. The qualifications are consistent, of course, with Eliot's view that Milton and Dryden together represent the two halves of the divided, or dividing, English sensibility—that they mark the moment at which 'the English mind altered'.[21] But this undertone seems remarkably close to Arnold, from whom the essay ostensibly parted company—Arnold who was always willing to concede that Dryden was a 'master in letters', a man of 'admirable talent', 'a man, on all sides, of such energetic and genial power', but whose 'verse' lacks 'high seriousness', lacks 'poetic largeness, freedom, insight, benignity' and whose language is essentially the language of prose.[22]

There is, then, at least some common ground between Eliot and Arnold on the subject of Dryden. What of Milton? We are most likely to remember that Eliot said 'Milton writes English like a dead language',[23] while Arnold said that in the matter of style Milton is superior even to Shakespeare—'the one artist of the highest rank in the great style whom we have'.[24] But to discover in more detail what Arnold thought of Milton, and of Milton's epic, we have to go back a few years before the essay 'Milton' (which was no more than an address delivered at the unveiling of a memorial window) to one called 'A French Critic on Milton', where Arnold asserts equally firmly that Milton 'is our great artist in style, our one first-rate master in the grand style',[25] but allows the French critic, Scherer, to say for him, or to support him in saying, what is unsatisfactory in Milton.

Milton the man is 'unamiable'; 'his want of sweetness of temper, of the Shakespearean largeness and indulgence, are undeniable'.[26] Much of *Paradise Lost* awakens merely 'languid interest'.[27] Indeed its subject 'has no special force or effectiveness'.[28] In substance it is 'a false poem, a grotesque poem, a tiresome poem';[29] yet in style it is 'the very essence of poetry'. Milton's 'power both of diction and of rhythm is unsurpassable.'[30]

Why then is Milton important? It is because, in an age when few readers learn at first hand the greatness of style of the best of Latin and Greek literature, his poetry, in its 'flawless perfection of . . . rhythm and diction'[31] gives us the sense of that ancient greatness, recreates it in our own tongue, and thus acts as a bulwark against 'the Anglo-Saxon contagion, all the flood of Anglo-Saxon commonness'.[32]

Is not Arnold saying what Eliot says—that 'Milton writes English like a dead language'—but saying it approvingly? In the case of Milton, as in that of Dryden, Arnold and Eliot are nearer agreement than appears at first sight to be the case. Neither likes Milton the man, nor the substance of Milton's epic. Both see him chiefly in terms of style. The differences in what they choose to emphasise and to value depend, not on a difference of seeing, but on what each feels the needs of the present moment to be. And ten years after his first essay on Milton Eliot is prepared to acknowledge that even to a poet of the twentieth century Milton may, after all, be useful:

> . . . it is his ability to give a perfect and unique pattern to every paragraph . . . and his ability to work in larger musical units than any other poet—that is to me the most conclusive evidence of Milton's supreme mastery. The peculiar feeling, almost a physical sensation of a breathless leap, communicated by Milton's long periods, and by his alone, is impossible to procure from rhymed verse. Indeed, this mastery is more conclusive evidence of his intellectual power, than is his grasp of any *ideas* that he borrowed or invented.[33]

Arnold's later essays restated and confirmed the view of English literary history that had served as the foundation of what we now recognize as the Romantic revolution in English poetry. Eliot put forward a new view which served the Modernist revolution. Neither of these men were literary historians. They were critics, not scholars; and like all the great critics before them, they were poet-critics. It is not in fact the literary historian who can radically alter our perspective on literary history. He sees too many exceptions to commit himself to the broad sweep; and his evaluations are usually tentative and always relative. You need to have some clear notion of how the poetry of the past will bear upon the poetic practice of the present before you can say confidently that one kind of poetry is a more vital force than another. The literary historian's tasks most often prove to be menial. He follows behind the major critic, confirming, completing, complaining, correcting.

It is difficult to be sure how much Arnold or Eliot knew in depth and in detail about the eighteenth century (on which both had a good deal to say and in which neither was primarily interested); but it is certain that the instinct for generalizing usefully from relatively small areas of reading and knowledge was highly developed in both of them. One cannot be sure, for example, whether either of them quite recognized that in the mid-eighteenth century poets were committing themselves to one or another of two styles (which meant in effect to a total poetic stance) by acknowledging Milton and Spenser on the one hand, or Dryden and Pope on the other, as their great fore-bears.[34] Yet with or without this knowledge, both Arnold and Eliot inherited the terms of the argument, Arnold favouring Milton, Eliot committing himself to Dryden. For Arnold the difference between Milton and Dryden, between 'genuine poetry' and the poetry of 'an age of prose', was to be located in its genesis—its source in the 'wits' or the 'soul' of the poet. True poetry was in some sense a poetry of 'inspiration', which the 'unamiable' Milton could produce and the 'genial' Dryden could not. I have tried to show elsewhere[35] that Eliot, for all his presentation of himself as anti-Romantic, understood these 'Romantic' distinctions perfectly well from his own experience of writing poetry. Poetry which drew a part of its strength from 'below the levels of consciousness' offered resonances of meaning and of music which more consciously crafted verse could not match: hence the lack of 'suggestiveness' in Dryden's words; hence too, perhaps, the lack of a fundamental 'seriousness' in his wit.

But for Eliot there was another consideration—that of diction; and it is this which accounts for the pre-eminence given to Dryden over Milton in Eliot's criticism. It was one of the tenets of the Pound-Eliot revolution that poetry ought to have the virtues of good prose, and that it should be free to employ vernacular language and to work into its texture the music of contemporary speech. It was in this respect that it seemed to Eliot in the 1936 Milton essay 'easier to get back to healthy language from Dryden than . . . from Milton', because 'it was Dryden who preserved, so far as it was preserved at all, the tradition of conversational language in poetry':

Milton does . . . represent poetry at the extreme limit from prose; and it was one of our tenets that verse should have the virtues of prose, that diction should become assimilated to cultivated contemporary speech, before aspiring to the elevation of poetry . . . And the study of Milton could be of no help here: it was only a hindrance.[36]

The problem of 'poetic diction' is complex and can only be touched upon here. In the eighteenth century Gray believed that 'the language of the age' was 'never the language of poetry'.[37] Johnson censured Gray for this—for having 'thought his language more poetical as it was more remote from common use',[38] and censured Milton's diction in the same terms;[39] yet Johnson also complained of Shakespeare using words which had been made 'low by the occasions to which they [were] applied, or the general character of them who use them'.[40] Wordsworth in his Preface to the *Lyrical Ballads* announced a new poetry that would employ 'the real language of men',[41] and insisted that 'there neither is, nor can be, any essential difference between the language of prose and metrical composition'.[42] Arnold appreciated and praised this 'perfect plainness'[43] of Wordsworth's, yet condemned Dryden and Pope as poets of 'an age of *prose*', elevated the ornate Gray above them, and described Milton as the greatest master of style in the language. In Eliot's essay on Dryden we can see this history of confusion and misunderstanding continuing when he quotes Hazlitt saying 'Dryden and Pope are the great masters of the artificial style of poetry in our language as . . . Chaucer, Spenser, Shakespeare and Milton . . . [are] of the natural'; and Eliot comments on the 'absurdity' of this 'contrast of Milton, our greatest master of the artificial style, with Dryden, whose *style* . . . is in a high degree natural'.[44]

What is surprising perhaps is not the misunderstandings (deliberate or otherwise) but the continuity of the debate and the consistency of its terms. There is, of course (and this is what Eliot implies), an element of contradiction in the Romantic movement declaring itself to be in revolt against artificiality while maintaining Milton at the centre of the English poetic tradition. Yet the contradiction is more apparent than real.

There are different kinds of 'artificiality'. There is the artificiality of decorum—the total decorum Johnson stood for,
of which a plain (but not 'low') poetic diction was merely a
part. And there was the other, more particular, and purely
literary artificiality—that of the Miltonic style, the Miltonic
high sentence, which was only one of several means used
by poets in the mid-eighteenth century (Collins, Gray, and
others) in their attempts to penetrate beneath the polished surfaces of wit and propriety. In this sense Wordsworth's 'simple'
poetry can be seen as another weapon, a powerful new agent
joining forces with Gray's and Collins's most complex odes, to
break down that total decorum of which Johnson was the last
great spokesman. It was not 'the real language of men' Wordsworth wished to represent so much as their real *passions*. And if
the Miltonic music as it revived in the eighteenth century had
served a purpose it was that of permitting the poet once again to
express a passionate commitment to his subject and to his own
role as poet, which Dryden's and Pope's worldly couplets seemed
to preclude:

> Cold is Cadwallo's tongue,
> That hush'd the stormy main:
> Brave Urien sleeps upon his craggy bed.[45]

This is (to employ Eliot's terms again) the 'magniloquence' of
Milton revived in an age of 'wit'; it has (to employ Arnold's
term) the Miltonic 'movement'; and it was because of this
quality of passionate, committed, bardic utterance that the nineteenth century (and Arnold) could see Gray as a true poet, and
Dryden and Pope, for all their relatively plain diction, as 'artificial'.

If what Eliot had to say about Milton and Dryden had been at
the centre of his criticism it could not have had quite the effect
that it did. But by pushing the Metaphysicals to the centre and
inviting us to see that as their rightful place, he brought about
a critical revolution. He did not discover the Metaphysicals. His
article on them was a review of a selection of their poems by Sir
Herbert Grierson—evidence of an interest which already
existed. But Eliot made very large claims for these poets, claims

which were both new and difficult to refute, and in writing about them he put them into a framework of three centuries of English poetry. Here, at its best, in the best poems of Donne and Marvell (and in some of the Jacobean dramatists) was a poetry of wit which was not merely analytical but passionate as well. The poet was not engaged in rending others but in rendering himself, or a mask of himself. Why the ears of English readers had been closed so long to the music of Metaphysical poetry would be difficult to decide; but it is certain that Eliot taught twentieth-century readers to hear it, and in doing so significantly altered our conception of the possibilities of poetry in the language. The lyrical and beautiful became less interesting than the dramatic and authentic. The poet capable of committing his passion to the hilt without losing a precise sense of the nature of that passion, including its defects and absurdities, commanded more respect than the poet who, in the full flood of rhetorical confidence, could be seen, by a slight twist of the reader's perspective, as the victim of his own feelings. What was to be admired in Marvell, for example, was 'not cynicism' but 'a constant inspection and criticism of experience . . . a recognition, implicit in the expression of every experience, of other kinds of experience which are possible'.[46] 'Irony', 'ambiguity', 'paradox', though not terms Eliot himself used very much, followed naturally upon his criticism as terms of approbation.

Eliot is at his best in writing about these poets, and at his most genuine. He is less satisfactory in the criticism of later ages, partly perhaps because he gets entangled in the terms of an old debate, and because he seems to take sides less from the promptings of innocent critical feeling than from a sense of how his statements will bear upon the literary politics of the moment. In his Preface to *Homage to John Dryden*, for example, he writes:

> I have long felt that the poetry of the seventeenth and eighteenth centuries, even much of that of inferior inspiration, possesses an elegance and a dignity absent from the popular and pretentious verse of the Romantic Poets and their successors.

A few years earlier he had written:

Because we have never learned to criticize Keats, Shelley and
Wordsworth (poets of assured though modest merit), Keats,
Shelley and Wordsworth punish us from their graves with
the annual scourge of the Georgian Anthology.[47]

In each of these statements (and in many more like them) we
can see that Eliot's primary target is his contemporary enemies
the Georgian poets and critics, but that he strikes at them
through the great Romantics, whose heirs they claim to be. For
this reason Eliot never comes properly to terms with the
Romantic movement. At the end of his essay on Marvell he
admits that 'wit' of the kind he has been discussing is 'irrelevant' to the best poems of Wordsworth, Shelley and Keats; but
he never extends the terms of his own criticism to take in or
appreciate the best of their poetry. Consequently the expansion
of our sense of poetic possibilities which his criticism offers in
one area is achieved at the cost of contraction in another.

In *The Use of Poetry and the Use of Criticism*, a series of lectures given at Harvard in 1932–3, Eliot proposed to make a survey of the relation of criticism to poetry from the Elizabethan
age to the twentieth century. Such a survey might have been
expected to offer some clarification and expansion of his already
stated view of the history of three centuries of English poetry,
and to bring the Romantic movement into clearer definition
within the overall picture. In the chapter on Dryden the idea of
a 'dissociation of sensibility' seems to be reaffirmed:

It is not so much the intellect, but something superior to
intellect, which went for a long time into eclipse; and this
luminary, by whatever name we may call it, has not yet
wholly issued from its secular obnubilation. The age of
Dryden was still a great age, though beginning to suffer a
death of the spirit, as the coarsening of its verse rhythms
shows . . .

In the succeeding chapters, however, Eliot does not make full
use of the opportunity to 'place' the Romantics. He is elusive,
even defensive, seeming to recognize the special claims that
might be made in particular for Wordsworth, but perhaps finding it still undesirable, in terms of the politics of contemporary

poetry and criticism, to acknowledge them: '... much of the poetry of Wordsworth and Coleridge', he writes, 'is just as turgid and artificial and elegant as any eighteenth century die-hard could wish' (p. 72)—thus trapping himself into writing about the eighteenth century in pejorative terms that would have suited Arnold, and into acknowledging that there is some, at least, of the poetry of Wordsworth and Coleridge, to which these terms do not apply. Then, surprisingly, he writes a few pages later:

> In Wordsworth and Coleridge we find not merely a variety of interests, even passionate interests; it is all one passion expressed through them all: poetry was for them the expression of a totality of unified interests ... (p. 81)

—a statement which strongly suggests some kind of 'unified sensibility'. But at the end of the chapter there is this:

> What I see, in the history of English poetry, is ... the split-ting up of personality. If we say that one of these partial per-sonalities which may develop in a national mind is that which manifested itself in the period between Dryden and Johnson, then what we have to do is to re-integrate it ... (pp. 84–5)

In the chapters which follow we are told that Wordsworth and Shelley are guilty of an 'abuse of poetry' (p. 89) in that they use poetry as a vehicle for ideas rather than using ideas to make poetry. Keats, on the other hand, did not abuse poetry in this way. Nor was he guilty of any 'withdrawal' in not propa-gating ideas: 'he was merely about his business' (p. 102)—the business of making poetry. This much is consistent with Eliot's argument, in other essays of the same period, that the poet's use of language has to be clearly distinguished from that of the philo-sopher or 'thinker'.[48] The philosopher makes the language serve his thought or idea; the poet makes an idea serve his poetry; and the Romantics, or at least Wordsworth and Shelley, 'abused' poetry by making it serve rather than use ideas. In the case of Wordsworth this may not matter too much; but in Shelley's case it sets up a barrier, because Shelley's ideas were 'ideas of adolescence' (p. 89), 'bolted whole and never assimilated' (p. 92).

One might have thought that Eliot would have found common ground with Arnold here. But when he comes to Arnold it is only to repeat what he said a few years earlier[49]—that Arnold was partly to blame for the decadence of the 1890s. Though Wordsworth's use of poetry as a vehicle for ideas was an 'abuse', nevertheless Arnold is condemned for inviting readers to set Wordsworth's 'philosophy' aside. Arnold had written of Wordsworth: 'His poetry is the reality, his philosophy the illusion', adding that one day we might learn to make this proposition general and to say 'Poetry is the reality, philosophy the illusion.' Eliot describes this as 'a striking, dangerous and subversive assertion' (p. 113).

It is no more 'striking, dangerous and subversive' than several assertions on the same subject made by Eliot himself;[50] and Arnold's essay on Wordsworth (one of his best if carefully and sympathetically read) rejects only the extravagant claims of 'the Wordsworthians' that their hero's poetry should be read for its 'scientific system of thought'. But one can see the line of Eliot's thinking. 'For Wordsworth and for Shelley poetry was a vehicle for one kind of philosophy or another'; this was bad, but at least 'the philosophy was something believed in' (p. 113). For Arnold the 'poetry' is not merely a thing in itself, distinct from the religion and philosophy it may be said to 'contain'; it becomes a *substitute* for religion and philosophy—it 'supersedes both' (p. 113); and it is this elevation of poetry which Eliot cannot accept and which seems to him to lead to some of the excesses of aestheticism.

Once again one notices the complications of an argument that takes place across decades and generations. Arnold, who was aware of the drift towards aestheticism, and who tried to counter it (in the essay on Keats, for example, or in the passage on Leopardi in the Byron essay) by arguing that style is not enough, that it must be accompanied by an adequate interpretation of life, is here found guilty of promoting aestheticism by giving poetry too high a place and by asking too much of it.

For the purpose of this essay I have been concerned almost exclusively with Eliot's early criticism. His later criticism, though it is full of interest and has many virtues, lacks the programme and consequently the coherence of the earlier. It is less decided, less emphatic, more demure, less original. It has no particular point of view other than that of the reasonable man of letters. It is not broadly influential in the way the early criticism was. The Eliot who has remained a force in modern criticism is the Eliot of those early essays.

Thus in putting Eliot's most influential criticism alongside, or against the backdrop of, Arnold's, it is a matter of putting early Eliot against late Arnold. Arnold found his way gradually towards the general view articulated most clearly in *Essays in Criticism, Second Series*, which remained influential—almost 'standard'—long after his death. Eliot articulated the new general view when he was still relatively young, and lived long enough to look back on it and comment on it (while it continued to have its effect) almost as if it had been produced by someone else.

The men who have come to be recognized as the great critics in English—Sidney, Dryden, Johnson, Coleridge, Arnold, Eliot—have been poets and their criticism has related almost exclusively to poetry and poetic drama. Each of them, at least since Dryden, has offered or implied a view of the development of English poetry—a view which accounted for the poetry of the critic's own age, and which was so broad as to be at once compelling and unsatisfactory. They are views which cannot properly be thought of as 'right' or 'wrong' but only as more or less persuasive, more or less serviceable in focussing the expectations of readers and the ambitions of poets upon the practice of poetry in the present age.

Arnold's position in relation to his age was not unlike Johnson's, in that he reformulated a view of English literature which had been established before him and which was already in some degree being challenged. Eliot's position was nearer to that of Wordsworth (the Wordsworth of the Preface to the *Lyrical Ballads*)—making way for something new in poetry, something apparently revolutionary, yet for which the ground was already well prepared. Thus Eliot's criticism animates a new poetry as Arnold's does not. Chiefly, of course, it animates his own, and in particular *The Waste Land*.

I have argued elsewhere[51] that *The Waste Land* has to be seen,

not as the work of an anti-Romantic, but as a poem whose ante-
cedents are unmistakeably Romantic; and that a great deal of
Eliot's criticism, particularly as it bears upon the important
question of poetic composition, is likewise Romantic, despite its
eye-catching anti-Romantic declarations and neo-classical catch-
phrases. Eliot wore the ribbons of one party while in the secrecy
of the polling booth compulsively voting for the other. But he
tried very hard to believe himself to be a witty poet and to act
as if he had inherited the neo-classical 'line of wit' rather than
the soul music of Romanticism. He wrote homage to John Dryden, but, as we have seen, his doubts about Dryden crept in. He
praised the Metaphysicals, but for their passionate wit, not for
wit alone. He complained of Milton and found him unamiable,
but knew perfectly well (as shown by the quotation above about
the 'almost . . . physical sensation of a breathless leap communicated by Milton's long periods') how central Milton's musical
qualities were to the strongest elements in the English poetic
tradition. And this conflict in Eliot, discernible in his criticism,
is now clearly revealed in the manuscripts of *The Waste Land*.

Even a casual glance at Mrs Valerie Eliot's edition of *The
Waste Land* manuscripts shows that the poem in its draft form
was quite different from the poem we have come to know as
probably the greatest single item in the history of the Modernist
movement in poetry. In its early stages the poem was an
uneven, often indifferent, attempt at a neo-Augustan satire
(much of it in heroic couplets), in which the predominating
voice was too personal for comfort, its feelings of superiority and
disgust too naked, over-riding the deeper and more humane
notes of lyricism and despair.

How those early drafts were transformed into the poem we
know has been traced particularly closely by Professor Hugh
Kenner,[52] who sees their possible beginning in Eliot's writing of
the review which became his essay on Dryden. 'To enjoy
Dryden', Eliot wrote hopefully in that essay, 'means to pass
beyond the limitations of the nineteenth century into a new
freedom'—and Professor Kenner sees Dryden's presence in the
earliest conception of the poem, and in particular in the first
version of the 'The Fire Sermon'. In the course of the revisions,
however, 'all identifiable trace of Dryden vanished . . . Also

gone was the long opening of "The Fire Sermon" which had imitated Pope. Of this there was nothing left at all, not a line, and there was no way to tell that the whole central section of Eliot's long poem had moved through modes of Augustan imitation.'[53] Thus the poem's original conception bore little relation to the identity and form it finally acquired; and the whole composition lacked shape and direction until pulled together at a late stage by the writing of 'What the Thunder Said', which had 'little ... to do with what seems to have been the poem's working plan. "What the Thunder Said" was virtually a piece of automatic writing. Eliot more than once testified that he wrote it almost at a sitting ... and the rapid handwriting of the holograph ... bears him out. False starts and second thoughts are few, and later retouching was insignificant.'[54]

The Waste Land, then, was 'reconceived from the wreckage of a different conception'.[55] In the extraordinary, exciting, and complex process by which not one creative mind but two went to work on the original material and transformed it, the centre of the poem had shifted from 'the urban panorama refracted through Augustan styles' to 'the urban apocalypse, the great city dissolved into a desert where voices sang from exhausted wells'. In this transformation was achieved 'the visionary unity that has fascinated two generations of readers'.[56]

Now let us consider for a moment Eliot's position as poet and critic during the years with which I have been chiefly concerned —the months immediately following the First World War. Born a few years after the death of Arnold, Eliot read the Romantics avidly as an adolescent but felt he had outgrown them with his young manhood. The conventions of Romanticism, in their several forms, had been debased and diluted by repetition and by the end of the first decade of the century the landscape seemed as cluttered with indifferent neo-Romantics as it seems now cluttered with indifferent neo-Modernists. Eliot was looking for 'a new freedom' and thought perhaps he had found it, or a way to it, in 'the line of wit'. Acerbity appealed especially, because it was a way of setting himself apart from the sentimentalism and weak lyricism of so many of his contemporaries.

In the writing of *The Waste Land* Augustan imitation gave Eliot at least material—a start, an impulse, something like a plan, and in due course lines of verse—to work on. After that it was a matter of creative instinct, his own abetted by Pound's, pruning, expunging, shifting the fragments about and spawning new ones, the excitement of shaping the poem itself creating the impulse for further writing, until in due course the unforeseeable because entirely new masterpiece was born.

What was Eliot to make of what he had done? He was bound to be conscious of what had happened consciously, and uncertain about the rest—and what had been conscious, and remained so, was some sense of a debt to 'the line of wit', and a belief that his poetry came forth in reaction against something that could be called Romanticism. In some ways Eliot was less well placed to see what he had done than we are fifty years later—just as Coleridge, among the prevailing literary conventions of his time, was incapable of recognizing that *Kubla Khan* was a finished poem and not a fragment. *The Waste Land* must have seemed as strange to Eliot as it was to seem to its first readers—strange, yet compelling. In presenting it to the public Eliot nervously added the now famous notes, which in turn encouraged a generation of critics to treat the work as a conscious and orderly construction whose hidden 'meaning' could be unlocked with aids like Jessie Weston and Sir James Frazer. In fact the poem was something quite different. Fragmentary in form yet also complete and self-sufficient, it was essentially a musical structure, playing upon certain themes and motifs taken, many of them, from a context of ideas, but not used as such in the poetry.

That Eliot in *The Waste Land* was more truly the heir of the Romantic movement than his Georgian contemporaries who laid claim to the inheritance is something I suspect many more critics would now be willing to recognize than was the case ten or fifteen years ago. The Augustan tradition—in particular the tradition of mock-heroic satire that passed from Dryden to Pope —maintained its surfaces at all costs. It was the poetry of a determined because precarious social sanity. It was beneath those surfaces that Romantic poetry in its finer moments successfully probed. The probing was instinctive and the results often obscure and fragmentary, like the salvaging of something from the ocean —and Eliot's recurrent image of things brought up, transformed, from the depths is central to his writing at this time. In composing *The Waste Land* he created a mock-heroic surface and then broke it, plunging beneath to sources of feeling which lay deeper. In this process he lived out his own neo-Romantic revolt against his own neo-classicism.

The form of the poem which resulted is organic. It grows from within, dictated by its own materials and history. Elements of the orginal satire remain, but these are (in both senses) *contained* within the total form. They are part of the total consciousness, but they are subdued by a larger charity, just as their couplets are subdued by a form which is larger, more expansive, more generous.

'Modernism', like *The Waste Land*, defined itself not according to this or that programme or plan but only as it came into being. It inherited everything that was revolutionary in Romanticism, yet it was no dead repetition of Romantic themes and surfaces. But if it was to understand itself it needed to understand Romanticism, and it is here that its critical consciousness can be seen in retrospect to have been inadequate.

I come back now to Matthew Arnold, and to Eliot's criticism seen alongside Arnold's. Eliot called his first book of criticism *The Sacred Wood*, taking his title, no doubt, from the first pages of Sir James Frazer's *The Golden Bough*, which describes an ancient ritual whereby a priest occupies a sacred wood as long as he can kill or drive off any contender for his priesthood. But whoever kills the priest assumes the role himself until he in turn is murdered. 'The post which he held by this precarious tenure carried with it the title of king.'[57] It is difficult to see what else Eliot could have meant by this title than that, as critic, or as critic and poet, he was entering the sacred wood in order to challenge the reigning priest; and if that is the case the title can be seen in retrospect as an oblique yet daring declaration of an intent that was in due course carried out. If the old priest, Arnold, 'died', it was Eliot who 'killed' him; and if Eliot no longer breaths, as he once did, in virtually every piece of criticism written on the subject of poetry in England, no full-scale contender for his priesthood has yet made an effective challenge.

Sustaining the metaphor for a moment one may add, however, that none of the old priests really 'dies'. They form, rather, a 'familiar compound ghost' with whom the new priest conducts his dialogues. Arnold in some degree still speaks in Eliot; and some of the questions he asks remain to be answered.

What is confusing and makes any attempt to sort out the historical strands at once difficult and interesting in this particular case is that in some significant respects Arnold is more 'modern' than Eliot. Arnold's criticism did not, and could not, animate a new poetry. It did not animate his own. It was, much of it, an unhappy substitute for the poetry he would like to have written. His essay on Gray is partly an essay on himself—a man who did not write more because he could not, and who could not because he was born at the wrong time: '. . . a man born in 1759 could profit by that renewing of men's minds of which the great historical manifestation was the French Revolution . . . If Gray . . . had been just thirty years old when the French Revolution broke out, he would have shown, probably, productiveness and animation in plenty.'

I think it is safe to say that Eliot could never have written such sentences. He could not have seen the French Revolution as 'the great historical manifestation' of a 'renewing of men's minds'. When he looked back it was with the nostalgia of the reactionary temperament to a time before 'something happened to the mind of England'. Yet Eliot lived to demonstrate Arnold's point, that a true poet, even one of deeply conservative temperament, could be animated by the spirit of his time if the time was right for the appearance of something new. Eliot set out in *The Waste Land* to imitate Dryden and Pope and to castigate his age, but without quite knowing what he was about he passed beyond his satiric intention into a new depth and a new freedom; and in this transformation of the neo-Augustan satire into the neo-Romantic visionary poem, Eliot offered a strange practical corroboration of the most central, and the most contentious, of Arnold's critical statements. 'Their poetry', to repeat what Arnold wrote of Dryden and Pope, 'was conceived and composed in their wits; true poetry is conceived and composed in the soul.' Arnold's terms, if they are less than satisfactory, remain intelligible. *The Waste Land* was conceived in the wits but it was composed in the soul.

Thus a study of Eliot's poetry can lead one to precisely the same kinds of questions that arise from placing alongside one another Arnold's and Eliot's respective statements on the history of English poetry, and it is appropriate now to return where we began. Once one has recognized, for example, the tentativeness of Eliot's 'homage' to Dryden, and the lack of any developed criticism of Pope, it becomes apparent that no major critic since Johnson has spoken unequivocally for these figures whom Arnold described as 'classics of our prose'. Can Arnold's criticism, then, be said to have been effectively answered? Can it be answered? Or does the combination of satiric substance and couplet form place such restrictions on the range of feeling that such poetry is, even when written by masters like Dryden and Pope, of a second order? Is the couplet itself, which breaks the flowing verse sentence that characterizes Shakespeare, Milton and Wordsworth at their best, alien to the finest of the English genius in poetry? And on the other front, does not Eliot's failure to come clearly to terms with the Romantic poets leave Arnold's late assertions on their behalf—in particular that they revived a greatness lost after Milton—still *critically* unchallenged?

These are large questions—so large as to seem impertinent. It is my point that they are questions raised but not answered by re-reading Eliot's criticism against the background of Arnold's. Eliot's most original contribution lay in what he had to say about the Metaphysicals and about the verse of the Jacobean dramatists. But this is something *added on to* the traditional appreciation of English poetry, without quite answering the questions raised in the late eighteenth century or rebutting the assertions made in the nineteenth.

The problems which the Romantic poets were the first to confront head-on remain. Science, technology, the fact, continue to advance at the expense of the mythologies on which poetry was traditionally founded. But while the mythologies recede literally, their imaginative truth becomes more and more essential to the preservation of our humanity. We grow nearer to, not further from, an understanding of Keats's 'I know nothing but the truth of imagination and the holiness of the heart's affections'.

Modernism inherited, by whatever by-paths and indirections, the Romantic commitment to the 'truth of imagination', adding new claims for the freedom of poetry to range widely and to create boldly in the search for that truth. Yet because in clearing the ground it had to skirmish with an indifferent poetry that already identified itself with the Romantic tradition, the Modernist movement perhaps lost the proper sense of its own inheritance. At least it seems to me that if there is to be a criticism capable of animating the genuinely new in poetry today, it must look once again to those areas of English poetry—and chiefly the Romantic area—which Eliot's most influential criticism failed to look at squarely. And in this task it may prove that there is still something to be learned from Arnold.

Notes

1. CRITICISM'S LOST LEADER

1 *Selected Essays* (1951), p. 368.
2 *To Criticize the Critic* (1965), p. 15.
3 Valerie Eliot, the second wife, has prefixed to her indispensable edition of *The Waste Land* (1971) a statement ascribed to Eliot by his friend Theodore Spencer, which she presumably knew to be authentic. It runs: 'Various critics have done me the honour to interpret the poem in terms of criticism of the contemporary world, have considered it, indeed, as an important bit of social criticism. To me it was only the relief of a personal and wholly insignificant grouse against life; it is just a piece of rhythmical grumbling.' From what I remember of Ted Spencer, whom I knew at Harvard, I am inclined to suspect that these are not all the *ipsissima verba* of Eliot, but some scraps of conversation that Spencer has cobbled together. Their general gist, however, need not be disputed, though in other moods Eliot certainly regarded *The Waste Land* as his masterpiece.
4 *Selected Essays*, p. 127.
5 *Essays in Criticism*, July 1952; April 1969. See also F. W. Bateson, *Essays in Critical Dissent* (1972), 'Variations on Some Eliot Themes', pp. 129–62.
6 The exact date of Verdenal's death was in fact 2 May 1915 (see George Watson, *Sewanee Review*, lxxxiv (Summer 1976), 3, p. 467). The heaviest English, French and Anzac losses in the whole Gallipoli operation were in April 1915. Eliot must have known this, even if he did not know *precisely* when Verdenal was killed or drowned. Some details about Verdenal—who was like Keats both a medical student and a poet when Eliot met him in Paris in 1910—will be found in Robert Sencourt's *T. S. Eliot: A Memoir* (1971).
7 She had been christened Vivienne but generally preferred to use the anglicized form. Sencourt acknowledges 'a particular debt of gratitude' for the information supplied by Vivien's family, who were also helpful to T. S. Matthews for his *Great Tom* (1974).
8 *The Waste Land*, ed. Valerie Eliot, p. xxii.
9 Ibid., p. xxvi.
10 Ibid.
11 Ibid., p. 129
12 *TLS*, 2 December 1920.
13 Pound confirmed this judgement (*Letters*, ed. D. D. Paige, p. 226).
14 *Selected Essays*, p. 30.
15 Rivière was the close friend and later the brother-in-law of Henri Alain-Fournier, the author of *Le Grand Meaulnes*, rightly described by Sencourt as 'a classic novel of adolescence'. Alain-Fournier gave Eliot lessons in French and French literature.

16 *To Criticize the Critic*, p. 185.
17 E. M. W. Tillyard and C. S. Lewis, *The Personal Heresy: A Controversy* (1939), p. 69.
18 *The Sacred Wood* (1920), p. 132.
19 *The Hound and Horn*, 1 (1928), 294.

3. THE POET AS CRITIC

1 'To Criticize the Critic', *To Criticize the Critic* (1965), p. 26.
2 Ibid., p. 25.
3 'The Music of Poetry', *On Poetry and Poets* (1957), p. 26.
4 In *T. S. Eliot: the Man and his Work*, ed. Allen Tate (1967).
5 Both are reprinted in *To Criticize the Critic*.
6 'John Dryden', *Selected Essays* (1951), p. 305.
7 'Andrew Marvell', *Selected Essays*, p. 304. The final sentence is a slightly ungrammatical adaptation of the last line of Laforgue's 'Complainte du pauvre jeune homme': *C'était une belle âme comme on n'en fait plus aujourd' hui*. An unlikely source for a tag applicable to Marvell; not so inappropriate to Eliot himself at this stage of his career.
8 *To Criticize the Critic*, p. 184.
9 'Some Notes on the Blank Verse of Christopher Marlowe', *The Sacred Wood* (1920), p. 79.
10 'Philip Massinger', *Selected Essays*, p. 209.
11 *On Poetry and Poets*, p. 89.
12 Ibid., p. 97.
13 Ibid., p. 98.

4. THE TRIALS OF A CHRISTIAN CRITIC

1 See for example Eliot's 'Introduction to *The Sacred Wood*', 'Arnold and Pater' and 'Francis Herbert Bradley' in *Selected Essays*, and 'Matthew Arnold' in *The Use of Poetry and the Use of Criticism*.
2 *The Sacred Wood* (1920), pp. xi–xii.
3 *The Sacred Wood*, p. ix; 'Francis Herbert Bradley', *Selected Essays* (1951), p. 449.
4 'Bradley', *Selected Essays*, p. 449.
5 'Preface to the 1928 Edition', *The Sacred Wood* (1928), pp. viii and x.
6 I. A. Richards, 'A Background for Contemporary Poetry', *The Criterion*, iii (July 1925), 520.
7 'A Note on Poetry and Belief', *The Enemy*, i (Jan. 1927), 16.
8 Ibid., p. 16.
9 *Science and Poetry* (New York, 1926), pp. 71–2.
10 'Dante', *Selected Essays*, p. 259.
11 Ibid., pp. 269 and 270.
12 Poetry and Propaganda', *The Bookman*, lxx (Feb. 1930), 598.
13 Ibid., pp. 601–2.
14 Ibid., p. 599.
15 *The Dial*, lxxxii, 5 (May 1927) 427. The essay was reprinted as 'Baudelaire in Our Time' in *For Lancelot Andrewes* (1928), p. 91.

16 'Baudelaire', *Selected Essays*, p. 421.
17 *Selected Essays*, p. 270.
18 *The Use of Poetry and the Use of Criticism* (1933), pp. 99–100.
19 Quoted in Roger Kojecky, T. S. Eliot's Social Criticism (New York, 1971), p. 78.
20 'Possum', 'The Use of Poetry', *New English Weekly*, v (14 June 1934), p. 215.
21 Quoted in Kojecky, p. 77.
22 Quoted in Ezra Pound, 'Mr. Eliot's Mare's Nest', *New English Weekly*, iv (8 March 1934), 500.
23 *After Strange Gods* (1934), pp. 23, 56.
24 Ibid., p. 18.
25 Ibid., p. 42.
26 Ibid., p. 38.
27 Ibid., pp. 54–5.
28 Ibid., pp. 60–1.
29 Ibid., p. 63.

5. ELIOT'S CONTRIBUTION TO CRITICISM OF DRAMA

1 *The Sacred Wood* (1920), p. 60.
2 *Selected Essays* (1951), p. 109.
3 Ibid., pp. 50–2.
4 Cf. for example the quotation from the 'obituary of the dead highwayman' in Byron's *Don Juan*, in *On Poetry and Poets* (1957), p. 204.
5 The relevant discussion is in the *Republic*, Bk. III.
6 *On Poetry and Poets*, p. 74.
7 Ibid., pp. 86–7.
8 *Selected Essays*, pp. 229–32.
9 A close comparison of Murray and Eliot would be a useful exercise.

6. THE 'PHILOSOPHICAL CRITIC'

1 Jean-Paul Sartre, interview in *Le Nouvel Observateur*, quoted from a translation in *New York Review of Books*, 7 August 1975.
2 'The Frontiers of Criticism' in *On Poetry and Poets* (1957), p. 106.
3 *To Criticize the Critic* (1965), p. 25.
4 *The Sacred Wood* (1928 edition), p. ix.
5 *To Criticize the Critic*, p. 25.
6 *The Sacred Wood*, p. x.
7 Ibid., p. 16.
8 Graham Hough, *Critical Quarterly*, 15 (1973), 108–9.
9 'Dante', *Selected Essays* (1951), p. 257.
10 'Shakespeare and the Stoicism of Seneca', ibid., p. 138.
11 Anne C. Bolgan, *What the Thunder Really Said* (Montreal, 1973), p. 99.
12 Richard Wollheim, *On Art and the Mind* (1973), p. 246.
13 *On Poetry and Poets*, p. 106.
14 Herbert Howarth, *Notes on Some Figures Behind T. S. Eliot* (1965), p. 215.
15 *The Use of Poetry and the Use of Criticism* (1933), p. 137, quoting Maritain.

16 'Religion and Literature' (1935) in *Selected Essays*, p. 399.
17 *The Use of Poetry and the Use of Criticism*, p. 136.
18 Ibid., p. 143.
19 'Charybde et Scylla', *Annales du Centre Universitaire Méditerranéan*, v, 1951–2 (Nice, 1952), pp. 71–82. I am grateful to Dr Newton-De Molina for some comments on this essay. He informs me that a typescript of this paper, in English, exists in the library of King's College, Cambridge. The source of the French text is unknown, but the French is very far from idiomatic and the English bones stick through the surface rather forcefully. Either it was felt necessary to stick very literally to the English, or perhaps Eliot's very style and method were not naturalizable into French.
20 'Charybde et Scylla', pp. 79–80.
21 Ibid., p. 80.
22 Donald Davie, *Pound* (1975), pp. 99–100.
23 'Charybde et Scylla', p. 81.
24 Cf., *To Criticize the Critic*, p. 19.
25 *On Poetry and Poets*, p. 115.
26 *The Use of Poetry and the Use of Criticism*, pp. 155–6.
27 Ibid., p. 35.
28 Ibid., p. 35 n. 1.
29 Fei-Pai Lu, *T. S. Eliot: the Dialectical Structure of His Theory of Poetry* (Chicago, 1966), p. 117.

8. ELIOT'S 'TONE'

1 This essay is derived from one on 'The Critical Revolution of T. S. Eliot', *Ariel: A Review of International English Literature* (1971), 26–42. A few paragraphs of the earlier essay have been adapted in a revised form by the kind permission of the present editor of *Ariel*, Professor George Wing.
2 Gotthold Ephraim Lessing, *Laokoön*, translated by W. A. Steel and A. Dent (1930).
3 For a philosophical critique of the tautology of aesthetic theory see Margaret Macdonald, 'Art and Imitation', *Proceedings of the Aristotelian Society* (New Series, liii, 1952–3). An even more trenchant attack on idealist aesthetics is Vincent Turner, S. J., 'The Desolation of Aesthetics' in *The Arts, Artists, and Thinkers*, edited by John M. Todd (1958), pp. 271–307. Collingwood's case is to be found in *The Principles of Art* (Oxford, 1938), in the chapters on 'Art as Magic' and 'Art as Amusement'.
4 T. S. Eliot, *Knowledge and Experience in the Philosophy of F. H. Bradley* (1964), p. 165.
5 T. S. Eliot, 'Francis Herbert Bradley' [1927] in *Selected Essays* (1951), p. 447.
6 T. S. Eliot, *On Poetry and Poets* (1957), p. 100.
7 Mallarmé was in raptures over Debussy's rendering of *L'Après Midi d'un Faune* and wrote to him of 'votre illustration ... qui ne présenterait de dissonance avec mon texte, sinon qu'aller plus loin, vraiment, dans la nostalgie et la lumière, avec finesse, avec malaise, avec richesse'. See Henri Mondor, *Vie de Mallarmé* (Paris, 1941), p. 370.
8 There is an interesting discussion of the Parisian *flâneur* of the nineteenth century in Walter Benjamin, 'On Some Motifs in Baudelaire', *Illuminations*, translated by Harry Zohn (1970), pp. 157–202. Benjamin, on the

basis of a passage in Gogol, suggests that the effort to adapt the eye to the lively crowds of the new cities produced a dazzle of images like the 'riot of dabs of colour' in Impressionist painting (op. cit., p. 199).

9 I. A. Richards, *Practical Criticism* (1929), p. 182.

10 The influence of Eliot's criticism has been discussed by George Watson, *Critical Quarterly*, vii (1965), 328–37. James Reeves has recorded how when he went up to Cambridge in 1928 he was handed two books, *Poems 1909–1925* and *The Sacred Wood*, much as 'the stranger who enters an Anglican church at service time is handed two books, *Hymns Ancient and Modern* and *The Book of Common Prayer*' (T. S. Eliot: A Symposium, compiled by Richard Marsh and Tambimuttu (1948), p. 38).

11 All references to *The Sacred Wood* are to the first edition of 1920.

12 Cyril Connolly, *The Condemned Playground: Essays 1927–1944* (1945), p. 140.

13 Cf. the judicious account of the biographical background of *The Waste Land* in Richard Ellmann, *Golden Codgers* (1974).

14 Gavin Bone, *Anglo-Saxon Poetry* (Oxford, 1943), p. 73.

15 Quoted in Hugh Kenner, *The Invisible Poet: T. S. Eliot* (1960), p. 83.

16 The chief indictment of Lawrence is in *After Strange Gods* (1934), pp. 58–61, a book which Eliot was later to regret; cf. Stephen Spender, *Eliot* (1975), p. 143.

17 F. H. Bradley, *Appearance and Reality* (1893), p. 172, quoted in Kristian Smidt, *Poetry and Belief in the Work of T. S. Eliot* (1961), p. 163. A phrase of Bradley in another work, *The Principles of Logic* (1883), 'a way of thinking in which the whole of reality was a system of differences immanent in each difference', seems to have a bearing on the treatment of unique moments of intense perception both in *Four Quartets* and the early essays.

18 There is a good summary account of de Gourmont's 'méthode antilivresque et concrète' in René Lalou, *Histoire de la littérature française contemporaine de 1870 à nos jours* (Paris, 1947), especially i. 225–8.

9. ELIOT, ARNOLD, AND THE ENGLISH POETIC TRADITION

1 *The Use of Poetry and the Use of Criticism* (1933), p. 129.

2 'Literature as Knowledge', *Essays of Four Decades* (1968), p. 76.

3 'Thomas Gray', *Essays in Criticism Second Series* (1888); reprinted 1960, pp. 54, 56–7.

4 *The Six Chief Lives from Johnson's 'Lives of the Poets'*, edited with a Preface by Matthew Arnold (1881), Preface, p. xx.

5 'Milton', *Essays in Criticism Second Series*, p. 38.

6 'Wordsworth', op. cit., pp. 88, 91, 93, etc.

7 'The Metaphysical Poets' (1921), *Selected Essays* (1951), pp. 286, 7, 8.

8 'The Metaphysical Poets', *Homage to John Dryden* (1924), p. 30, and *Selected Essays*, p. 288. An interesting textual confusion arises from this emendation. In his second essay on Milton (*On Poetry and Poets*, 1957, p. 152) Eliot quotes himself as having written 'in an essay on Dryden' that the dissociation of sensibility was 'due to' Milton and Dryden. He appears to have quoted himself from Tillyard's book on Milton, thus

mistaking the essay from which the quotation comes, and overlooking his own later emendation.

9 'Andrew Marvell' (1921), *Selected Essays*, p. 293.
10 Ibid., p. 301.
11 'Milton' (1936), *On Poetry and Poets* (1957), p. 142.
12 *Homage to John Dryden* (1924), p. 9.
13 'Andrew Marvell', *Selected Essays*, p. 302.
14 Ibid., p. 296.
15 Ibid., p. 301.
16 'Poetry in the 18th Century' (1930), *The Pelican Guide to English Literature 4: From Dryden to Johnson*, ed. Boris Ford (1963), p. 275.
17 'John Dryden' (1921), *Selected Essays*, p. 309.
18 Ibid., p. 305.
19 Ibid., pp. 314–15.
20 Ibid., p. 316.
21 'Andrew Marvell', *Selected Essays*, p. 297.
22 'The Study of Poetry', *Essays in Criticism Second Series*, pp. 22 and 24.
23 'Milton' (1936), *On Poetry and Poets*, p. 141.
24 'Milton', *Essays in Criticism Second Series*, p. 38.
25 *Mixed Essays* (1879), 1903 edition, p. 267.
26 Ibid., p. 244.
27 Ibid., p. 249.
28 Ibid., p. 261.
29 Ibid., p. 264.
30 Ibid., pp. 265, 266.
31 'Milton', *Essays in Criticism Second Series*, p. 37.
32 Ibid., p. 40.
33 'Milton' (1947), *On Poetry and Poets*, p. 158.
34 The obvious case is Collins who, like Joseph Warton, liked to make this distinction. In 'Ode on the Poetical Character' Collins imagines Milton 'From *Waller's* Myrtle Shades retreating', Waller exemplifying the smooth versifying tradition that reached its peak in Dryden and Pope. (Here again we can see a poet offering a view of literary history to justify his own practice.)
35 'Eliot's Dark Embryo', *The New Poetic* (1964).
36 'Milton' (1947), *On Poetry and Poets*, p. 160.
37 'Mr. Gray to Mr. West', *Gray's Poems, Letters and Essays*, with an introduction by John Drinkwater (1955), p. 136.
38 *The Works of Samuel Johnson . . . in twelve volumes* (1806), xi, *The Lives of the Poets*, p. 323.
39 '. . . through all his greater works there prevails an uniform peculiarity of Diction . . . far removed from common use . . .' Ibid., xii, p. 157.
40 *The Rambler* No. 168, *The Yale Edition of the Works of Samuel Johnson*, v, p. 126.
41 *The Lyrical Ballads 1798–1805*, with an introduction and notes by George Sampson (1965), p. 5.
42 Ibid., p. 17.
43 'Wordsworth', *Essays in Criticism Second Series*, p. 93.
44 *Selected Essays*, pp. 309–10.
45 Gray, 'The Bard'.
46 'Andrew Marvell', *Selected Essays*, p. 303.
47 'Observations', *The Egoist*, May 1918.

48 E.g. from 'Shakespeare and the Stoicism of Seneca': 'In truth neither Shake-speare nor Dante [as *poets*, the context implies] did any real thinking—that was not their job...The poet makes poetry, the metaphysician makes metaphysics, the bee makes honey, the spider secretes a filament; you can hardly say that any of these agents believes: he merely does', *Selected Essays*, pp. 136 and 138; and from 'Arnold and Pater': 'The theory...of "art for art's sake" is still valid in so far as it can be taken as an exhor-tation to the artist to stick to his job...The right practice of "art for art's sake" was the devotion of Flaubert or Henry James.' *Selected Essays*, pp. 442–3.

49 In 'Arnold and Pater' (1930).

50 See the quotations under note 48 above. And consider also the following from *The Use of Poetry and the Use of Criticism*, p. 151: 'The chief use of the "meaning" of a poem, in the ordinary sense, may be...to satisfy one habit of the reader, to keep his mind diverted and quiet, while the poem does its work upon him...This is a normal situation of which I approve.'

51 In *The New Poetic*.

52 'The Urban Apocalypse', in *Eliot in His Time: Essays on the Occasion of the Fiftieth Anniversary of 'The Waste Land'*, ed. A. Walton Litz (1973).

53 Ibid., p. 34.

54 Ibid., pp. 41–2.

55 Ibid., p. 48.

56 Ibid., p. 46.

57 Sir James G. Frazer, *The Golden Bough*, abridged edition (1923), p. 1. I thought I was the first to note this significance in Eliot's title but the editor of the present volume points out to me that it is made by George Watson in *The Literary Critics* (1964), p. 187.

Index

Note. Italicized numerals in the Eliot entry indicate quotations.